ROAD TO RIVERDALE®

VOLUME ONE

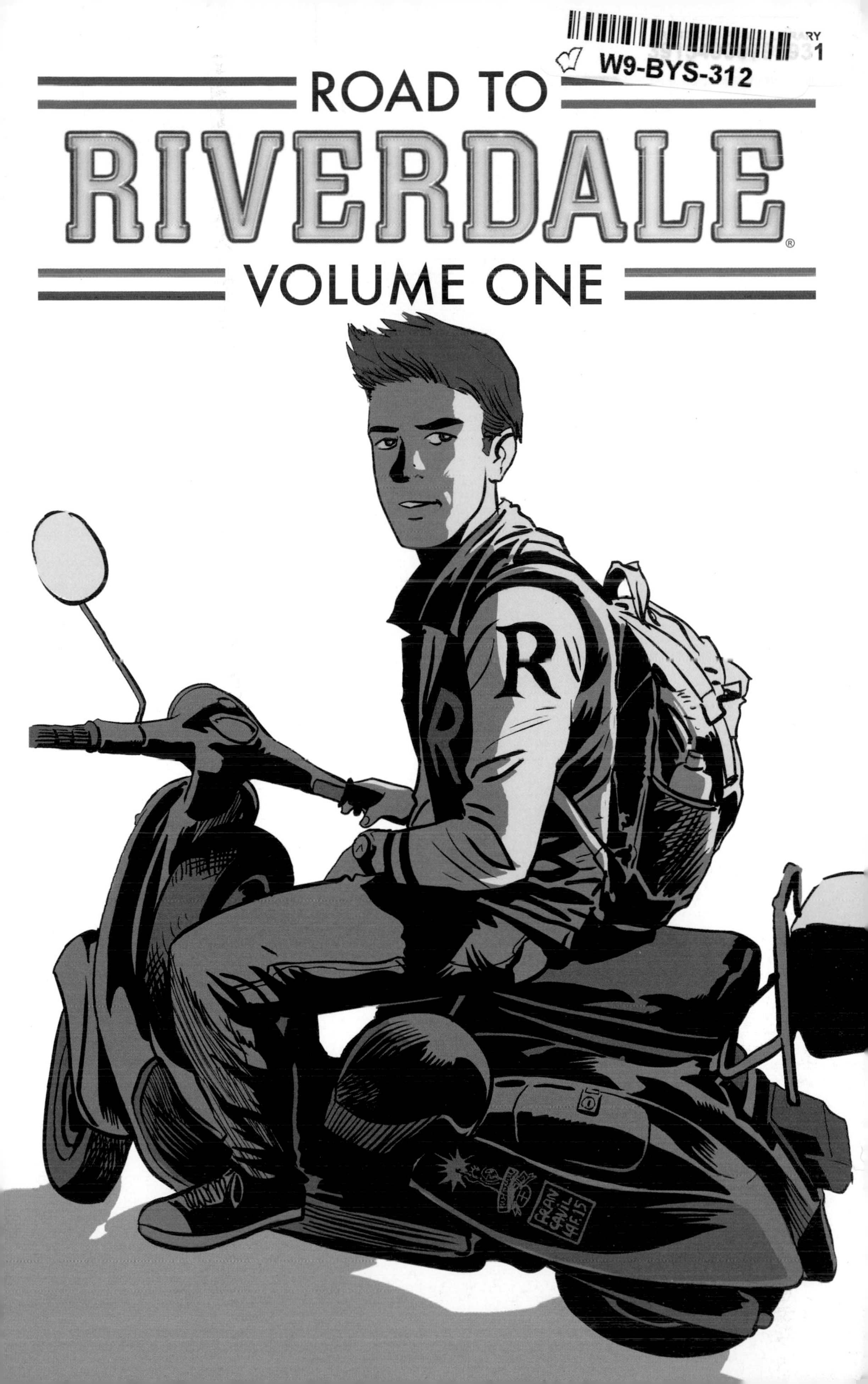

COVER ART BY
FRANCESCO FRANCAVILLA

FEATURING STORIES BY
MARK WAID, CHIP ZDARSKY,
ADAM HUGHES, MARGUERITE BENNETT,
CAMERON DeORDIO & TOM DeFALCO

WITH ART BY
FIONA STAPLES, ERICA HENDERSON,
ADAM HUGHES, AUDREY MOK, SANDY JARRELL,
ANDRE SZYMANOWICZ, JOSÉ VILLARRUBIA,
JEN VAUGHN, KELLY FITZPATRICK & JACK MORELLI

EDITOR
MIKE PELLERITO

CO-EDITOR (*JOSIE*)
ALEX SEGURA

ASSOCIATE EDITOR
STEPHEN OSWALD

ASSISTANT EDITOR
JAMIE LEE ROTANTE

EDITOR-IN-CHIEF
VICTOR GORELICK

GRAPHIC DESIGN BY
KARI McLACHLAN

PUBLISHER
JON GOLDWATER

ROAD TO
RIVERDALE
INTRODUCTION

Archie is for everyone and Archie is everywhere. Most importantly, Archie is today.

That's been my mandate and mantra since I took over the reins of Archie Comics. I wanted Archie to not only be something that people looked back on fondly, but also felt was a vibrant, must-read brand in the present. It wasn't an easy change to make, and it's one we're still seeing happen live.

There've been many turning points on that road — the introduction of Kevin Keller, Archie's wedding, *Afterlife with Archie* and the *Death of Archie* come to mind immediately. But the most overt and game-changing move came in 2015, when we relaunched our flagship title with a new ARCHIE #1, courtesy of, hands-down, the best creative team in comics in writer Mark Waid and artist Fiona Staples. That watershed moment opened the door for an entire line of 'New Riverdale' series, like JUGHEAD, BETTY & VERONICA and more. It was a daring, unexpected move for us as a company. It was risky. But Archie Comics hasn't succeeded by sitting pat and waiting for other companies to take the lead. We've made a name for ourselves by making history, not experiencing it. And, make no bones about it — ARCHIE #1 was a historic moment for this company and for comic books in general.

How do I know this? Well, take a minute and look at Fiona Staples's Archie from the cover of ARCHIE #1. Then take a look at the amazing KJ Apa, the actor playing Archie Andrews on the new CW series, *Riverdale*. They're not identical, but the feeling, tone and vibe are completely in sync. The characters you see on your TV screen portraying Archie, Jughead, Betty and Veronica and more have literally sprung from the pages of the New Riverdale books we create, month-in and month-out. There is no bigger compliment that can be paid to the work of talents like Waid, Staples, Chip Zdarsky, Adam Hughes, Marguerite Bennett, Cameron DeOrdio, Tom DeFalco and so many more. These stories have gone from print to reality because they're of the moment. They don't feel dated and they're compelling, funny, heartfelt and — not to put too fine a point on it — alive.

The *Riverdale* TV series is a work of cinematic art, and it's being brought to life by a team of people so completely invested in it — and in Archie — that I'm supremely confident you'll love it! Showrunner Roberto Aguirre-Sacasa, who is also our Chief Creative Officer and the mastermind behind horror hits like *Afterlife* and *Chilling Adventures of Sabrina*, has a passion for these characters that can be seen in every shot and scene he writes, whether it's a comic book page or on the show. Paired with Greg Berlanti, Sarah Schechter, The CW and Warner Bros., they've created a show that honors these pop culture icons but also moves them forward. And, as long as I've been running Archie Comics, that's what it's been all about: staying vibrant, staying engaged and moving these properties into the present and the future.

So, sit back with this veritable greatest hits package of comic book stories and enjoy a first-class tour of one of my proudest achievements: the New Riverdale. As you'll see when you tune into *Riverdale* on your TVs, these books have already begun to influence and inspire the world we live in.

— JON GOLDWATER

ROAD TO RIVERDALE

CONTENTS

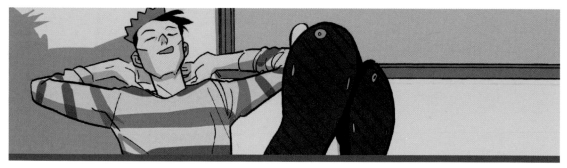

Where it all began!

In July 2015, the world was introduced to the NEW RIVERDALE with an all-new #1 issue of *Archie*, after a 666-issue run spanning over 70 years. The series launched with a bang thanks to the clever and charming story courtesy of legendary comics writer Mark Waid and the beautiful and striking art of artist Fiona Staples.

The new *Archie* re-introduced the characters to the world in a way that was groundbreaking while still paying homage to the years of classic comics that came before it. While the characters and settings may have updated looks, the heart of what makes them so likeable and accessible to readers is still there.

STORY BY
MARK WAID

ART BY
FIONA STAPLES

COLORING BY
ANDRE SZYMANOWICZ
WITH JEN VAUGHN

LETTERING BY
JACK MORELLI

ROAD TO RIVERDALE®

ARCHIE

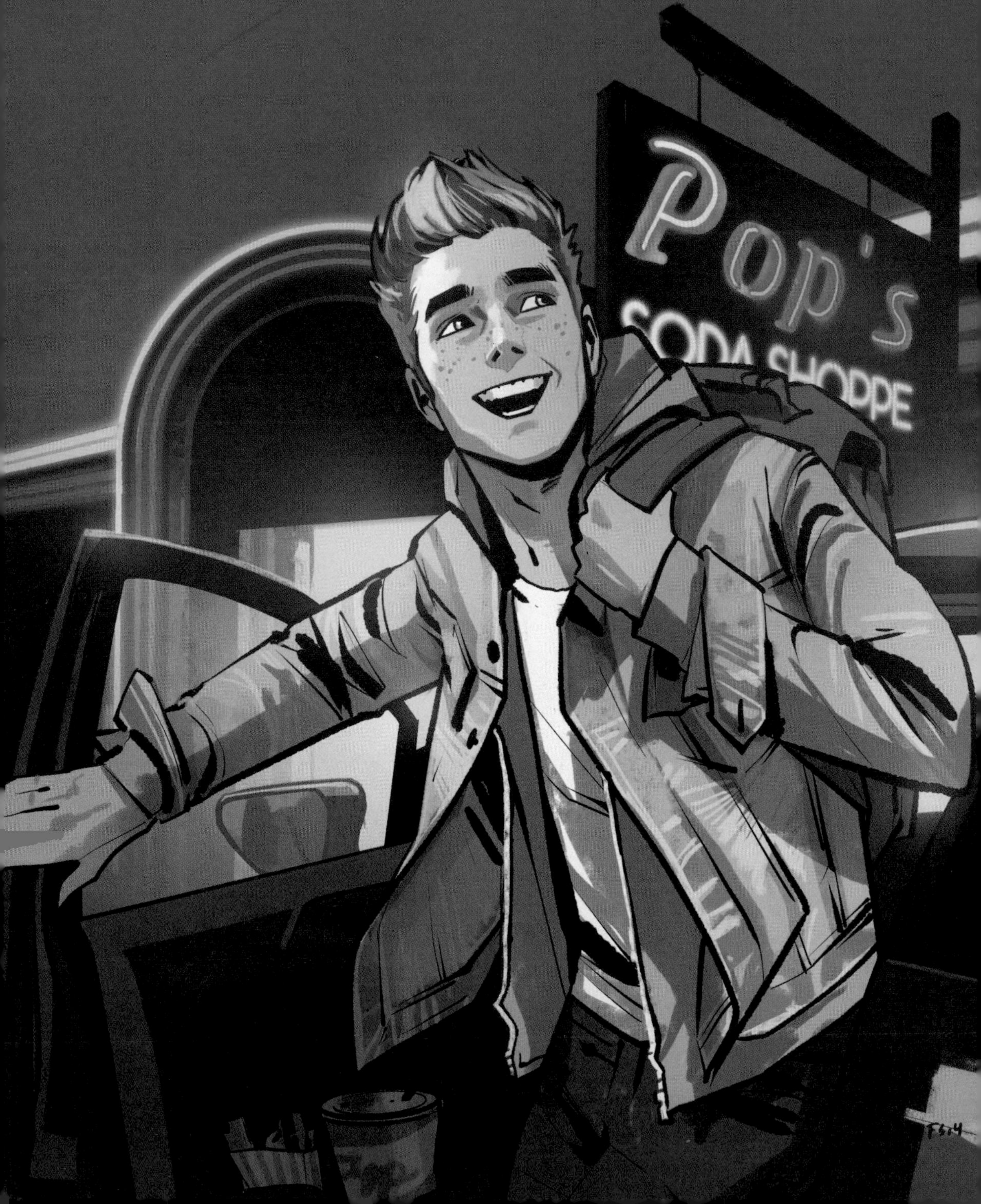

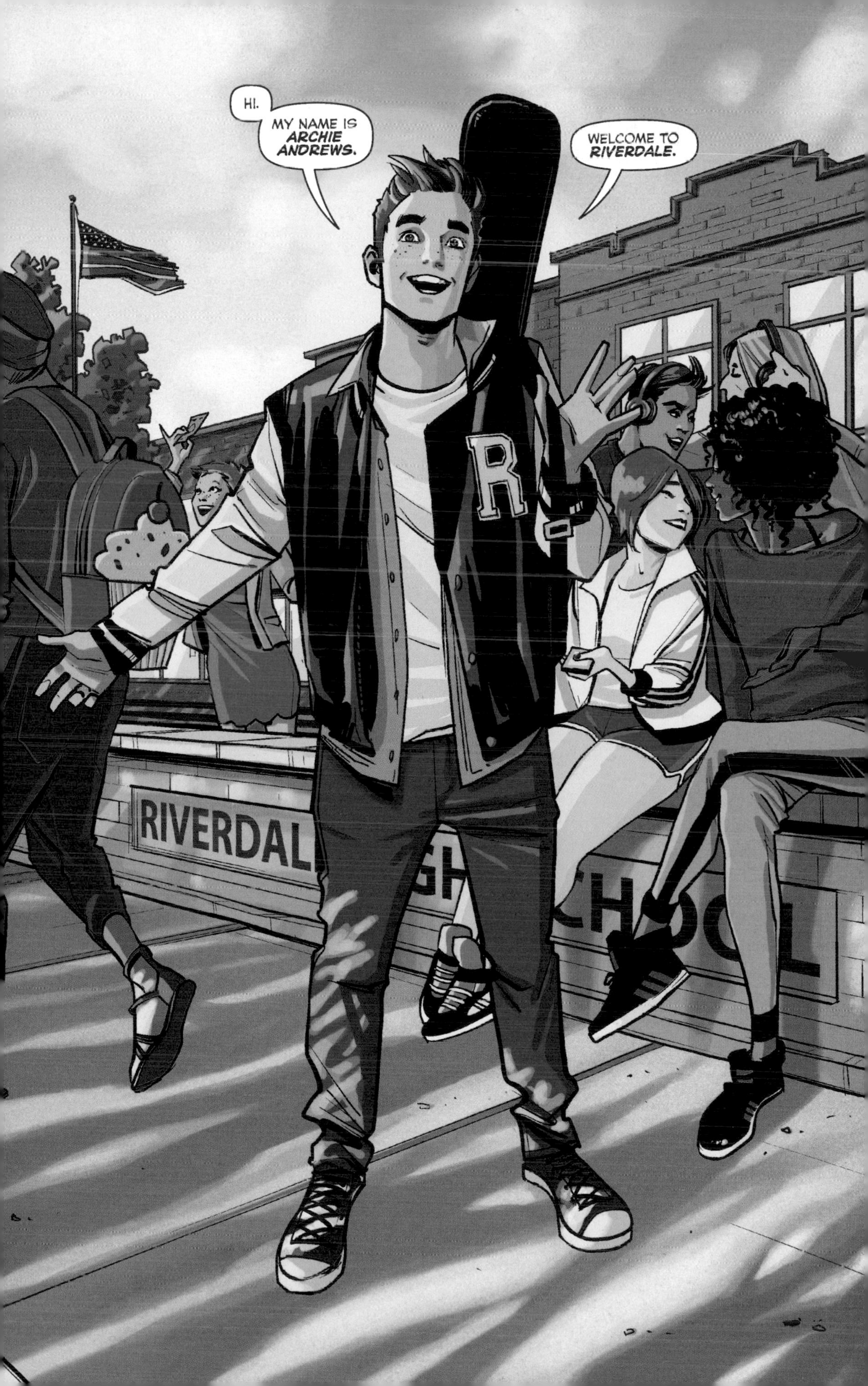
HI.
MY NAME IS ARCHIE ANDREWS.
WELCOME TO RIVERDALE.

CHAPTER ONE: There is this Girl

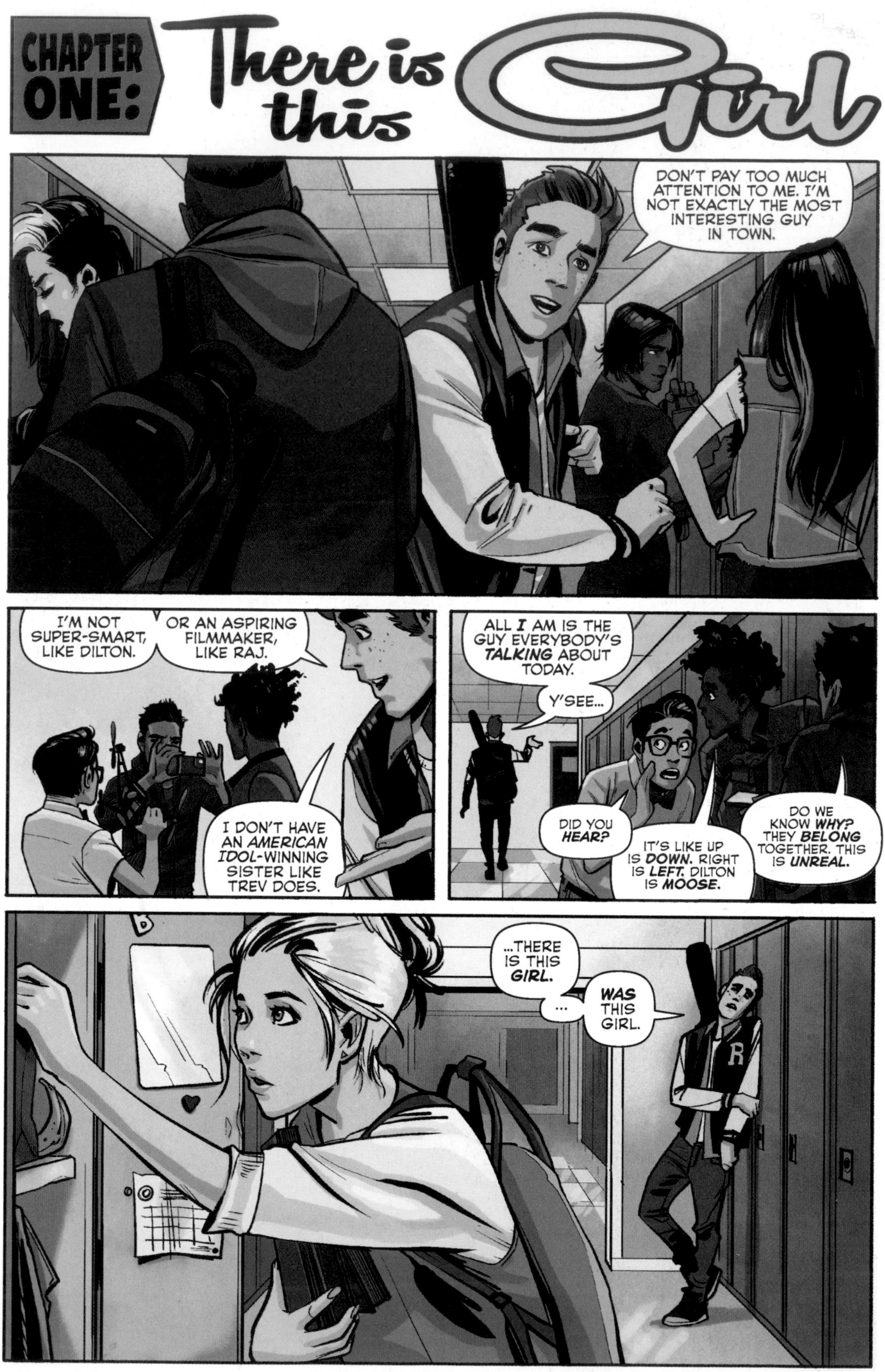
DON'T PAY TOO MUCH ATTENTION TO ME. I'M NOT EXACTLY THE MOST INTERESTING GUY IN TOWN.
I'M NOT SUPER-SMART, LIKE DILTON.
OR AN ASPIRING FILMMAKER, LIKE RAJ.
I DON'T HAVE AN *AMERICAN IDOL*-WINNING SISTER LIKE TREV DOES.
ALL *I* AM IS THE GUY EVERYBODY'S *TALKING* ABOUT TODAY.
Y'SEE...
DID YOU *HEAR?*
IT'S LIKE UP IS *DOWN*. RIGHT IS *LEFT*. DILTON IS *MOOSE*.
DO WE KNOW *WHY?* THEY *BELONG* TOGETHER. THIS IS *UNREAL*.
...THERE IS THIS *GIRL*.
...
WAS THIS GIRL.

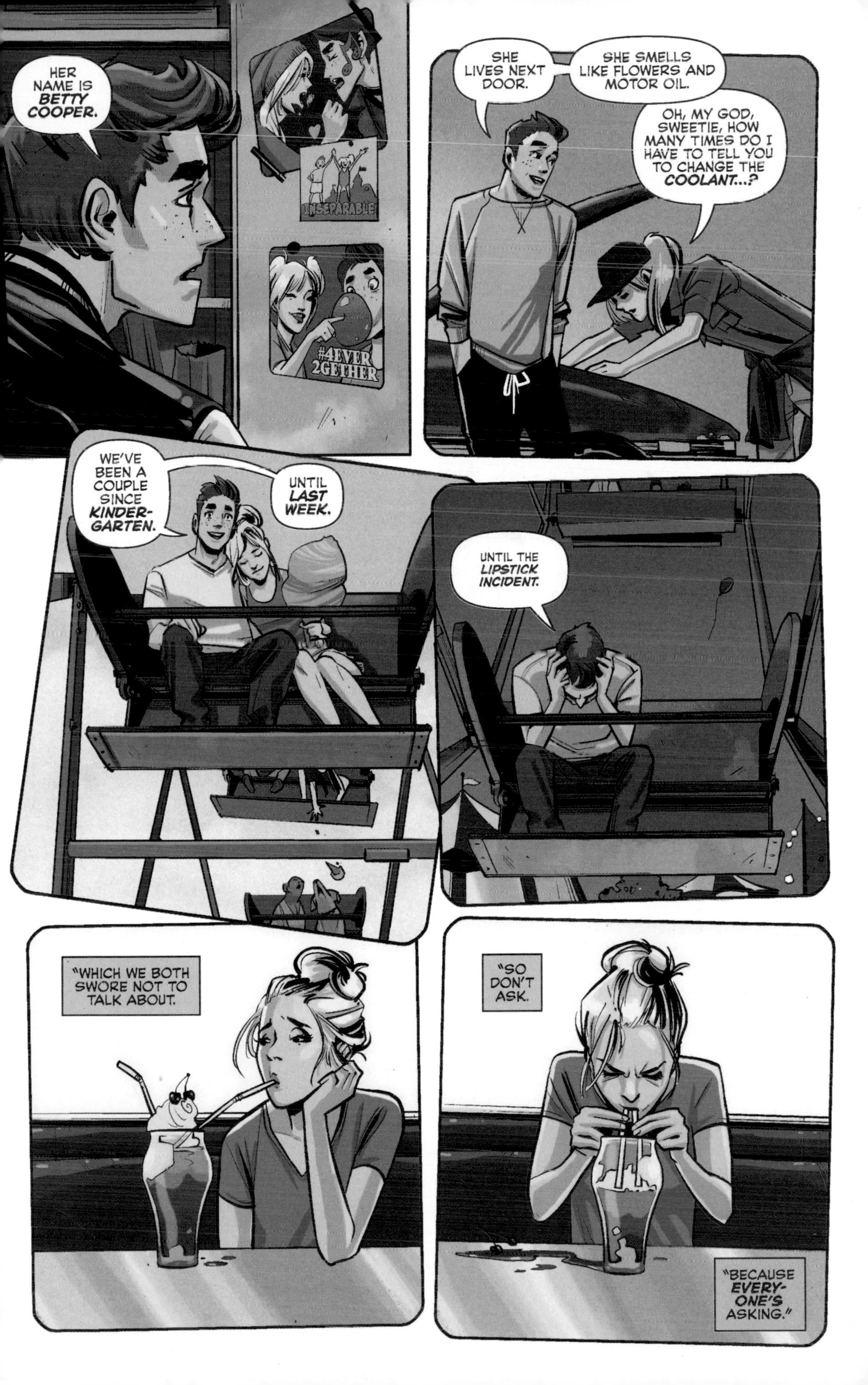
HER NAME IS BETTY COOPER.
UNSEPARABLE
#4EVER 2GETHER
SHE LIVES NEXT DOOR.
SHE SMELLS LIKE FLOWERS AND MOTOR OIL.
OH, MY GOD, SWEETIE, HOW MANY TIMES DO I HAVE TO TELL YOU TO CHANGE THE COOLANT...?
WE'VE BEEN A COUPLE SINCE KINDER-GARTEN.
UNTIL LAST WEEK.
UNTIL THE LIPSTICK INCIDENT.
"WHICH WE BOTH SWORE NOT TO TALK ABOUT.
"SO DON'T ASK.
"BECAUSE EVERY-ONE'S ASKING."

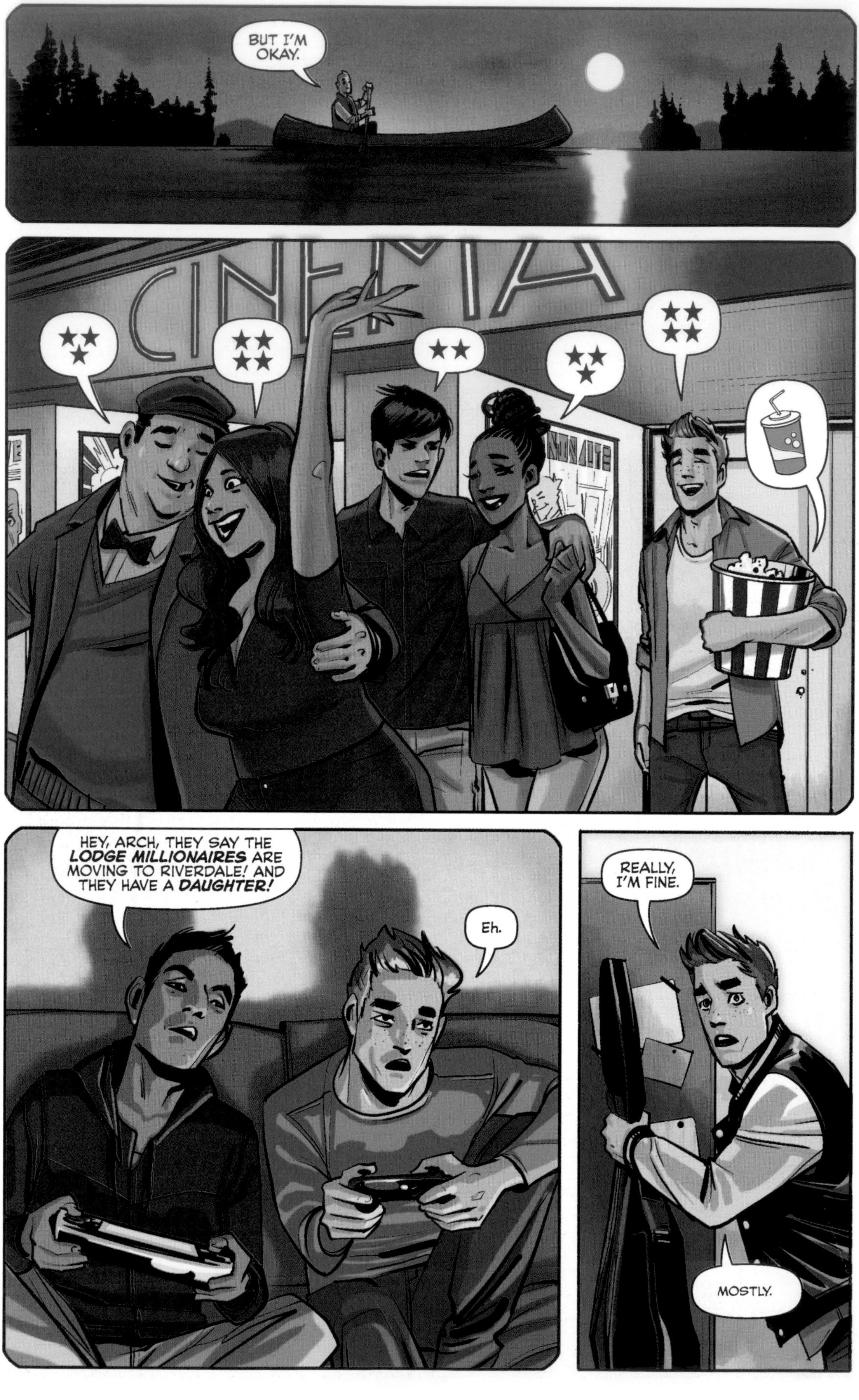

BUT I'M OKAY.
CINEMA
HEY, ARCH, THEY SAY THE LODGE MILLIONAIRES ARE MOVING TO RIVERDALE! AND THEY HAVE A DAUGHTER!
Eh.
REALLY, I'M FINE.
MOSTLY.

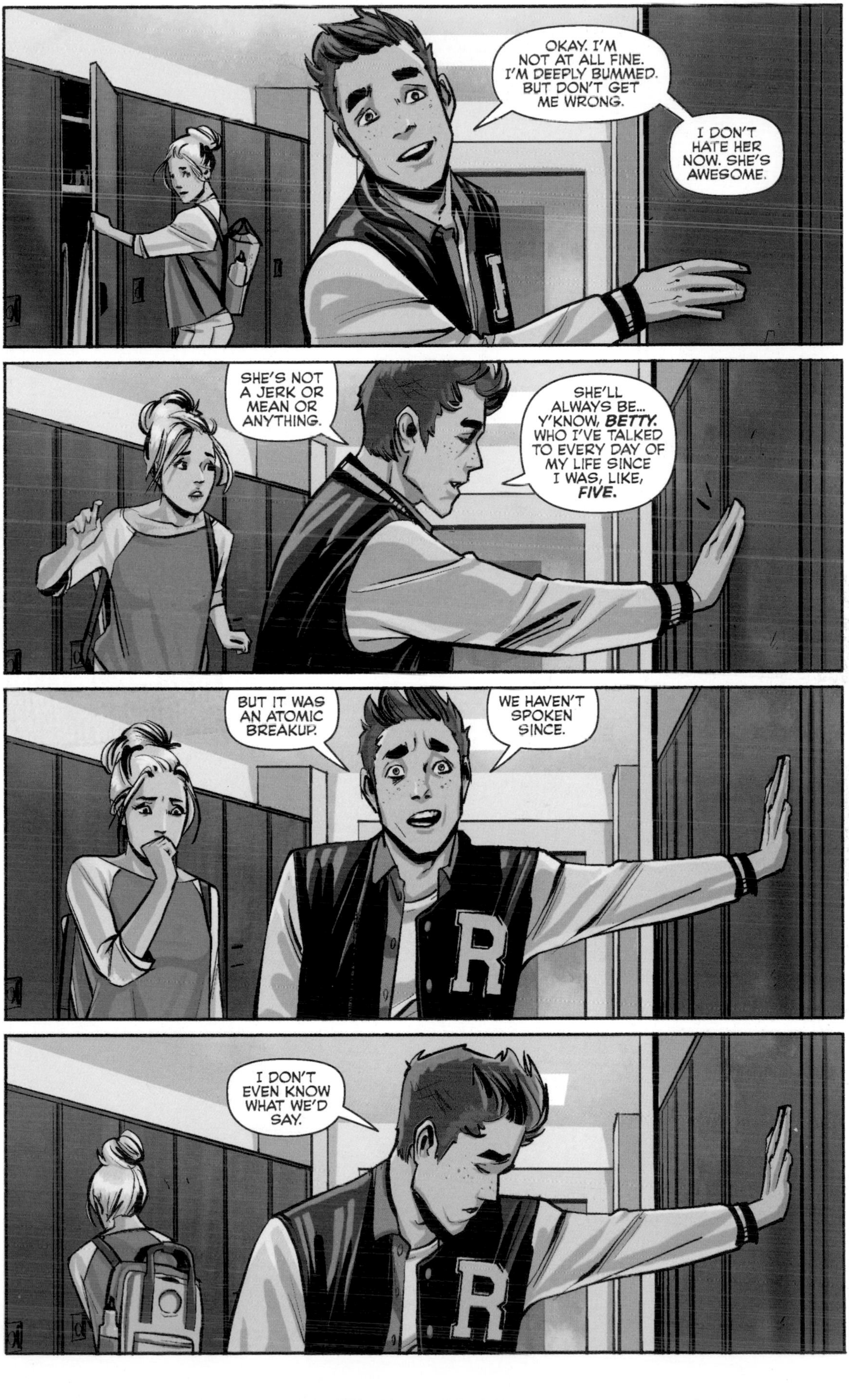
OKAY. I'M NOT AT ALL FINE. I'M DEEPLY BUMMED. BUT DON'T GET ME WRONG.
I DON'T HATE HER NOW. SHE'S AWESOME.
SHE'S NOT A JERK OR MEAN OR ANYTHING.
SHE'LL ALWAYS BE... Y'KNOW, ***BETTY.*** WHO I'VE TALKED TO EVERY DAY OF MY LIFE SINCE I WAS, LIKE, ***FIVE.***
BUT IT WAS AN ATOMIC BREAKUP.
WE HAVEN'T SPOKEN SINCE.
I DON'T EVEN KNOW WHAT WE'D SAY.

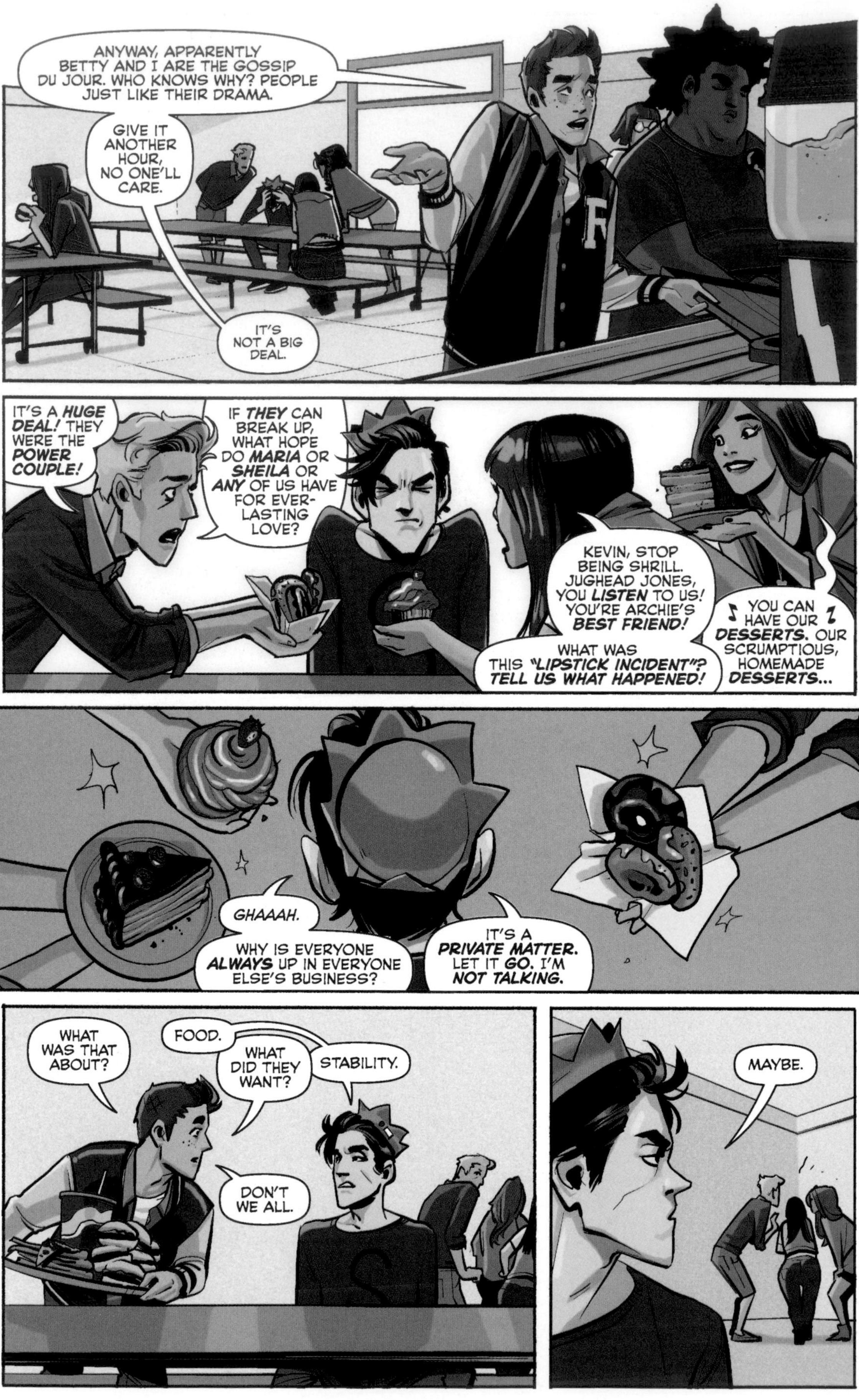
ANYWAY, APPARENTLY BETTY AND I ARE THE GOSSIP DU JOUR. WHO KNOWS WHY? PEOPLE JUST LIKE THEIR DRAMA.
GIVE IT ANOTHER HOUR, NO ONE'LL CARE.
IT'S NOT A BIG DEAL.
IT'S A HUGE DEAL! THEY WERE THE POWER COUPLE!
IF THEY CAN BREAK UP, WHAT HOPE DO MARIA OR SHEILA OR ANY OF US HAVE FOR EVER-LASTING LOVE?
KEVIN, STOP BEING SHRILL. JUGHEAD JONES, YOU LISTEN TO US! YOU'RE ARCHIE'S BEST FRIEND!
WHAT WAS THIS "LIPSTICK INCIDENT"? TELL US WHAT HAPPENED!
YOU CAN HAVE OUR DESSERTS. OUR SCRUMPTIOUS, HOMEMADE DESSERTS...
GHAAAH.
WHY IS EVERYONE ALWAYS UP IN EVERYONE ELSE'S BUSINESS?
IT'S A PRIVATE MATTER. LET IT GO. I'M NOT TALKING.
WHAT WAS THAT ABOUT?
FOOD.
WHAT DID THEY WANT?
STABILITY.
DON'T WE ALL.
MAYBE.

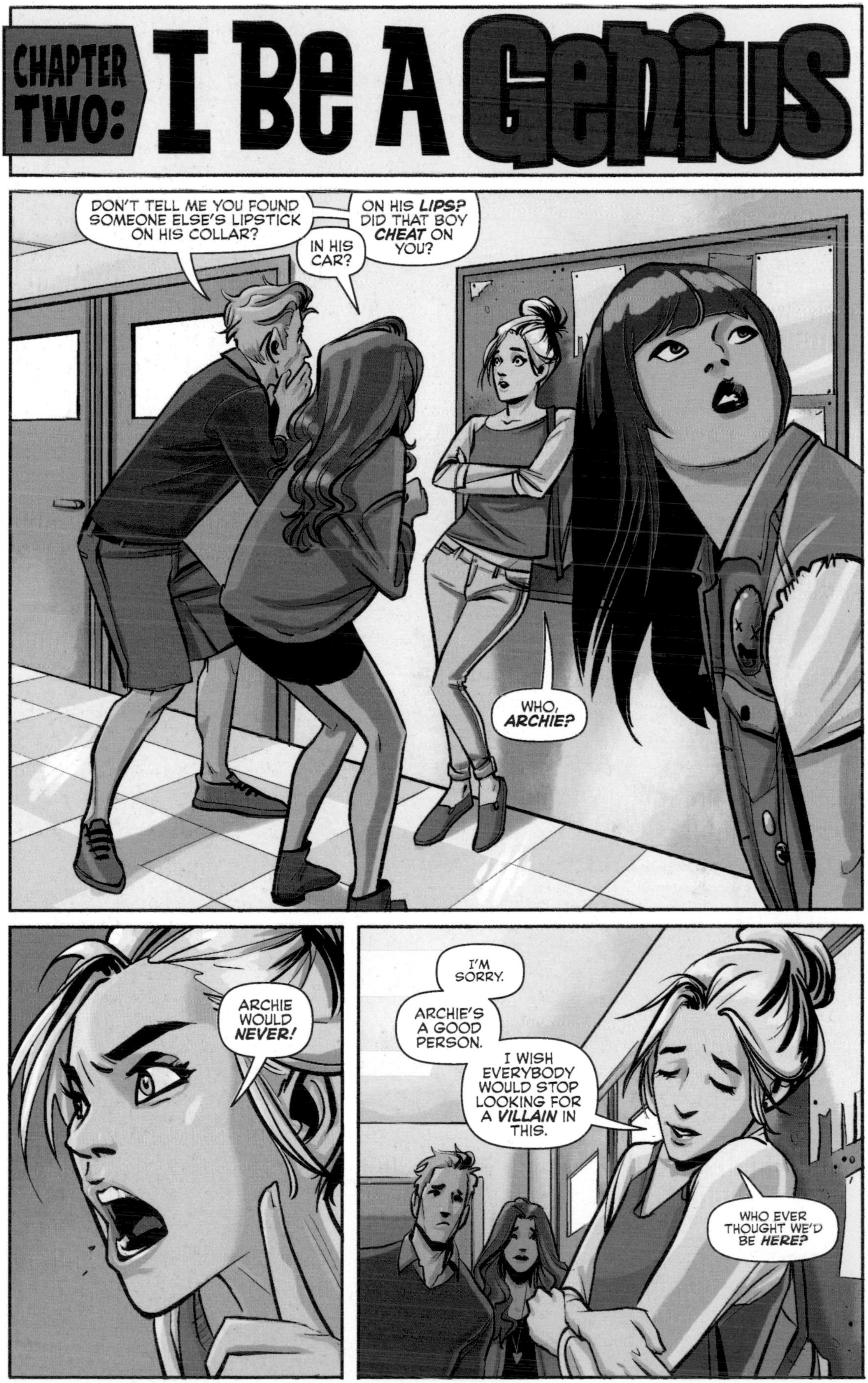
CHAPTER TWO: I Be A Genius
DON'T TELL ME YOU FOUND SOMEONE ELSE'S LIPSTICK ON HIS COLLAR?
IN HIS CAR?
ON HIS LIPS? DID THAT BOY CHEAT ON YOU?
WHO, ARCHIE?
ARCHIE WOULD NEVER!
I'M SORRY.
ARCHIE'S A GOOD PERSON.
I WISH EVERYBODY WOULD STOP LOOKING FOR A VILLAIN IN THIS.
WHO EVER THOUGHT WE'D BE HERE?

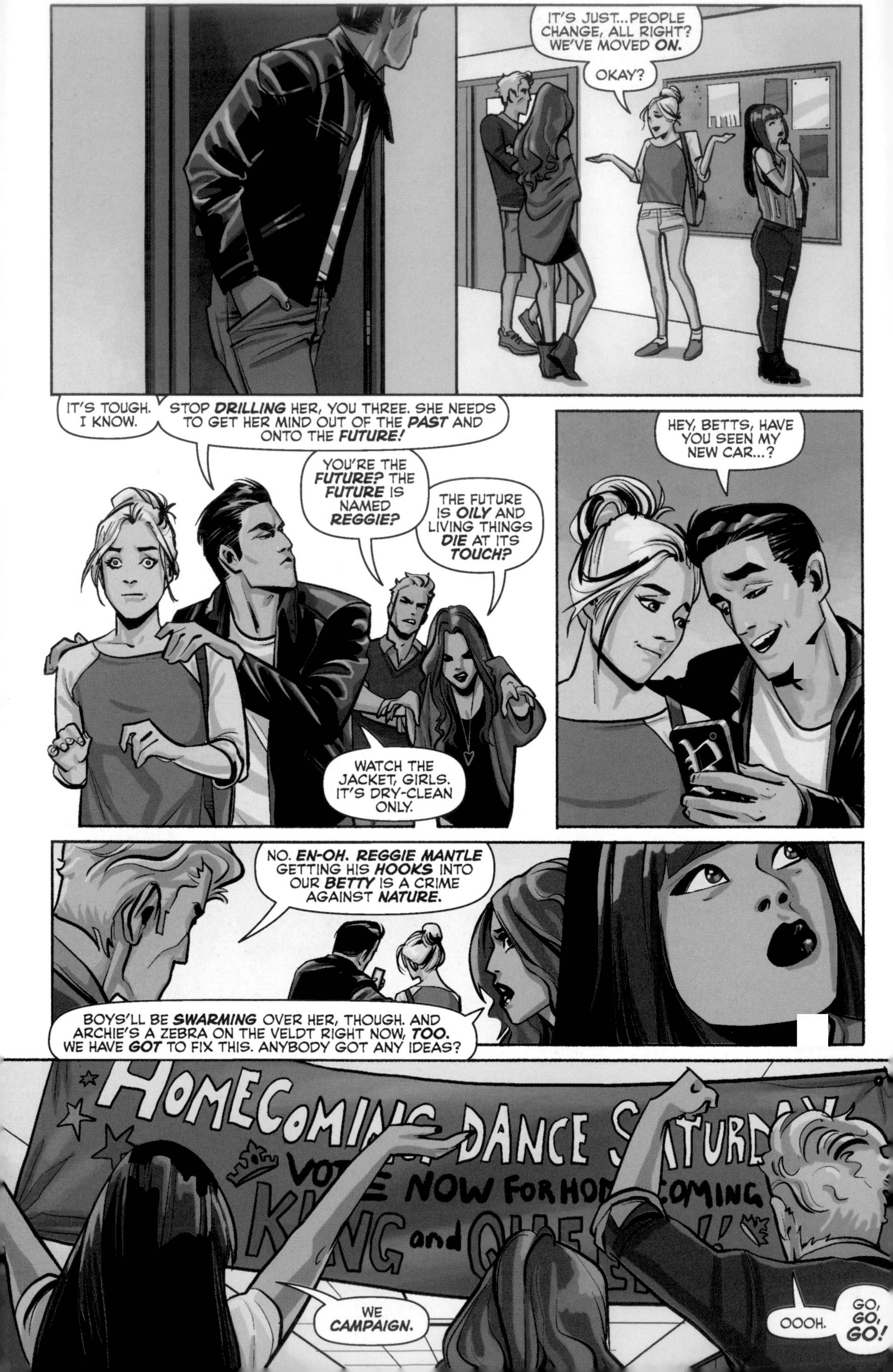
IT'S JUST...PEOPLE CHANGE, ALL RIGHT? WE'VE MOVED ON.
OKAY?
IT'S TOUGH. I KNOW.
STOP DRILLING HER, YOU THREE. SHE NEEDS TO GET HER MIND OUT OF THE PAST AND ONTO THE FUTURE!
YOU'RE THE FUTURE? THE FUTURE IS NAMED REGGIE?
THE FUTURE IS OILY AND LIVING THINGS DIE AT ITS TOUCH?
WATCH THE JACKET, GIRLS. IT'S DRY-CLEAN ONLY.
HEY, BETTS, HAVE YOU SEEN MY NEW CAR...?
NO. EN-OH. REGGIE MANTLE GETTING HIS HOOKS INTO OUR BETTY IS A CRIME AGAINST NATURE.
BOYS'LL BE SWARMING OVER HER, THOUGH. AND ARCHIE'S A ZEBRA ON THE VELDT RIGHT NOW, TOO. WE HAVE GOT TO FIX THIS. ANYBODY GOT ANY IDEAS?
WE CAMPAIGN.
OOOH.
GO, GO, GO!

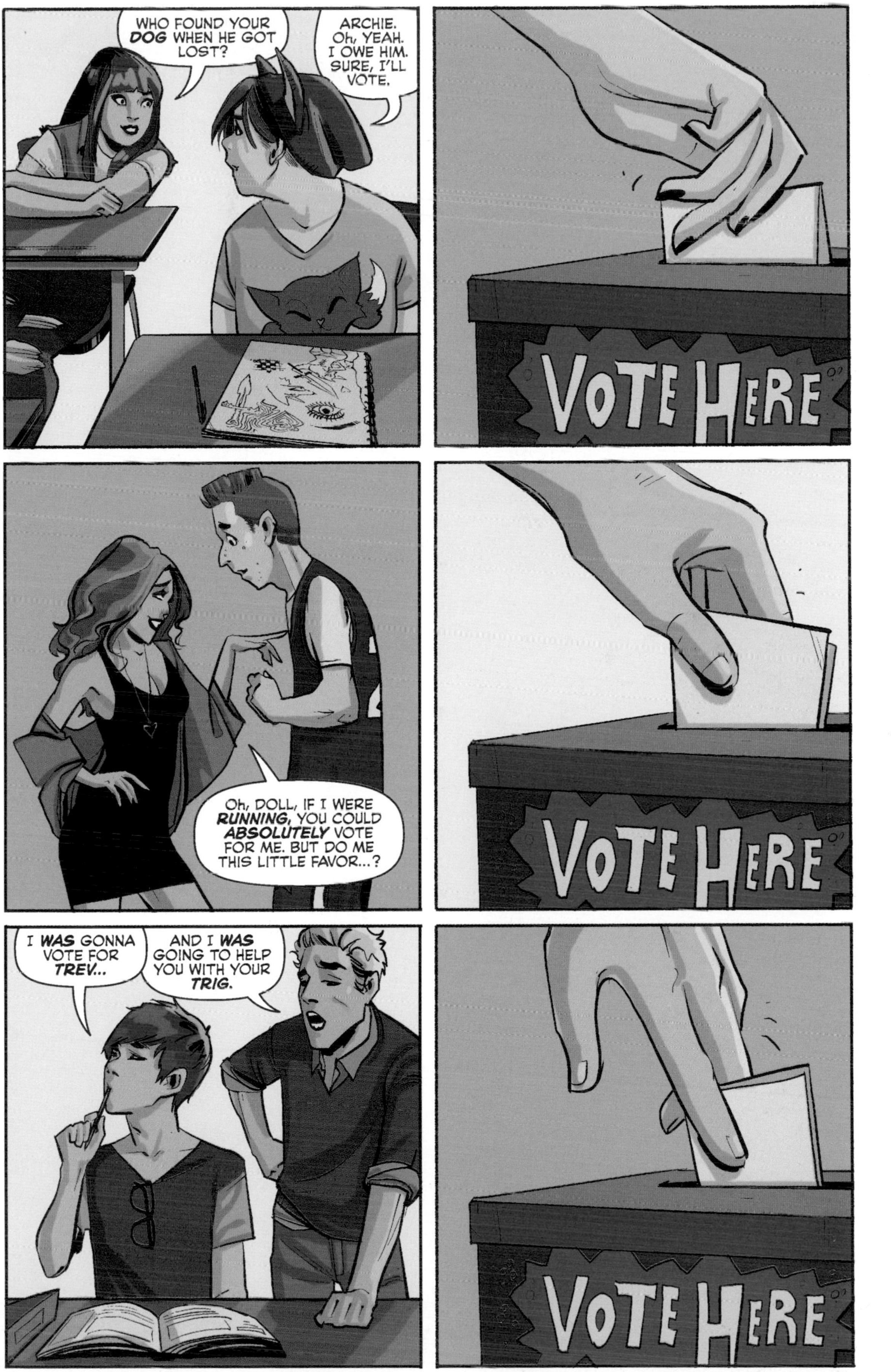
WHO FOUND YOUR DOG WHEN HE GOT LOST?
ARCHIE. Oh, YEAH. I OWE HIM. SURE, I'LL VOTE.
VOTE HERE
Oh, DOLL, IF I WERE RUNNING, YOU COULD ABSOLUTELY VOTE FOR ME. BUT DO ME THIS LITTLE FAVOR...?
VOTE HERE
I WAS GONNA VOTE FOR TREV...
AND I WAS GOING TO HELP YOU WITH YOUR TRIG.
VOTE HERE

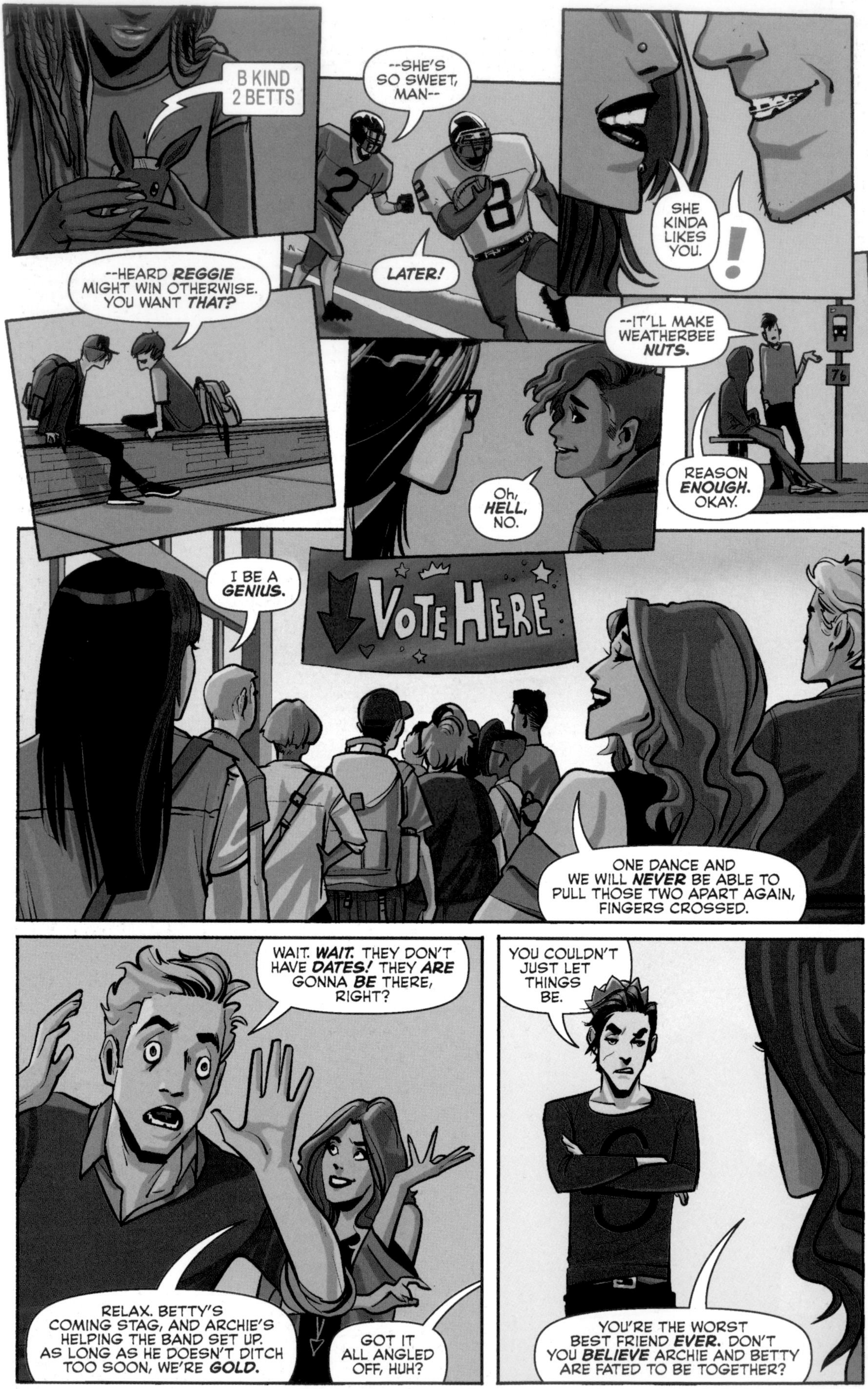
B KIND 2 BETTS
--SHE'S SO SWEET, MAN--
LATER!
SHE KINDA LIKES YOU.
!
--HEARD REGGIE MIGHT WIN OTHERWISE. YOU WANT THAT?
Oh, HELL, NO.
--IT'LL MAKE WEATHERBEE NUTS.
REASON ENOUGH. OKAY.
I BE A GENIUS.
VOTE HERE
ONE DANCE AND WE WILL NEVER BE ABLE TO PULL THOSE TWO APART AGAIN, FINGERS CROSSED.
WAIT. WAIT. THEY DON'T HAVE DATES! THEY ARE GONNA BE THERE, RIGHT?
RELAX. BETTY'S COMING STAG, AND ARCHIE'S HELPING THE BAND SET UP. AS LONG AS HE DOESN'T DITCH TOO SOON, WE'RE GOLD.
GOT IT ALL ANGLED OFF, HUH?
YOU COULDN'T JUST LET THINGS BE.
YOU'RE THE WORST BEST FRIEND EVER. DON'T YOU BELIEVE ARCHIE AND BETTY ARE FATED TO BE TOGETHER?

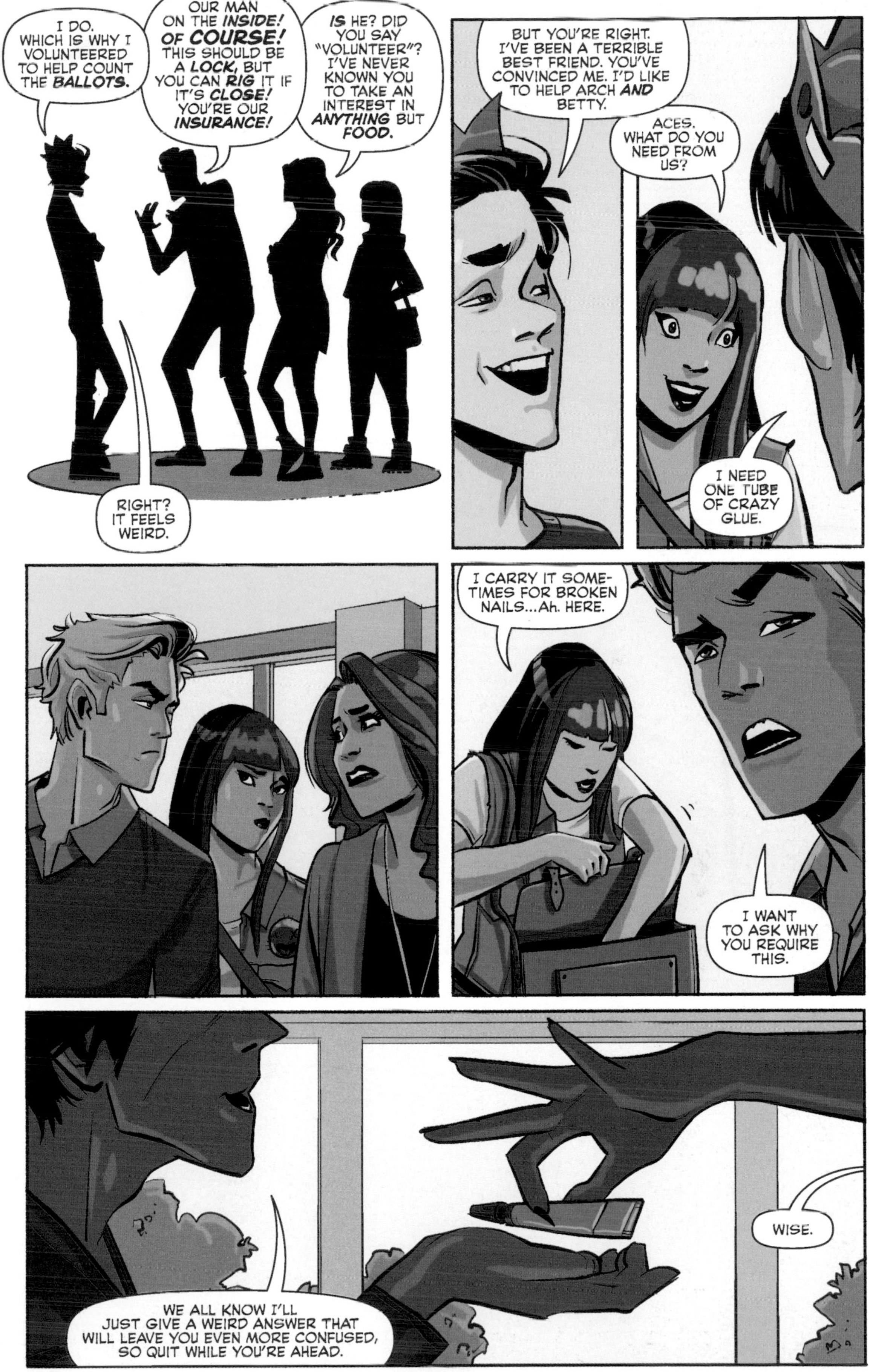
I DO. WHICH IS WHY I VOLUNTEERED TO HELP COUNT THE BALLOTS.
OUR MAN ON THE INSIDE! OF COURSE! THIS SHOULD BE A LOCK, BUT YOU CAN RIG IT IF IT'S CLOSE! YOU'RE OUR INSURANCE!
IS HE? DID YOU SAY "VOLUNTEER"? I'VE NEVER KNOWN YOU TO TAKE AN INTEREST IN ANYTHING BUT FOOD.
RIGHT? IT FEELS WEIRD.
BUT YOU'RE RIGHT. I'VE BEEN A TERRIBLE BEST FRIEND. YOU'VE CONVINCED ME. I'D LIKE TO HELP ARCH AND BETTY.
ACES. WHAT DO YOU NEED FROM US?
I NEED ONE TUBE OF CRAZY GLUE.
I CARRY IT SOMETIMES FOR BROKEN NAILS...Ah. HERE.
I WANT TO ASK WHY YOU REQUIRE THIS.
WE ALL KNOW I'LL JUST GIVE A WEIRD ANSWER THAT WILL LEAVE YOU EVEN MORE CONFUSED, SO QUIT WHILE YOU'RE AHEAD.
WISE.

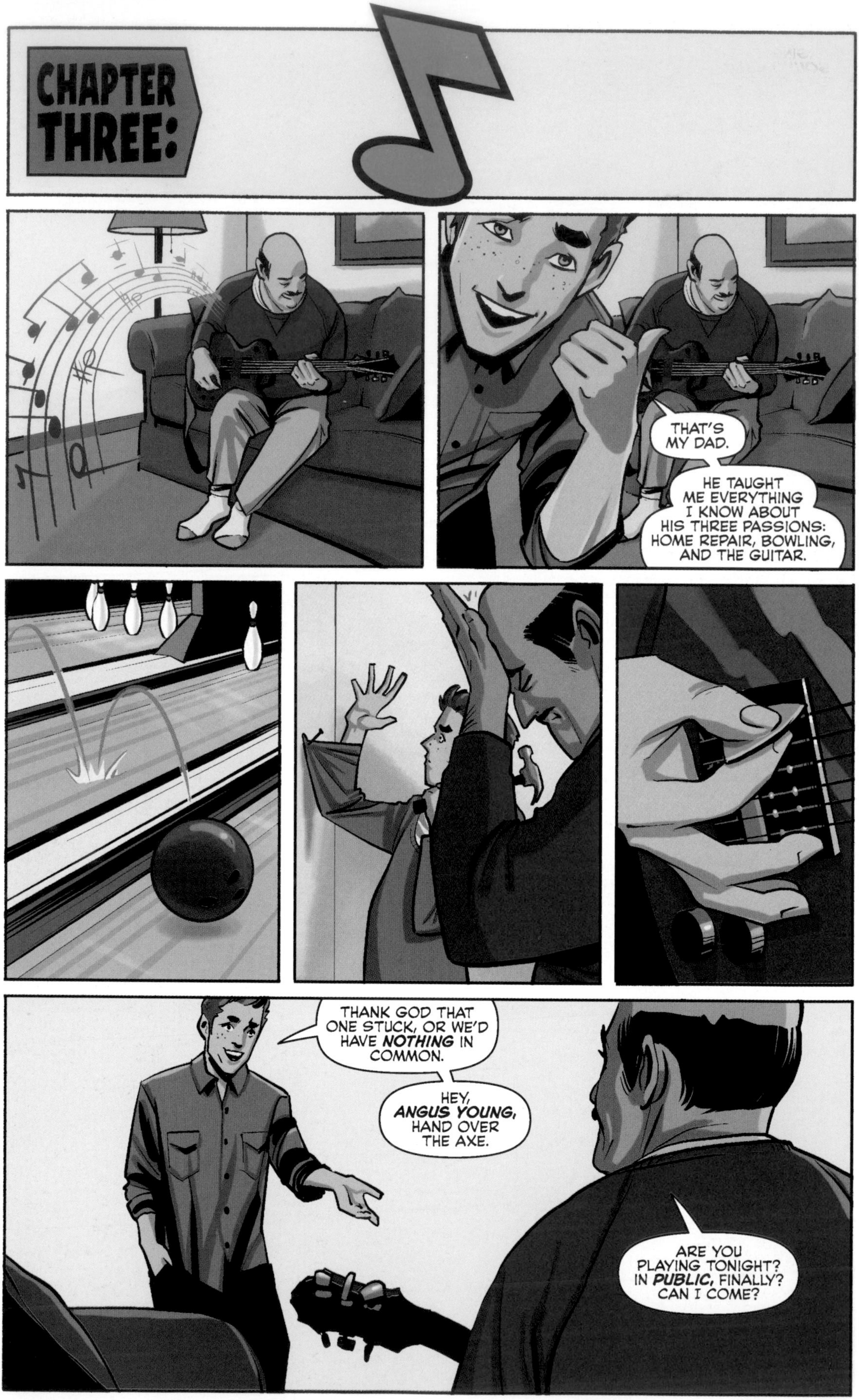
CHAPTER THREE:
THAT'S MY DAD.
HE TAUGHT ME EVERYTHING I KNOW ABOUT HIS THREE PASSIONS: HOME REPAIR, BOWLING, AND THE GUITAR.
THANK GOD THAT ONE STUCK, OR WE'D HAVE NOTHING IN COMMON.
HEY, ANGUS YOUNG, HAND OVER THE AXE.
ARE YOU PLAYING TONIGHT? IN PUBLIC, FINALLY? CAN I COME?

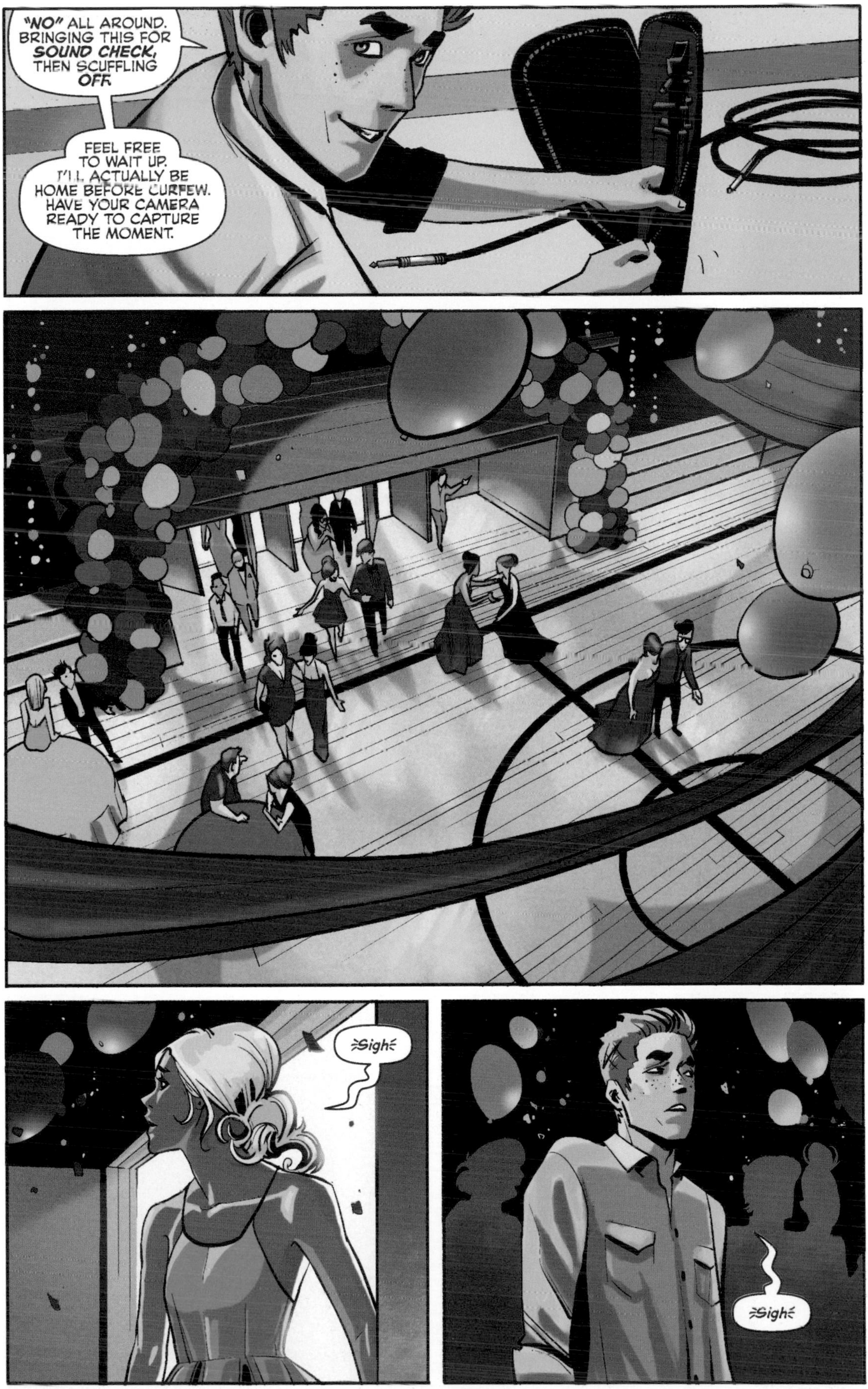
"NO" ALL AROUND. BRINGING THIS FOR SOUND CHECK, THEN SCUFFLING OFF.
FEEL FREE TO WAIT UP. I'LL ACTUALLY BE HOME BEFORE CURFEW. HAVE YOUR CAMERA READY TO CAPTURE THE MOMENT.
Sigh
Sigh

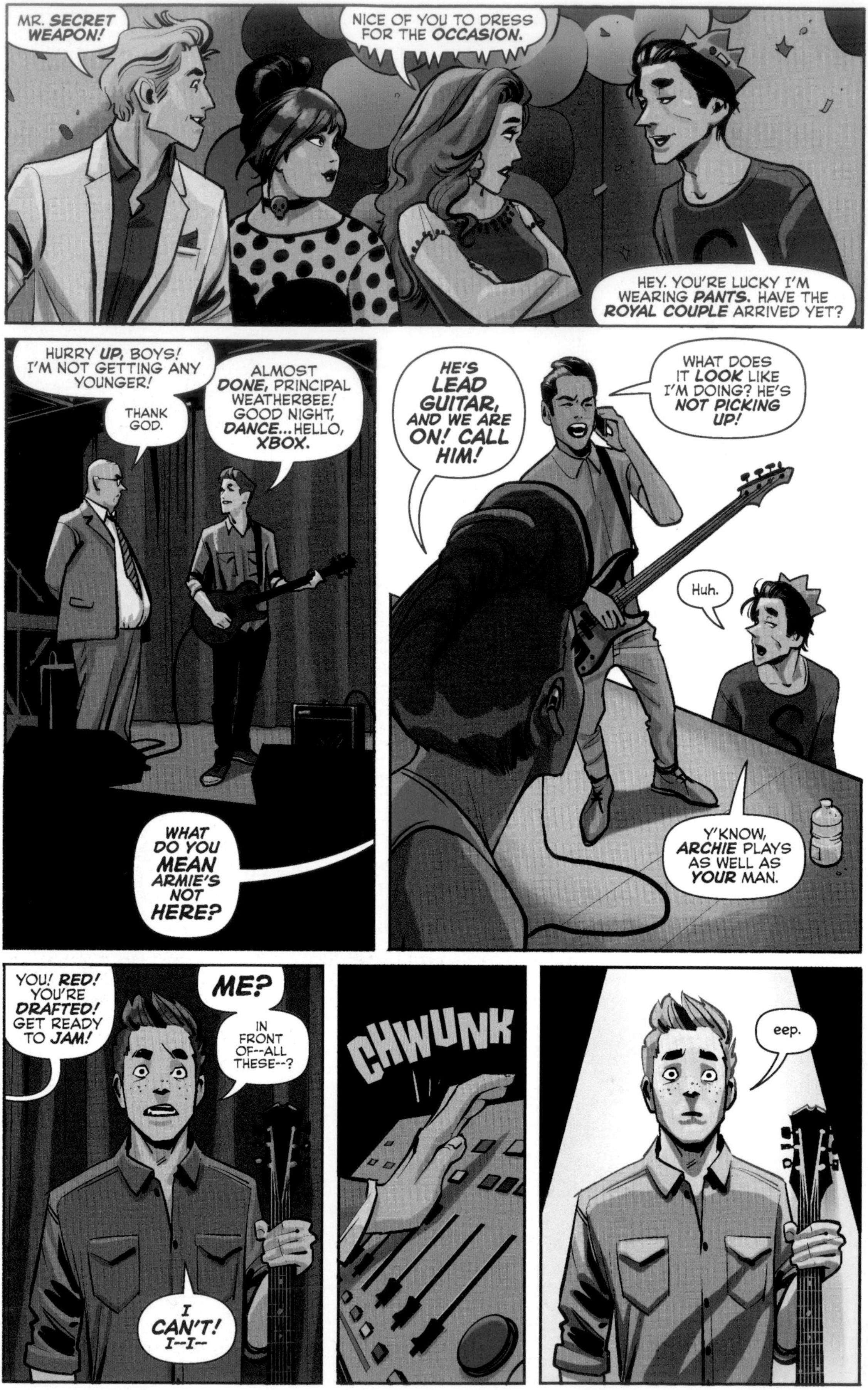
MR. SECRET WEAPON!
NICE OF YOU TO DRESS FOR THE OCCASION.
HEY. YOU'RE LUCKY I'M WEARING PANTS. HAVE THE ROYAL COUPLE ARRIVED YET?
HURRY UP, BOYS! I'M NOT GETTING ANY YOUNGER!
THANK GOD.
ALMOST DONE, PRINCIPAL WEATHERBEE! GOOD NIGHT, DANCE...HELLO, XBOX.
WHAT DO YOU MEAN ARMIE'S NOT HERE?
HE'S LEAD GUITAR, AND WE ARE ON! CALL HIM!
WHAT DOES IT LOOK LIKE I'M DOING? HE'S NOT PICKING UP!
Huh.
Y'KNOW, ARCHIE PLAYS AS WELL AS YOUR MAN.
YOU! RED! YOU'RE DRAFTED! GET READY TO JAM!
ME?
IN FRONT OF--ALL THESE--?
I CAN'T! I--I--
CHWUNK
eep.

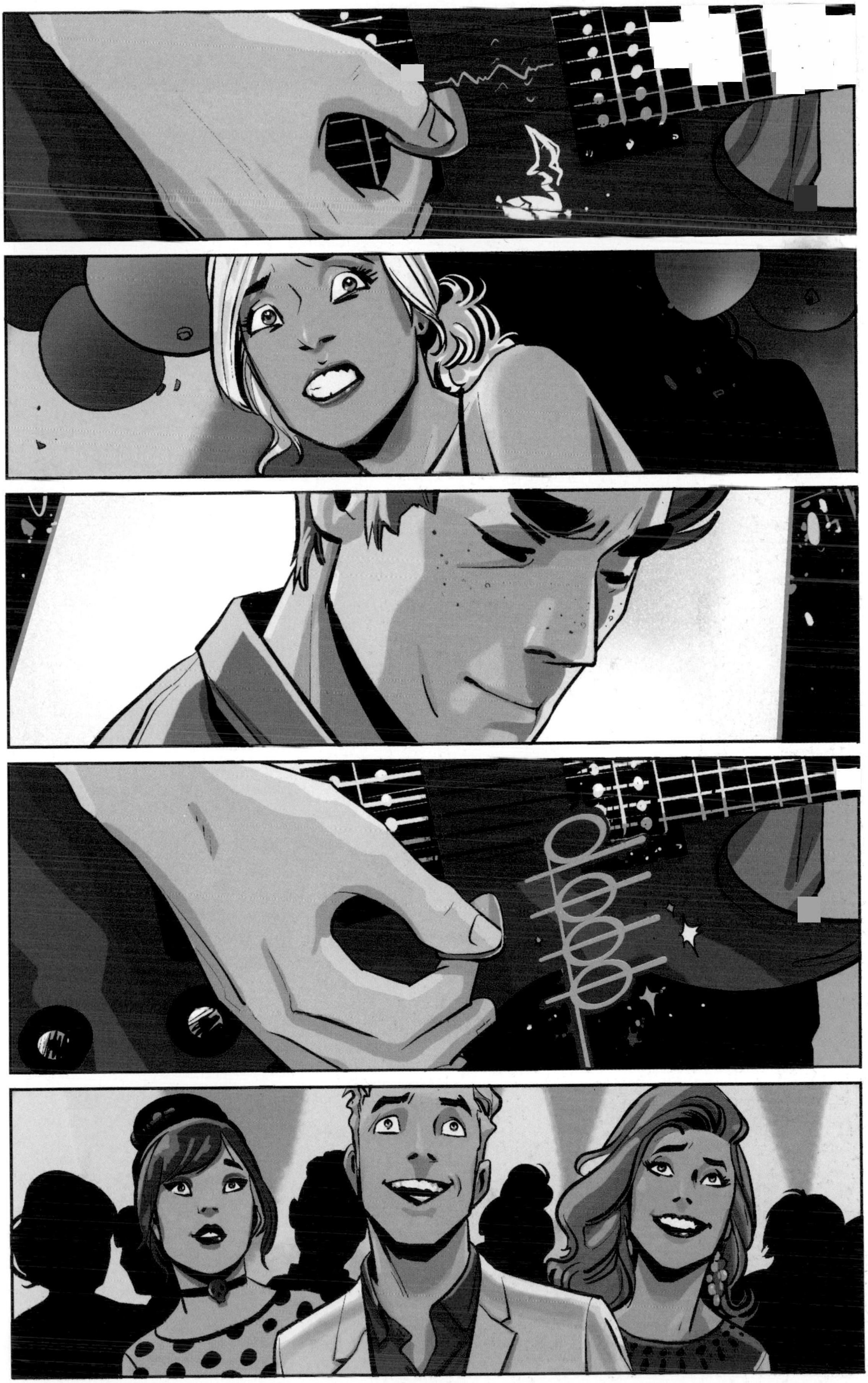

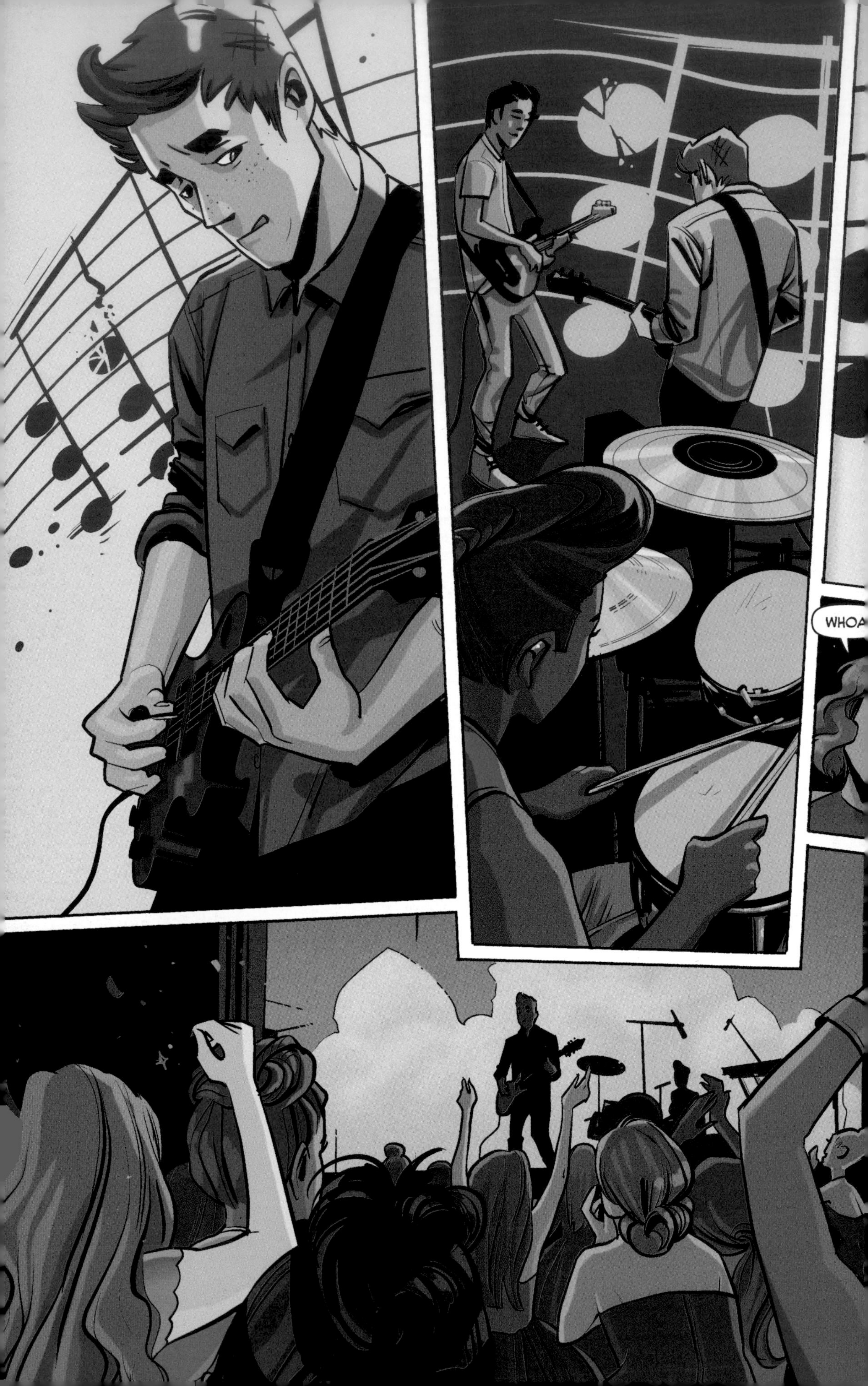
WHOA

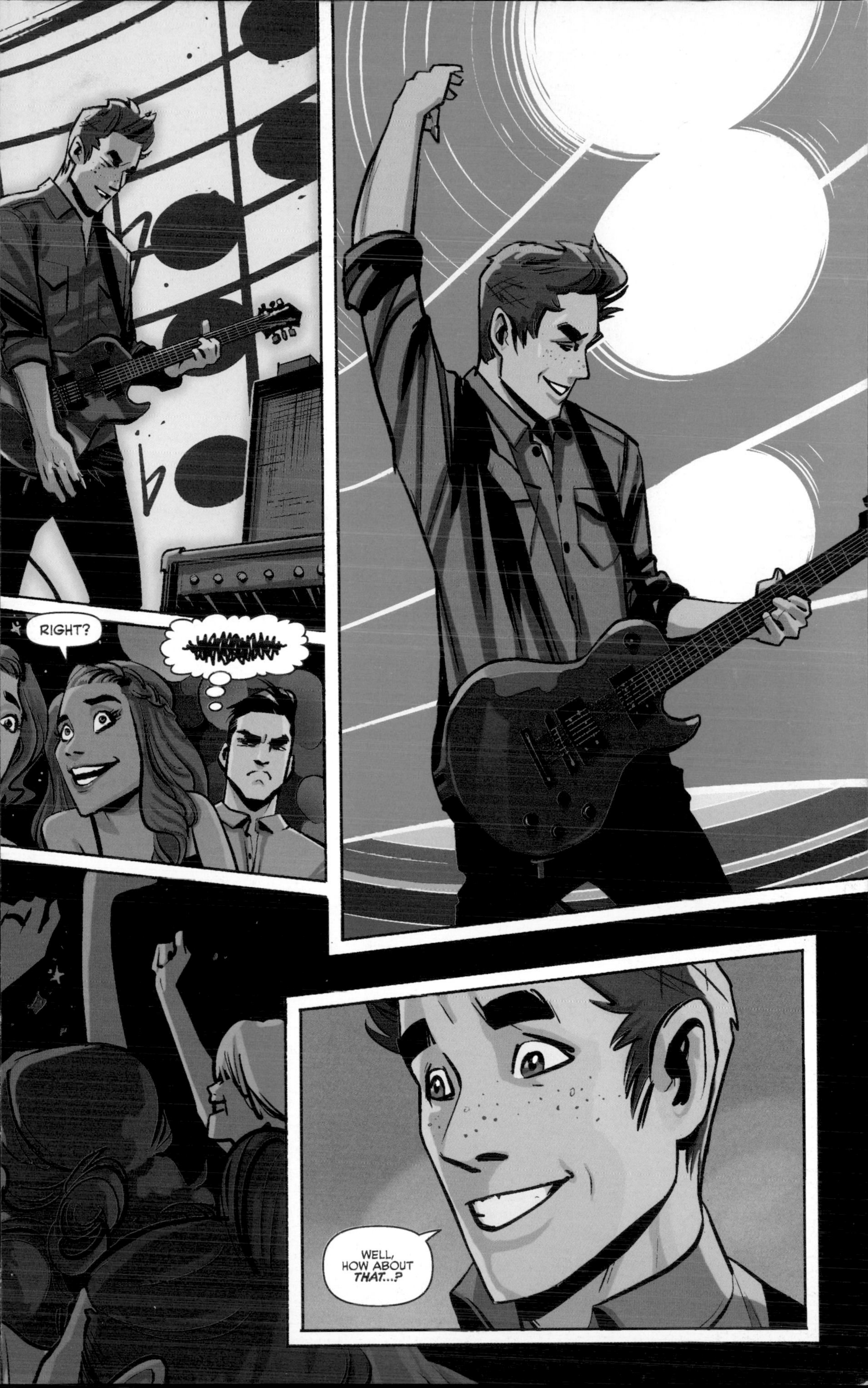
RIGHT?
WELL, HOW ABOUT THAT...?

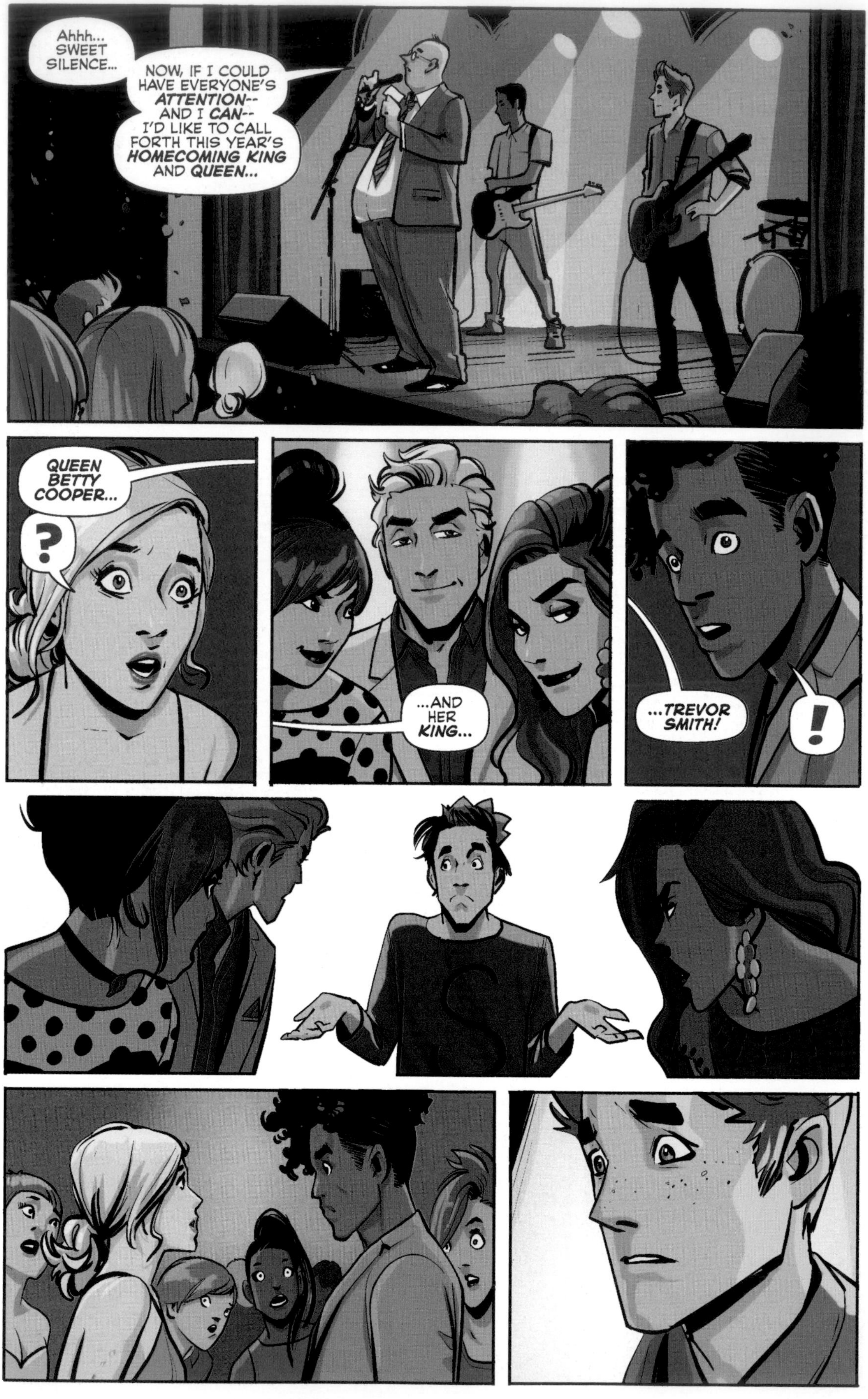
Ahhh... SWEET SILENCE...
NOW, IF I COULD HAVE EVERYONE'S ***ATTENTION***-- AND I ***CAN***-- I'D LIKE TO CALL FORTH THIS YEAR'S ***HOMECOMING KING*** AND ***QUEEN***...
QUEEN BETTY COOPER...
?
...AND HER ***KING***...
...***TREVOR SMITH!***
!

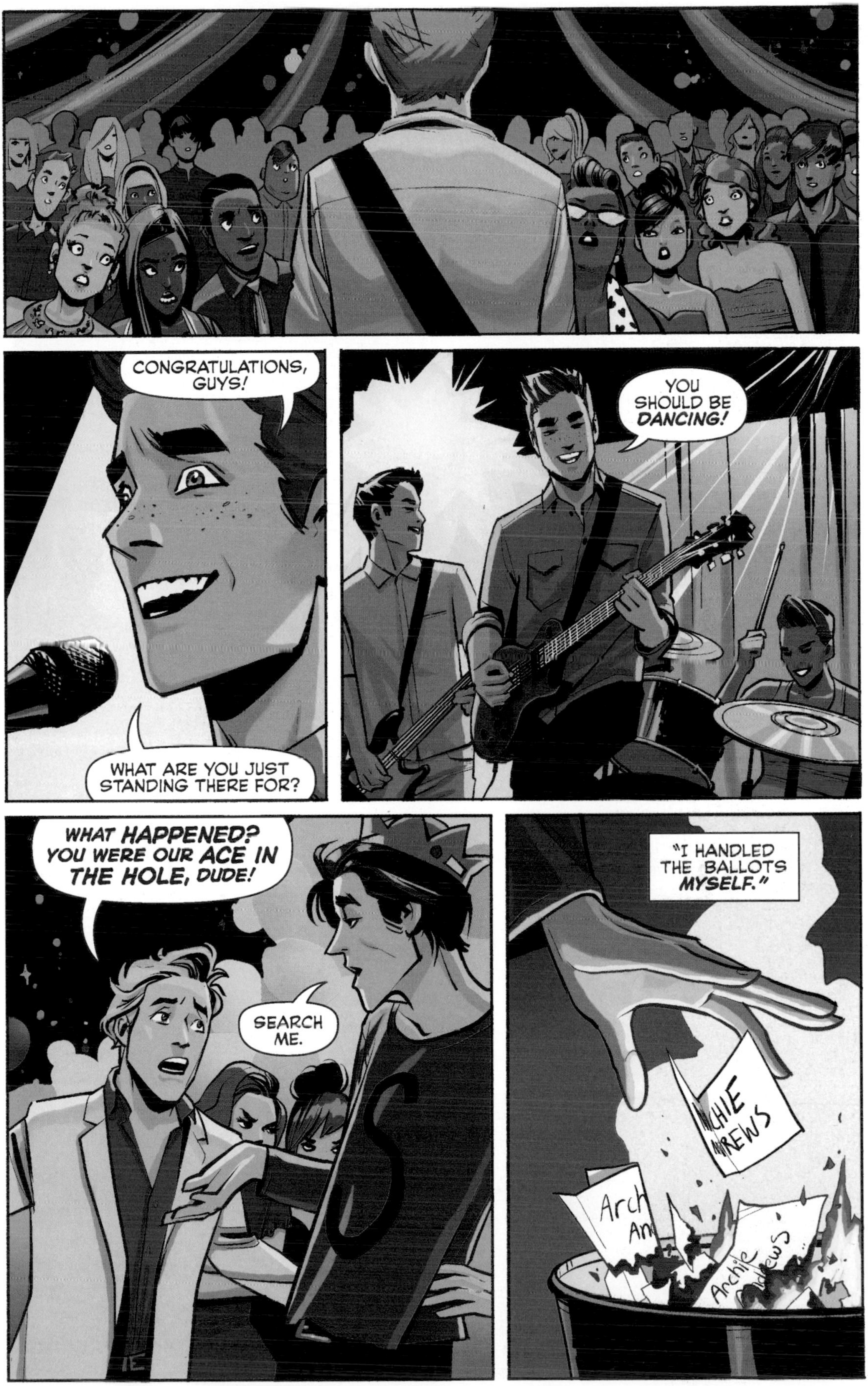
CONGRATULATIONS, GUYS!
WHAT ARE YOU JUST STANDING THERE FOR?
YOU SHOULD BE DANCING!
WHAT HAPPENED? YOU WERE OUR ACE IN THE HOLE, DUDE!
SEARCH ME.
"I HANDLED THE BALLOTS MYSELF."

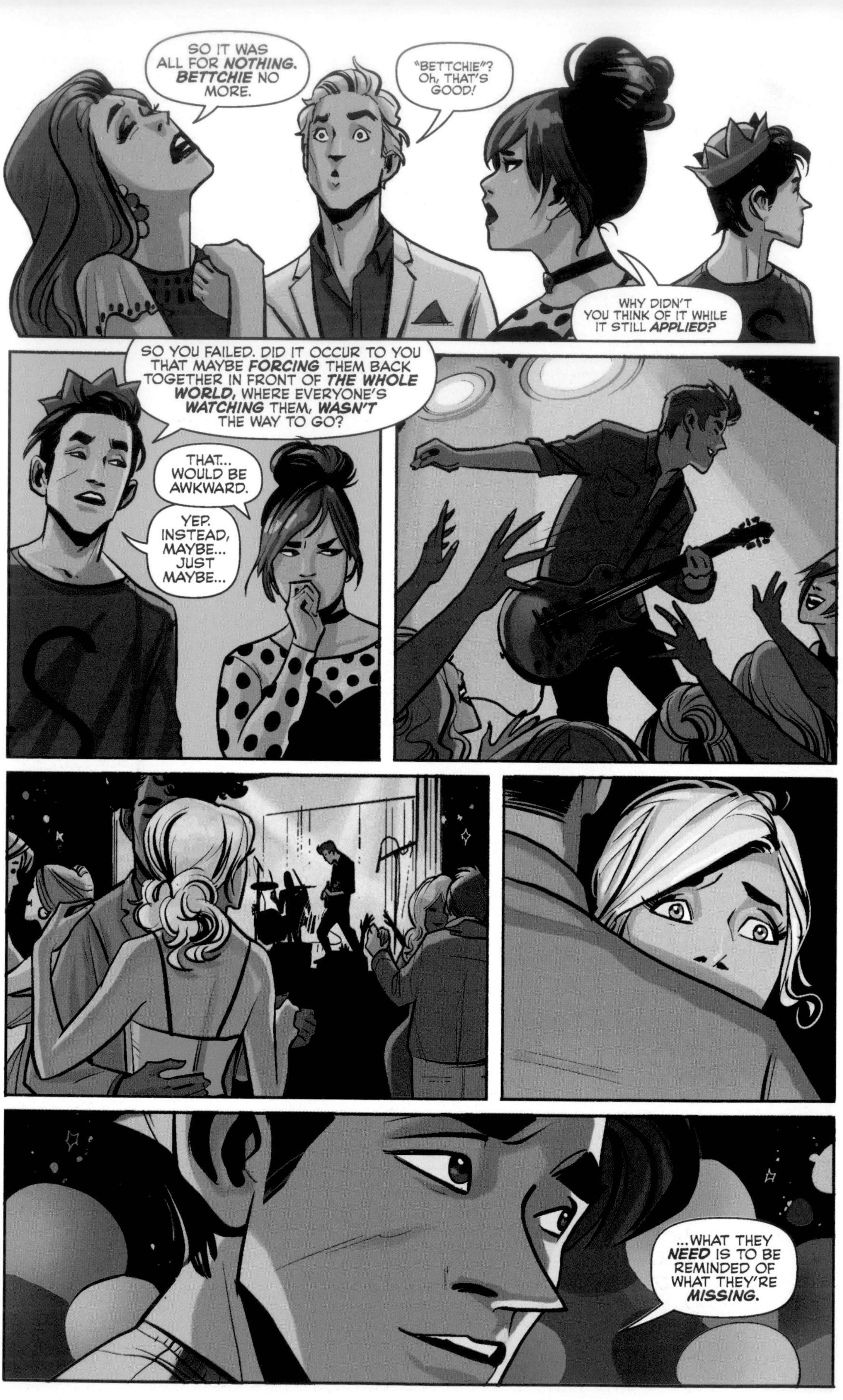
SO IT WAS ALL FOR NOTHING. BETTCHIE NO MORE.
"BETTCHIE"? Oh, THAT'S GOOD!
WHY DIDN'T YOU THINK OF IT WHILE IT STILL APPLIED?
SO YOU FAILED. DID IT OCCUR TO YOU THAT MAYBE FORCING THEM BACK TOGETHER IN FRONT OF THE WHOLE WORLD, WHERE EVERYONE'S WATCHING THEM, WASN'T THE WAY TO GO?
THAT... WOULD BE AWKWARD.
YEP. INSTEAD, MAYBE... JUST MAYBE...
...WHAT THEY NEED IS TO BE REMINDED OF WHAT THEY'RE MISSING.

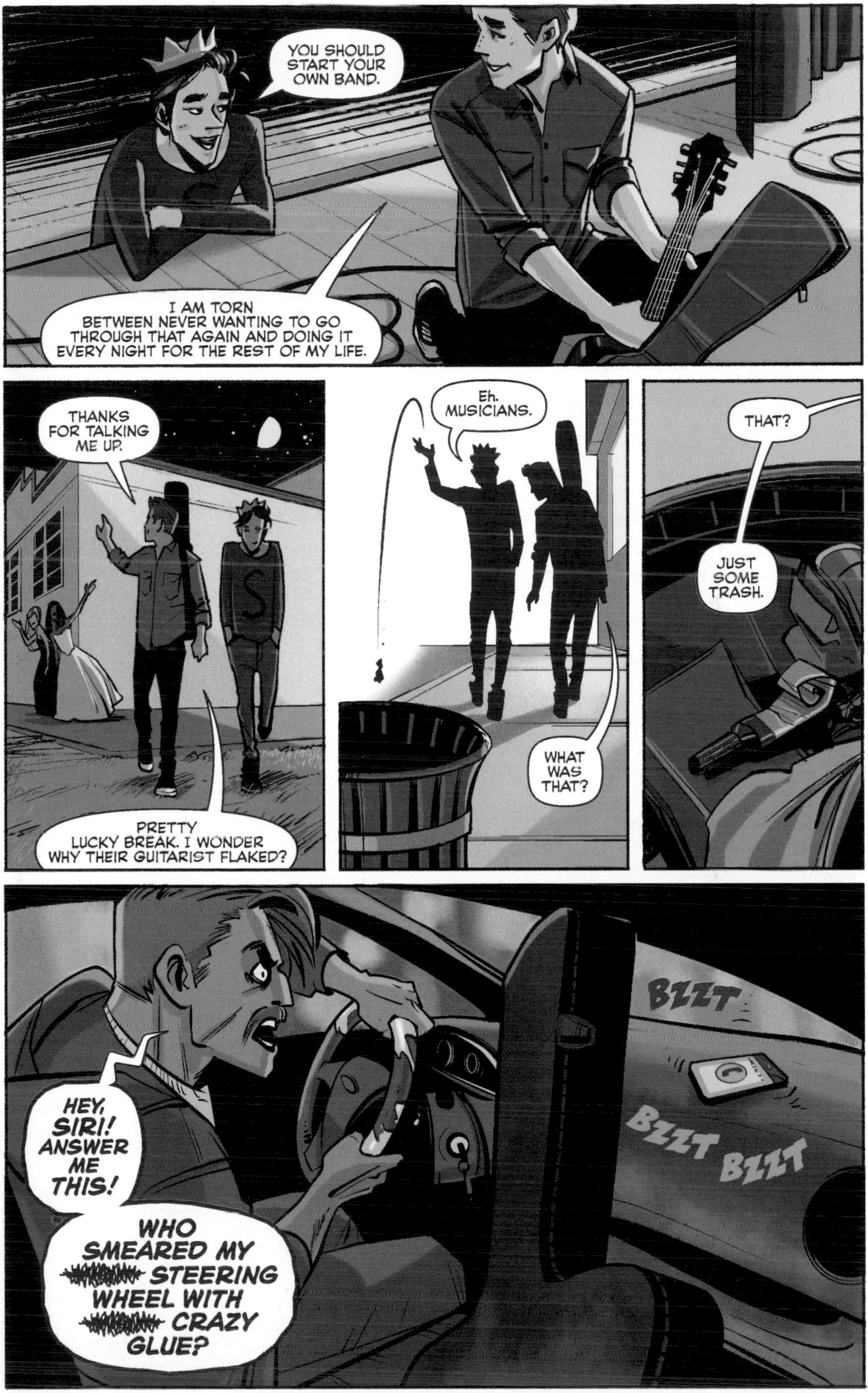
YOU SHOULD START YOUR OWN BAND.
I AM TORN BETWEEN NEVER WANTING TO GO THROUGH THAT AGAIN AND DOING IT EVERY NIGHT FOR THE REST OF MY LIFE.
THANKS FOR TALKING ME UP.
PRETTY LUCKY BREAK. I WONDER WHY THEIR GUITARIST FLAKED?
Eh. MUSICIANS.
WHAT WAS THAT?
THAT?
JUST SOME TRASH.
BZZT
HEY, SIRI! ANSWER ME THIS!
WHO SMEARED MY [censored] STEERING WHEEL WITH [censored] CRAZY GLUE?
BZZT BZZT

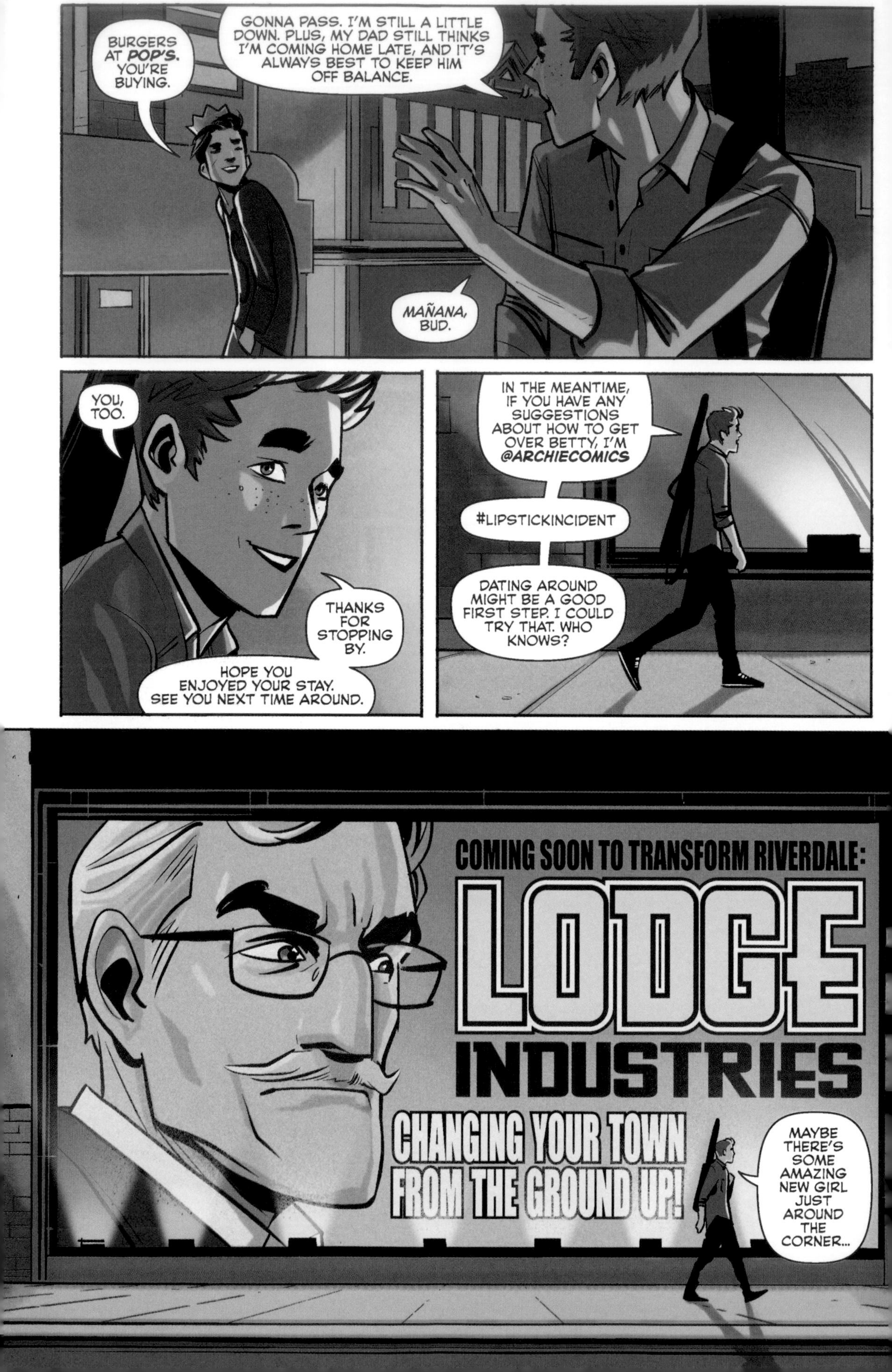
BURGERS AT POP'S. YOU'RE BUYING.
GONNA PASS. I'M STILL A LITTLE DOWN. PLUS, MY DAD STILL THINKS I'M COMING HOME LATE, AND IT'S ALWAYS BEST TO KEEP HIM OFF BALANCE.
MAÑANA, BUD.
YOU, TOO.
THANKS FOR STOPPING BY.
HOPE YOU ENJOYED YOUR STAY. SEE YOU NEXT TIME AROUND.
IN THE MEANTIME, IF YOU HAVE ANY SUGGESTIONS ABOUT HOW TO GET OVER BETTY, I'M @ARCHIECOMICS
#LIPSTICKINCIDENT
DATING AROUND MIGHT BE A GOOD FIRST STEP. I COULD TRY THAT. WHO KNOWS?
COMING SOON TO TRANSFORM RIVERDALE:
LODGE INDUSTRIES
CHANGING YOUR TOWN FROM THE GROUND UP!
MAYBE THERE'S SOME AMAZING NEW GIRL JUST AROUND THE CORNER...

After the hugely successful relaunch of *Archie*, it only made sense that his best friend get the same treatment.

Just a few months later *Jughead* re-emerged from a three-year long hiatus with an all-new #1 from the hilarious and entertaining team of writer Chip Zdarsky and artist Erica Henderson. The *Jughead* series modernizes the humor that people have come to associate with and love about Archie's burger-loving best friend, while also cultivating room for him to grow and develop as a person.

The series is full of big belly-laughs and comical situations, but still manages to make some important points and further develop Jughead's role within his group of friends.

STORY BY
CHIP ZDARSKY

ART BY
ERICA HENDERSON

LETTERING BY
JACK MORELLI

ROAD TO

RIVERDALE®

JUGHEAD

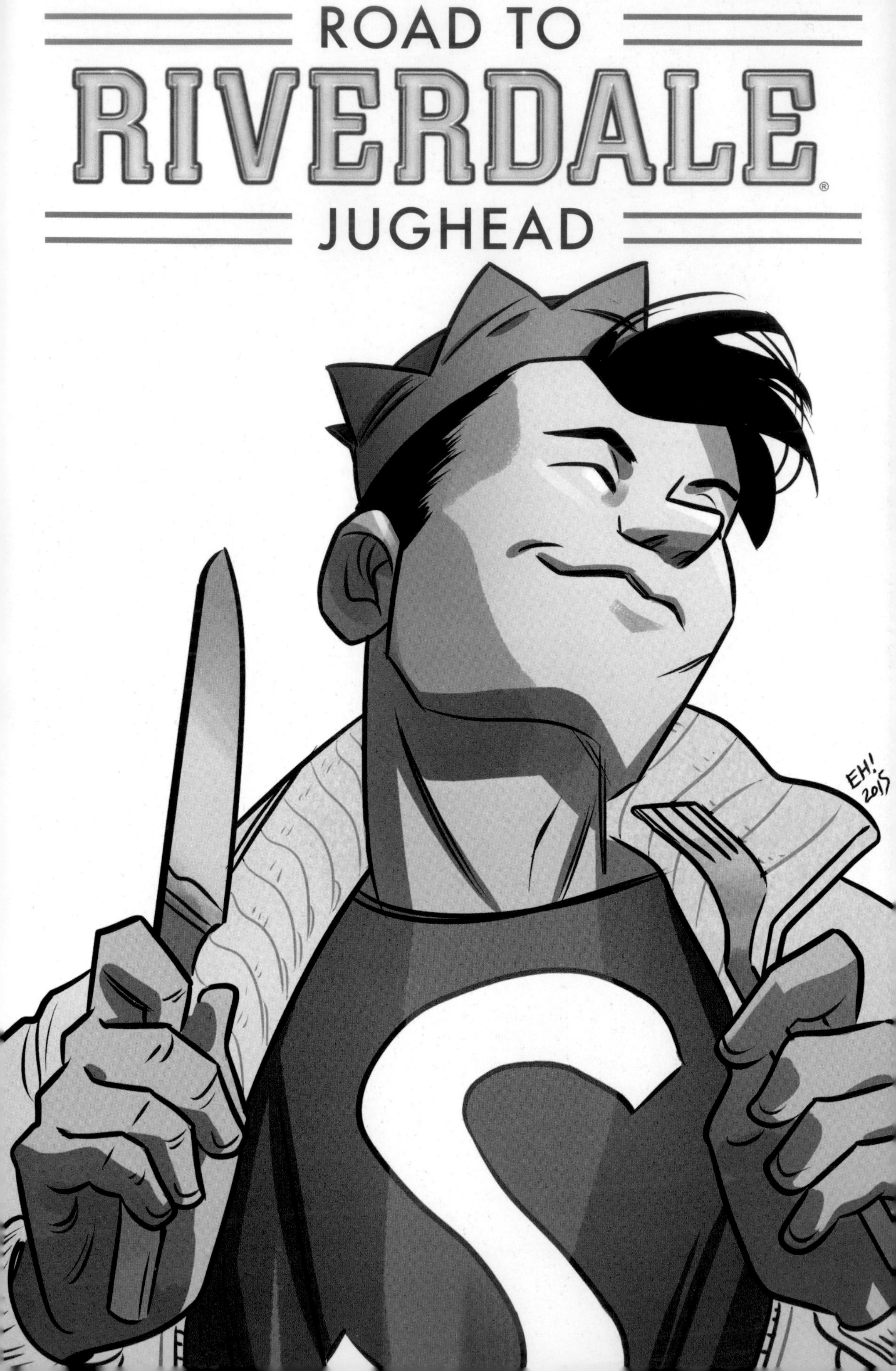
EH! 2015

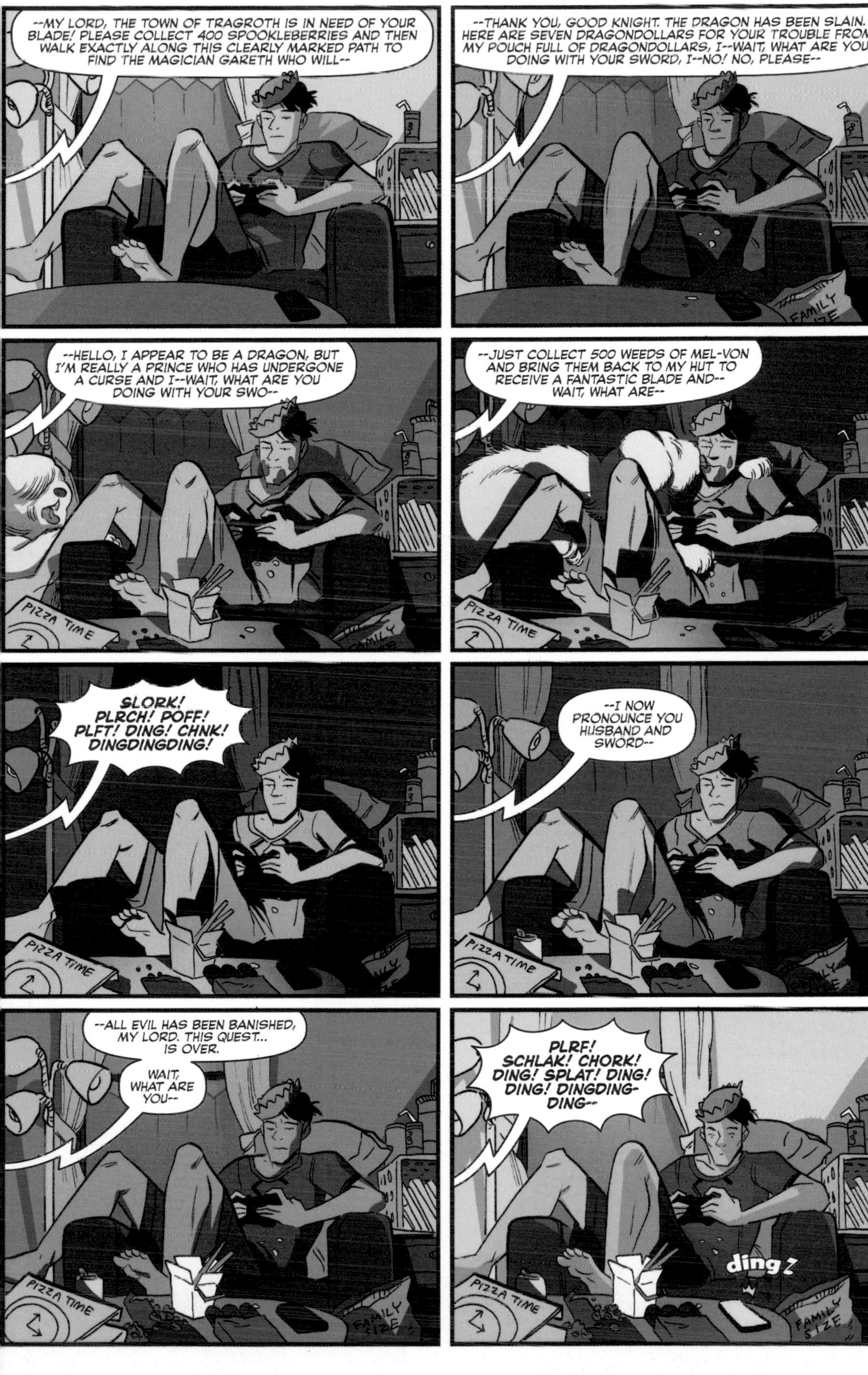
--MY LORD, THE TOWN OF TRAGROTH IS IN NEED OF YOUR BLADE! PLEASE COLLECT 400 SPOOKLEBERRIES AND THEN WALK EXACTLY ALONG THIS CLEARLY MARKED PATH TO FIND THE MAGICIAN GARETH WHO WILL--
--THANK YOU, GOOD KNIGHT. THE DRAGON HAS BEEN SLAIN. HERE ARE SEVEN DRAGONDOLLARS FOR YOUR TROUBLE FROM MY POUCH FULL OF DRAGONDOLLARS, I--WAIT, WHAT ARE YOU DOING WITH YOUR SWORD, I--NO! NO, PLEASE--
FAMILY SIZE
--HELLO, I APPEAR TO BE A DRAGON, BUT I'M REALLY A PRINCE WHO HAS UNDERGONE A CURSE AND I--WAIT, WHAT ARE YOU DOING WITH YOUR SWO--
PIZZA TIME
--JUST COLLECT 500 WEEDS OF MEL-VON AND BRING THEM BACK TO MY HUT TO RECEIVE A FANTASTIC BLADE AND-- WAIT, WHAT ARE--
PIZZA TIME
SLORK! PLRCH! POFF! PLFT! DING! CHNK! DINGDINGDING!
PIZZA TIME
--I NOW PRONOUNCE YOU HUSBAND AND SWORD--
PIZZA TIME
--ALL EVIL HAS BEEN BANISHED, MY LORD. THIS QUEST... IS OVER.
WAIT, WHAT ARE YOU--
PIZZA TIME
FAMILY SIZE
PLRF! SCHLAK! CHORK! DING! SPLAT! DING! DING! DINGDING-DING--
ding
PIZZA TIME
FAMILY SIZE

ARCHIE COMICS PROUDLY PRESENTS

JUGHEAD

LOVINGLY BROUGHT TO YOU BY CHIP & ERICA

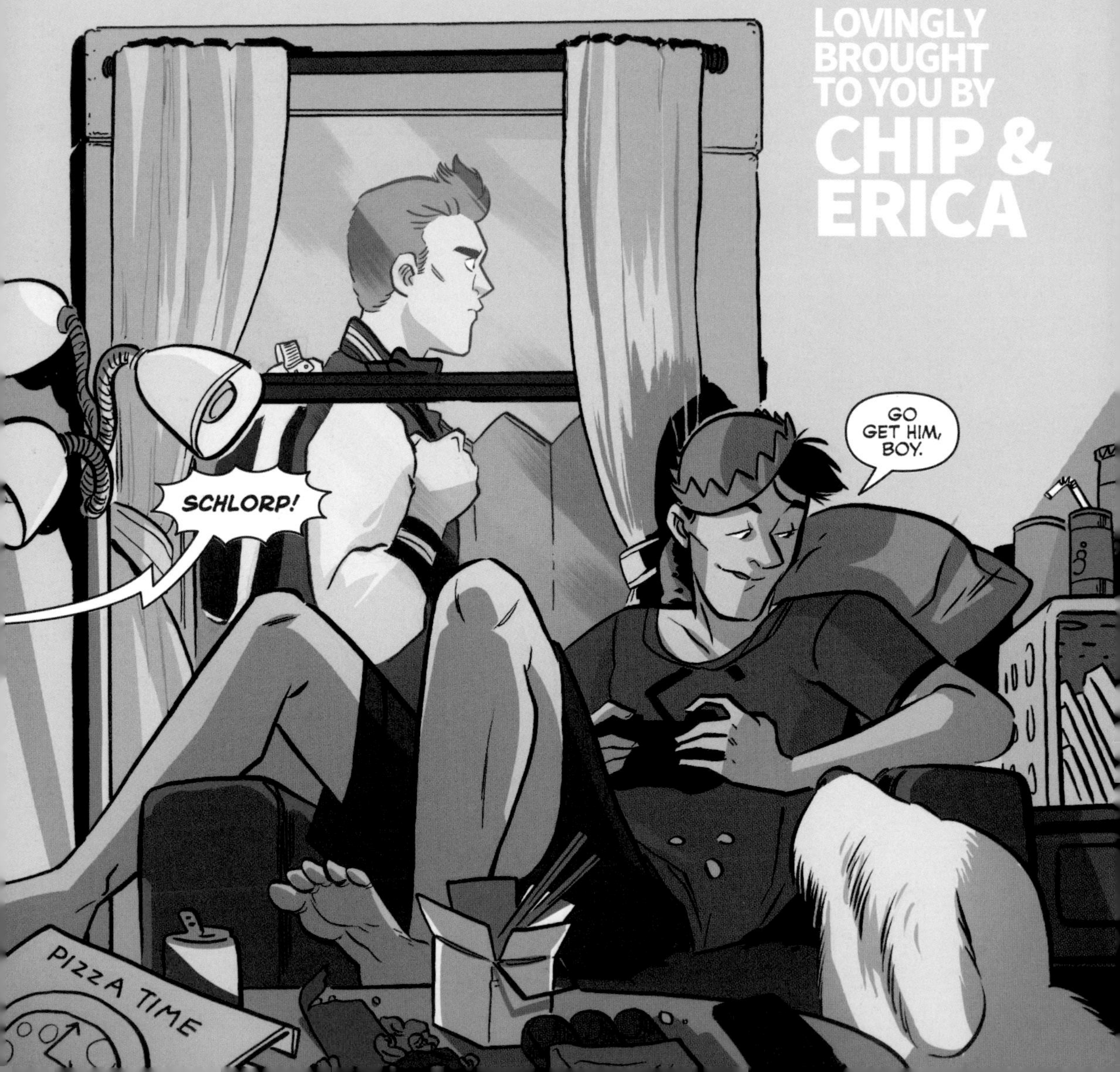
SCHLORP!
GO GET HIM, BOY.
PIZZA TIME

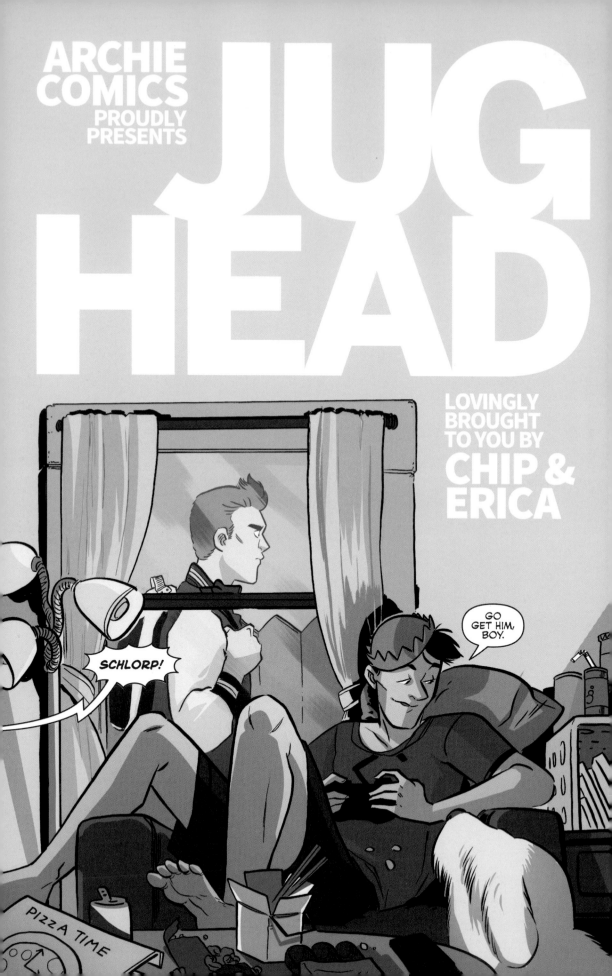

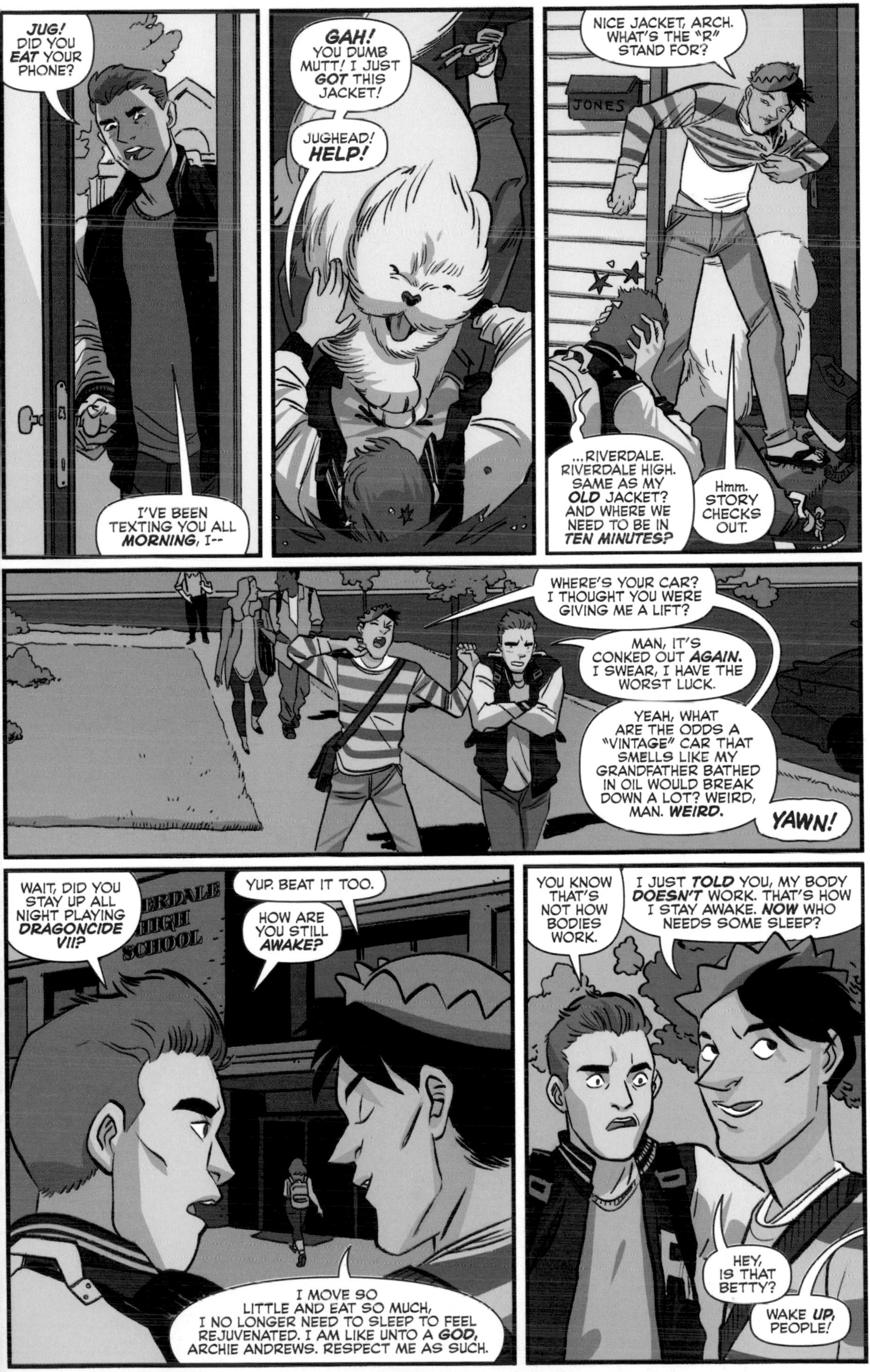

JUG! DID YOU EAT YOUR PHONE?
I'VE BEEN TEXTING YOU ALL MORNING, I--
GAH! YOU DUMB MUTT! I JUST GOT THIS JACKET!
JUGHEAD! HELP!
JONES
NICE JACKET, ARCH. WHAT'S THE "R" STAND FOR?
...RIVERDALE. RIVERDALE HIGH. SAME AS MY OLD JACKET? AND WHERE WE NEED TO BE IN TEN MINUTES?
Hmm. STORY CHECKS OUT.
WHERE'S YOUR CAR? I THOUGHT YOU WERE GIVING ME A LIFT?
MAN, IT'S CONKED OUT AGAIN. I SWEAR, I HAVE THE WORST LUCK.
YEAH, WHAT ARE THE ODDS A "VINTAGE" CAR THAT SMELLS LIKE MY GRANDFATHER BATHED IN OIL WOULD BREAK DOWN A LOT? WEIRD, MAN. WEIRD.
YAWN!
WAIT, DID YOU STAY UP ALL NIGHT PLAYING DRAGONCIDE VII?
YUP. BEAT IT TOO.
HOW ARE YOU STILL AWAKE?
I MOVE SO LITTLE AND EAT SO MUCH, I NO LONGER NEED TO SLEEP TO FEEL REJUVENATED. I AM LIKE UNTO A GOD, ARCHIE ANDREWS. RESPECT ME AS SUCH.
YOU KNOW THAT'S NOT HOW BODIES WORK.
I JUST TOLD YOU, MY BODY DOESN'T WORK. THAT'S HOW I STAY AWAKE. NOW WHO NEEDS SOME SLEEP?
HEY, IS THAT BETTY?
WAKE UP, PEOPLE!

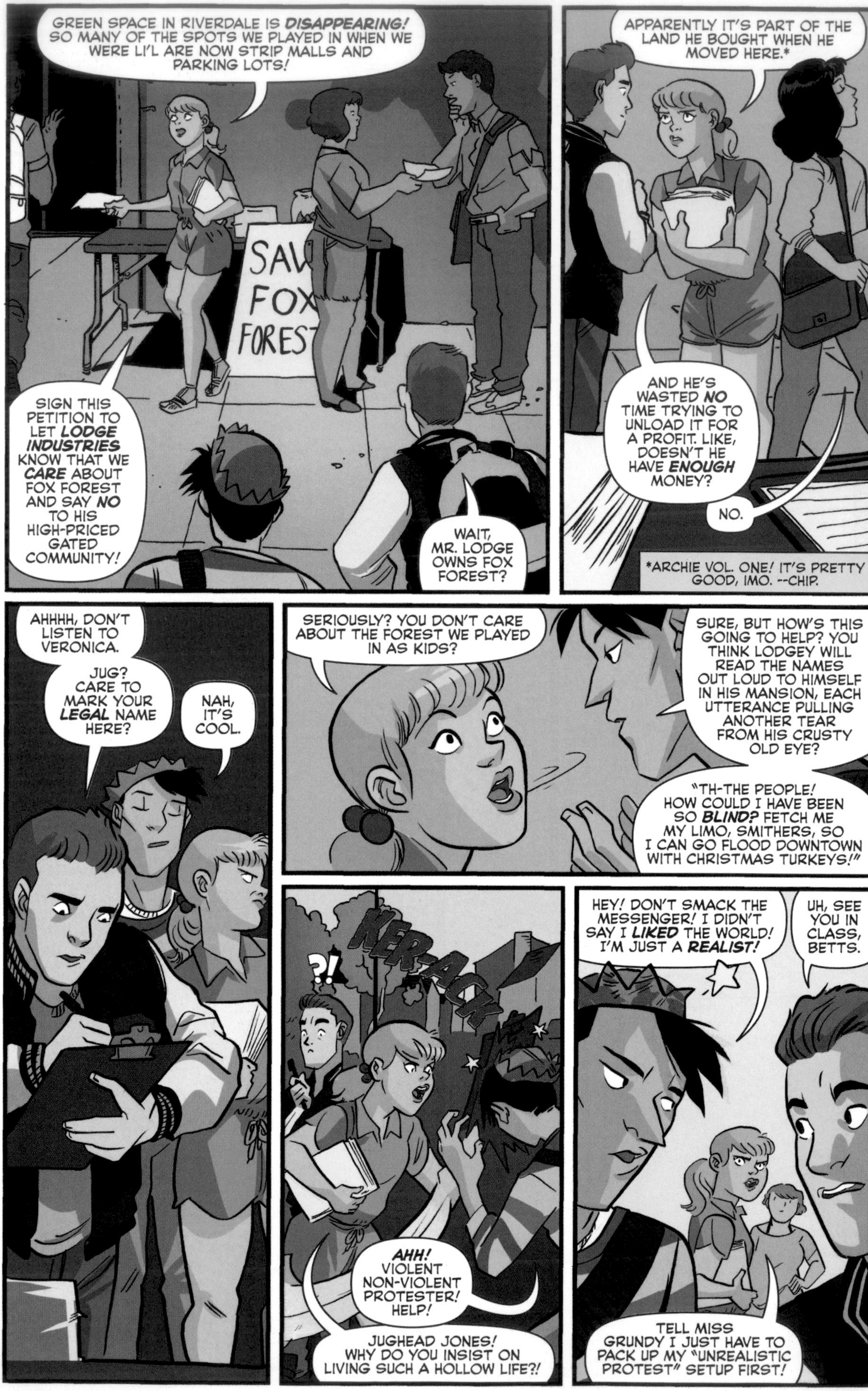
GREEN SPACE IN RIVERDALE IS *DISAPPEARING!* SO MANY OF THE SPOTS WE PLAYED IN WHEN WE WERE LI'L ARE NOW STRIP MALLS AND PARKING LOTS!
SAVE FOX FOREST
SIGN THIS PETITION TO LET *LODGE INDUSTRIES* KNOW THAT WE *CARE* ABOUT FOX FOREST AND SAY *NO* TO HIS HIGH-PRICED GATED COMMUNITY!
WAIT, MR. LODGE OWNS FOX FOREST?
APPARENTLY IT'S PART OF THE LAND HE BOUGHT WHEN HE MOVED HERE.*
AND HE'S WASTED *NO* TIME TRYING TO UNLOAD IT FOR A PROFIT. LIKE, DOESN'T HE HAVE *ENOUGH* MONEY?
NO.
*ARCHIE VOL. ONE! IT'S PRETTY GOOD, IMO. --CHIP.
AHHHH, DON'T LISTEN TO VERONICA.
JUG? CARE TO MARK YOUR *LEGAL* NAME HERE?
NAH, IT'S COOL.
SERIOUSLY? YOU DON'T CARE ABOUT THE FOREST WE PLAYED IN AS KIDS?
SURE, BUT HOW'S THIS GOING TO HELP? YOU THINK LODGEY WILL READ THE NAMES OUT LOUD TO HIMSELF IN HIS MANSION, EACH UTTERANCE PULLING ANOTHER TEAR FROM HIS CRUSTY OLD EYE?
"TH-THE PEOPLE! HOW COULD I HAVE BEEN SO *BLIND?* FETCH ME MY LIMO, SMITHERS, SO I CAN GO FLOOD DOWNTOWN WITH CHRISTMAS TURKEYS!"
KER-ACK
?!
AHH! VIOLENT NON-VIOLENT PROTESTER! HELP!
JUGHEAD JONES! WHY DO YOU INSIST ON LIVING SUCH A HOLLOW LIFE?!
HEY! DON'T SMACK THE MESSENGER! I DIDN'T SAY I *LIKED* THE WORLD! I'M JUST A *REALIST!*
UH, SEE YOU IN CLASS, BETTS.
TELL MISS GRUNDY I JUST HAVE TO PACK UP MY "UNREALISTIC PROTEST" SETUP FIRST!

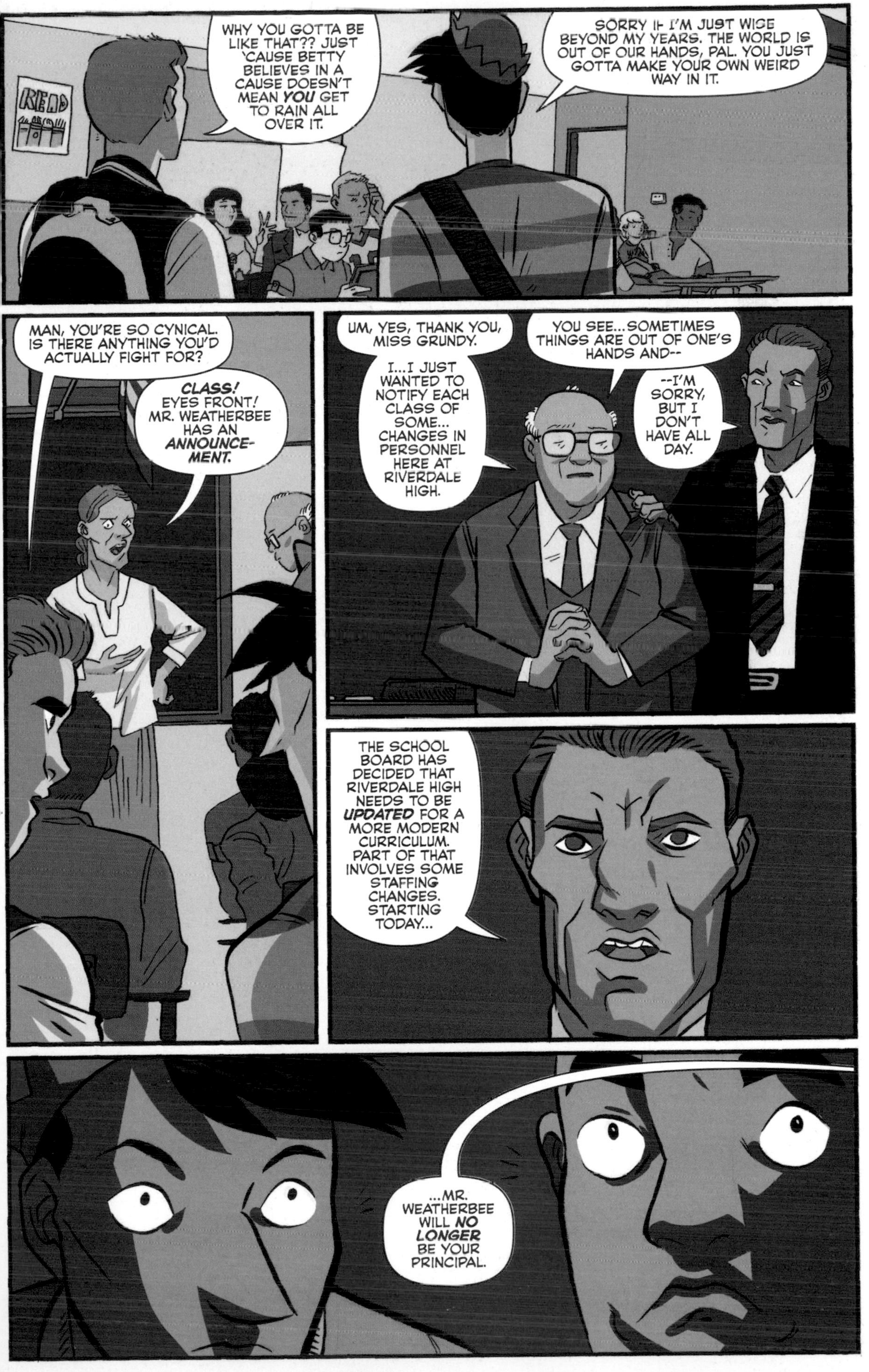

WHY YOU GOTTA BE LIKE THAT?? JUST 'CAUSE BETTY BELIEVES IN A CAUSE DOESN'T MEAN YOU GET TO RAIN ALL OVER IT.
SORRY IF I'M JUST WISE BEYOND MY YEARS. THE WORLD IS OUT OF OUR HANDS, PAL. YOU JUST GOTTA MAKE YOUR OWN WEIRD WAY IN IT.
READ
MAN, YOU'RE SO CYNICAL. IS THERE ANYTHING YOU'D ACTUALLY FIGHT FOR?
CLASS! EYES FRONT! MR. WEATHERBEE HAS AN ANNOUNCEMENT.
UM, YES, THANK YOU, MISS GRUNDY.
I...I JUST WANTED TO NOTIFY EACH CLASS OF SOME... CHANGES IN PERSONNEL HERE AT RIVERDALE HIGH.
YOU SEE...SOMETIMES THINGS ARE OUT OF ONE'S HANDS AND--
--I'M SORRY, BUT I DON'T HAVE ALL DAY.
THE SCHOOL BOARD HAS DECIDED THAT RIVERDALE HIGH NEEDS TO BE UPDATED FOR A MORE MODERN CURRICULUM. PART OF THAT INVOLVES SOME STAFFING CHANGES. STARTING TODAY...
...MR. WEATHERBEE WILL NO LONGER BE YOUR PRINCIPAL.

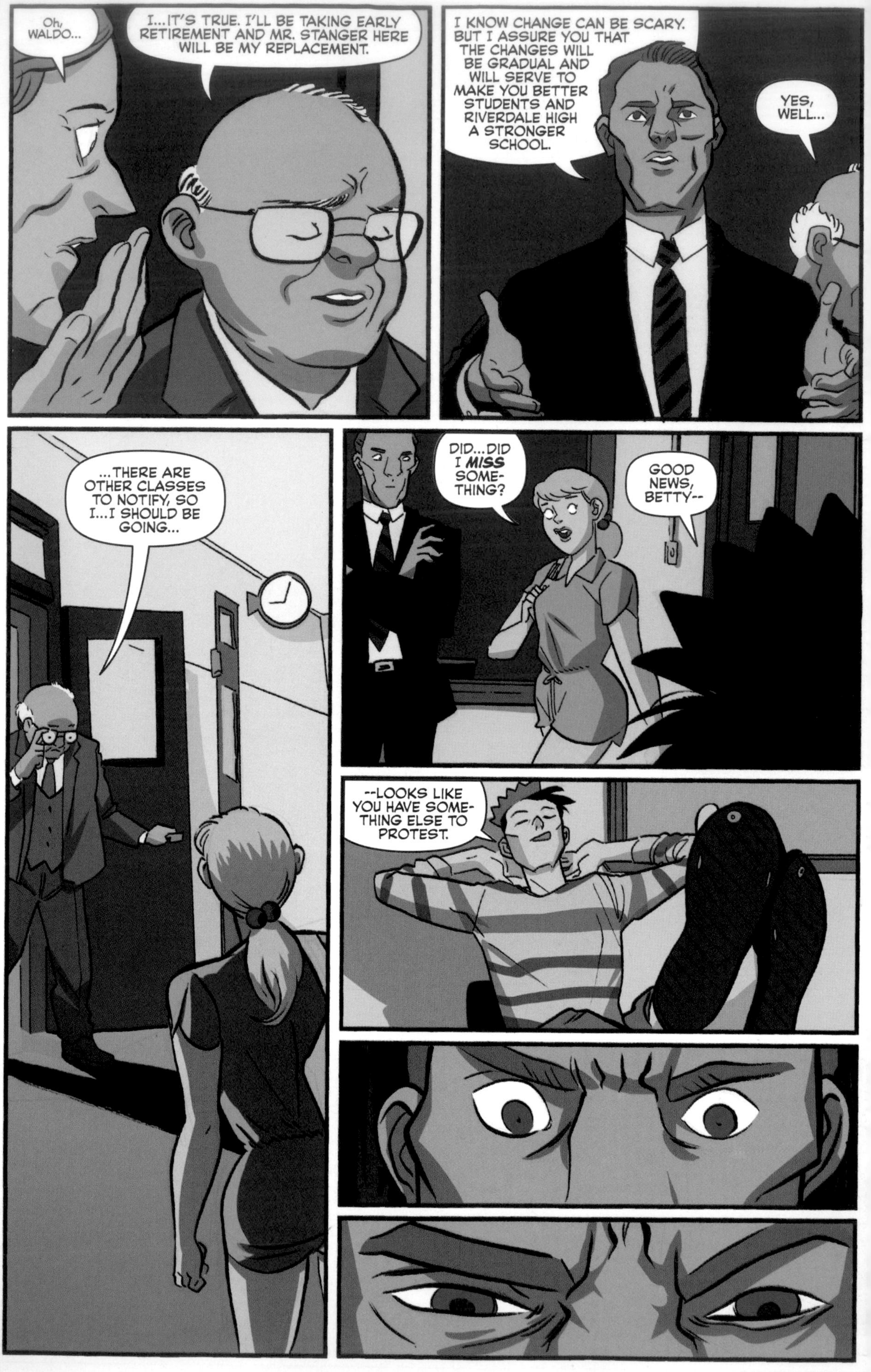
Oh, WALDO...
I...IT'S TRUE. I'LL BE TAKING EARLY RETIREMENT AND MR. STANGER HERE WILL BE MY REPLACEMENT.
I KNOW CHANGE CAN BE SCARY. BUT I ASSURE YOU THAT THE CHANGES WILL BE GRADUAL AND WILL SERVE TO MAKE YOU BETTER STUDENTS AND RIVERDALE HIGH A STRONGER SCHOOL.
YES, WELL...
...THERE ARE OTHER CLASSES TO NOTIFY, SO I...I SHOULD BE GOING...
DID...DID I MISS SOME-THING?
GOOD NEWS, BETTY--
--LOOKS LIKE YOU HAVE SOME-THING ELSE TO PROTEST.

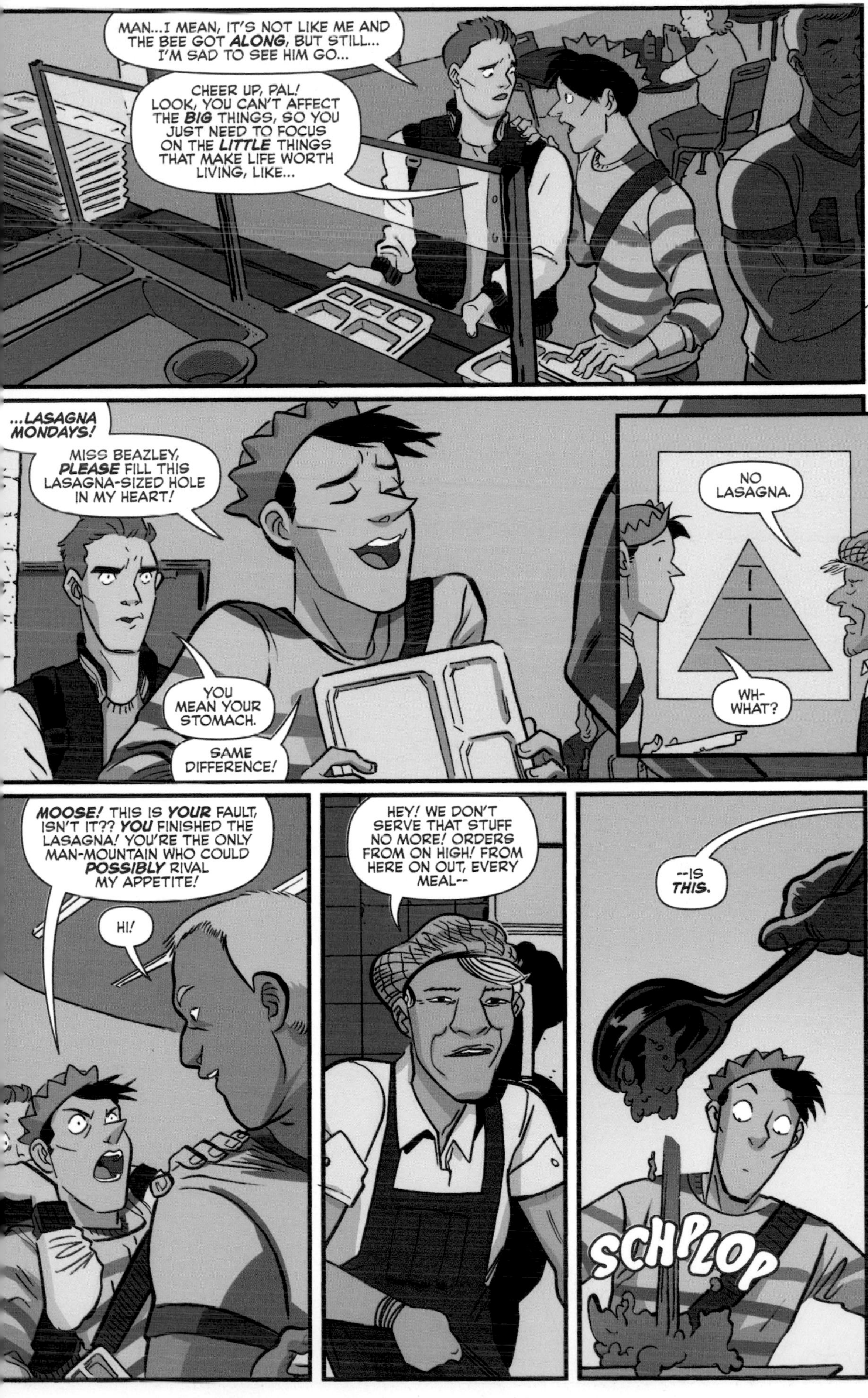
MAN...I MEAN, IT'S NOT LIKE ME AND THE BEE GOT ALONG, BUT STILL... I'M SAD TO SEE HIM GO...
CHEER UP, PAL! LOOK, YOU CAN'T AFFECT THE BIG THINGS, SO YOU JUST NEED TO FOCUS ON THE LITTLE THINGS THAT MAKE LIFE WORTH LIVING, LIKE...
...LASAGNA MONDAYS!
MISS BEAZLEY, PLEASE FILL THIS LASAGNA-SIZED HOLE IN MY HEART!
YOU MEAN YOUR STOMACH.
SAME DIFFERENCE!
NO LASAGNA.
WH-WHAT?
MOOSE! THIS IS YOUR FAULT, ISN'T IT?? YOU FINISHED THE LASAGNA! YOU'RE THE ONLY MAN-MOUNTAIN WHO COULD POSSIBLY RIVAL MY APPETITE!
HI!
HEY! WE DON'T SERVE THAT STUFF NO MORE! ORDERS FROM ON HIGH! FROM HERE ON OUT, EVERY MEAL--
--IS THIS.
SCHPLOP

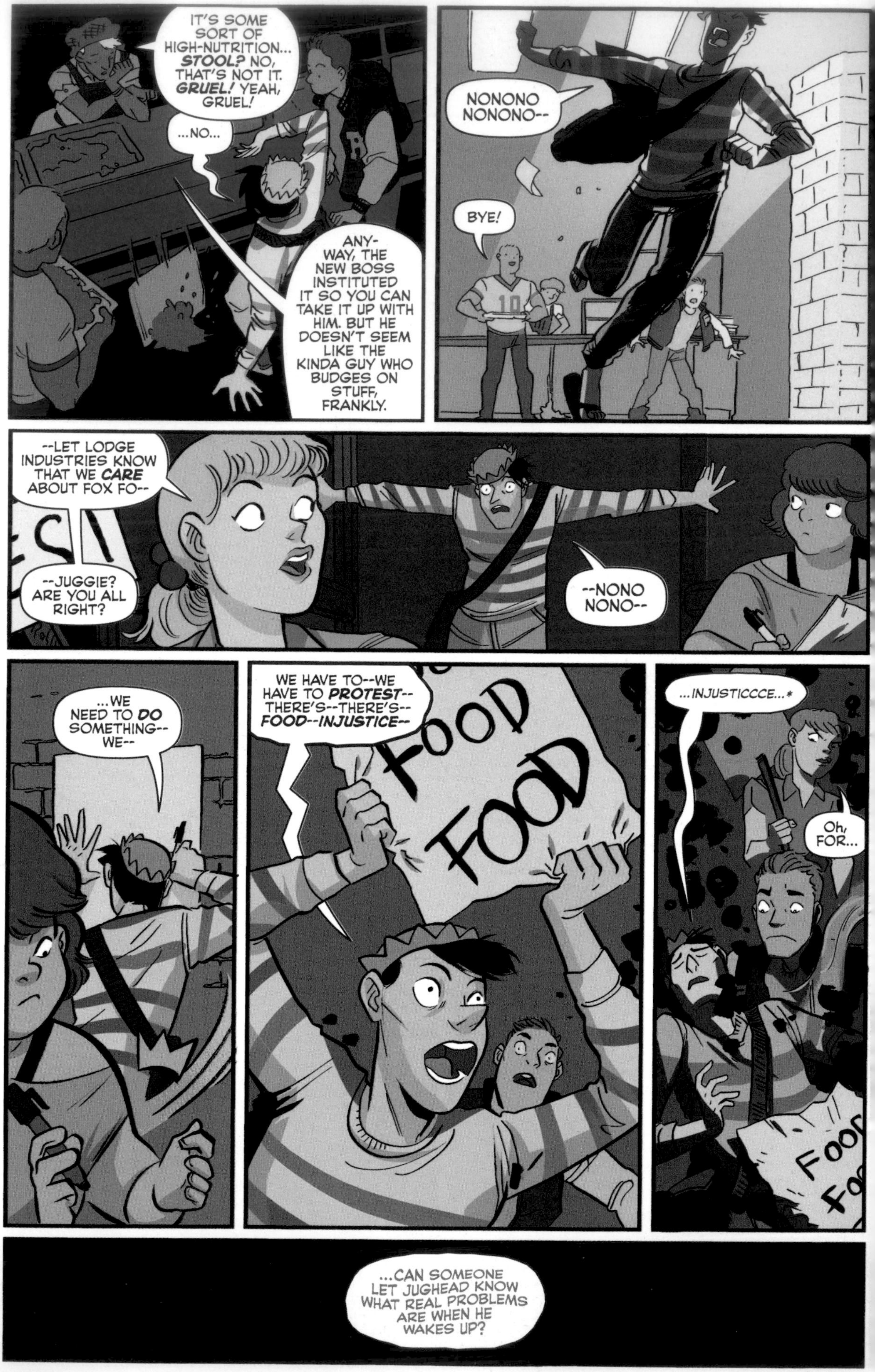
IT'S SOME SORT OF HIGH-NUTRITION... STOOL? NO, THAT'S NOT IT. GRUEL! YEAH, GRUEL!
...NO...
ANY-WAY, THE NEW BOSS INSTITUTED IT SO YOU CAN TAKE IT UP WITH HIM. BUT HE DOESN'T SEEM LIKE THE KINDA GUY WHO BUDGES ON STUFF, FRANKLY.
NONONO NONONO--
BYE!
--LET LODGE INDUSTRIES KNOW THAT WE CARE ABOUT FOX FO--
--JUGGIE? ARE YOU ALL RIGHT?
--NONO NONO--
...WE NEED TO DO SOMETHING-- WE--
WE HAVE TO--WE HAVE TO PROTEST-- THERE'S--THERE'S-- FOOD--INJUSTICE--
FOOD
FOOD
...INJUSTICCCE...*
Oh, FOR...
...CAN SOMEONE LET JUGHEAD KNOW WHAT REAL PROBLEMS ARE WHEN HE WAKES UP?

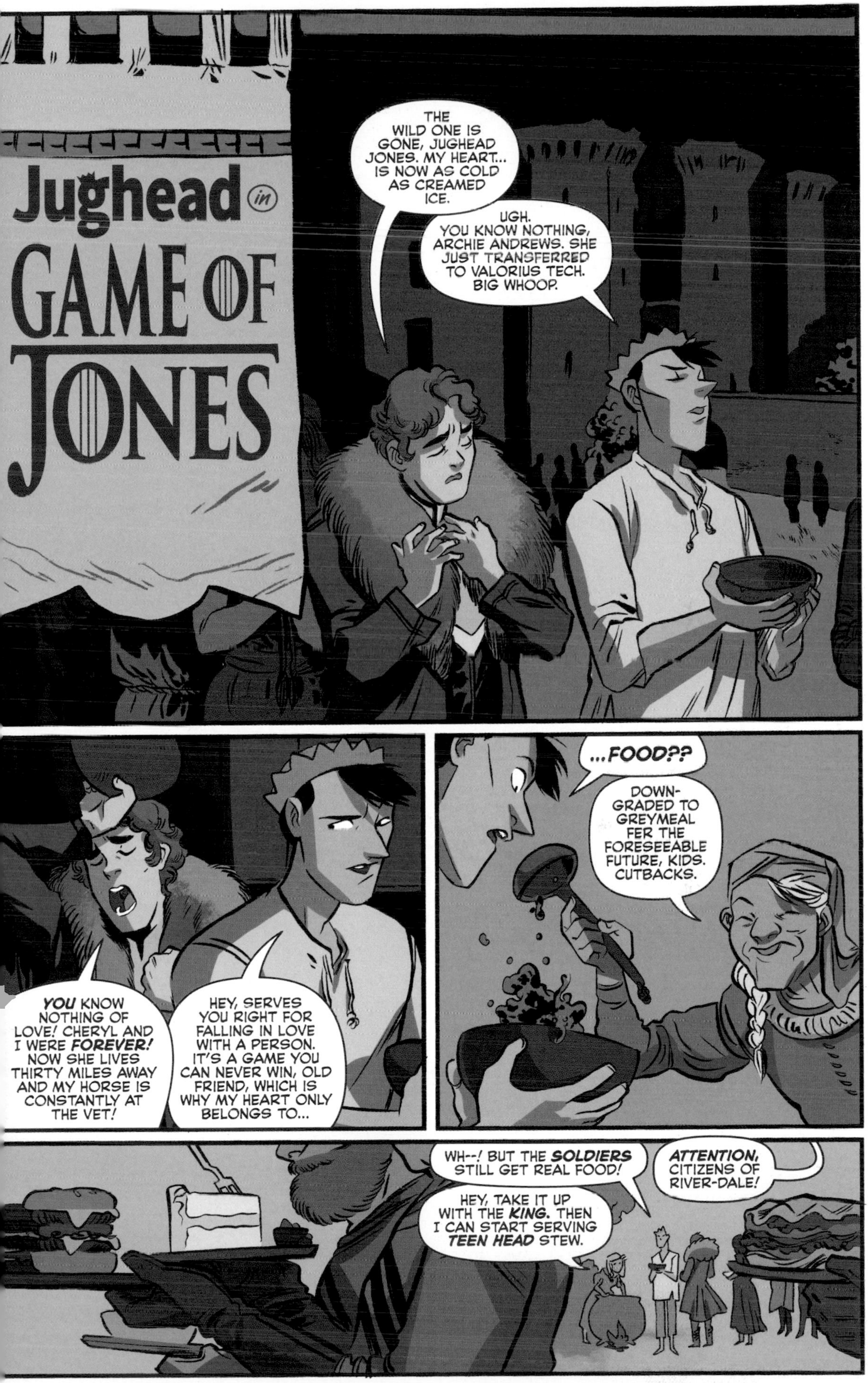
Jughead in
GAME OF JONES
THE WILD ONE IS GONE, JUGHEAD JONES. MY HEART... IS NOW AS COLD AS CREAMED ICE.
UGH. YOU KNOW NOTHING, ARCHIE ANDREWS. SHE JUST TRANSFERRED TO VALORIUS TECH. BIG WHOOP.
YOU KNOW NOTHING OF LOVE! CHERYL AND I WERE FOREVER! NOW SHE LIVES THIRTY MILES AWAY AND MY HORSE IS CONSTANTLY AT THE VET!
HEY, SERVES YOU RIGHT FOR FALLING IN LOVE WITH A PERSON. IT'S A GAME YOU CAN NEVER WIN, OLD FRIEND, WHICH IS WHY MY HEART ONLY BELONGS TO...
...FOOD??
DOWN-GRADED TO GREYMEAL FER THE FORESEEABLE FUTURE, KIDS. CUTBACKS.
WH--! BUT THE SOLDIERS STILL GET REAL FOOD!
HEY, TAKE IT UP WITH THE KING. THEN I CAN START SERVING TEEN HEAD STEW.
ATTENTION, CITIZENS OF RIVER-DALE!

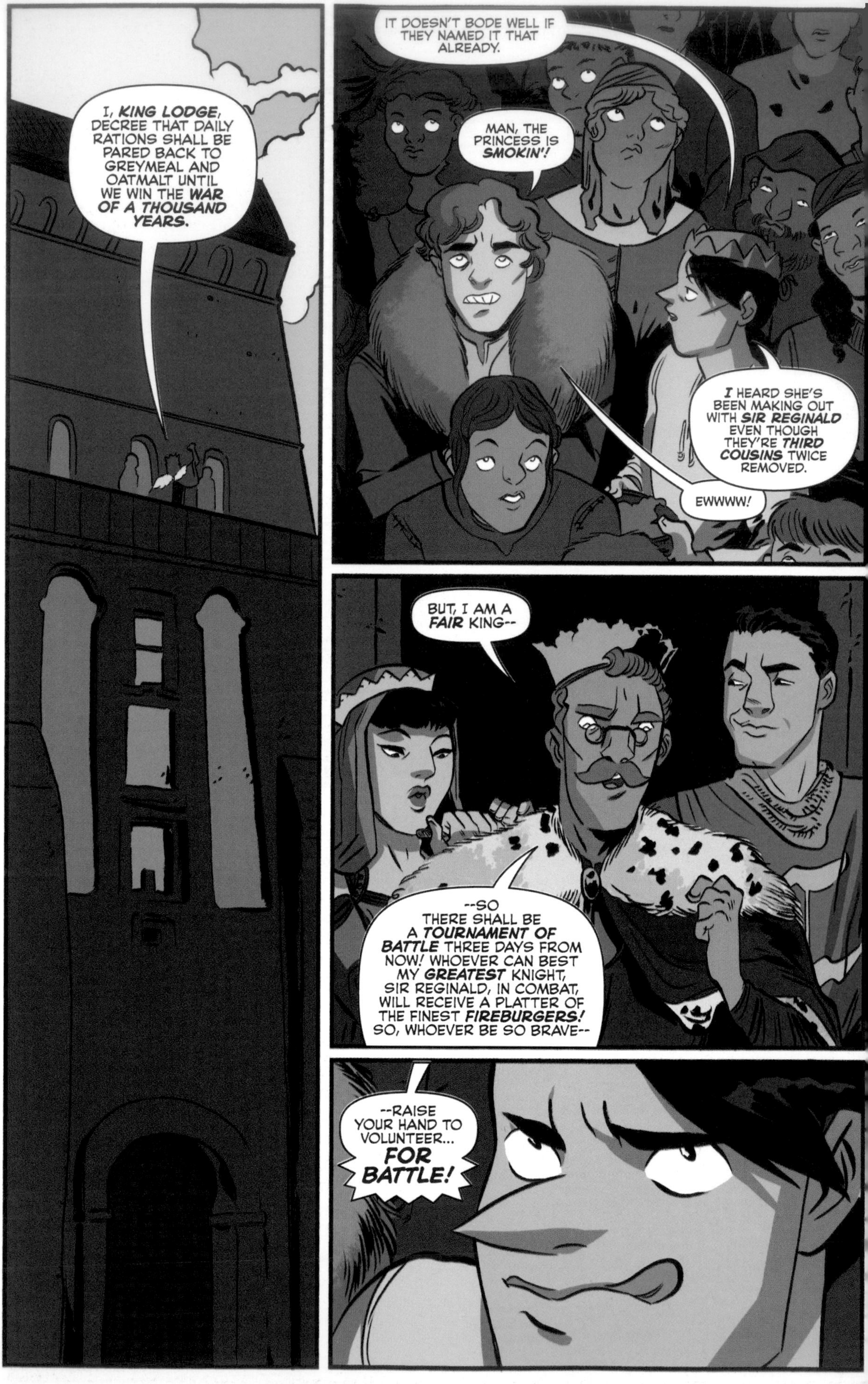
I, KING LODGE, DECREE THAT DAILY RATIONS SHALL BE PARED BACK TO GREYMEAL AND OATMALT UNTIL WE WIN THE WAR OF A THOUSAND YEARS.
IT DOESN'T BODE WELL IF THEY NAMED IT THAT ALREADY.
MAN, THE PRINCESS IS SMOKIN'!
I HEARD SHE'S BEEN MAKING OUT WITH SIR REGINALD EVEN THOUGH THEY'RE THIRD COUSINS TWICE REMOVED.
EWWWW!
BUT, I AM A FAIR KING--
--SO THERE SHALL BE A TOURNAMENT OF BATTLE THREE DAYS FROM NOW! WHOEVER CAN BEST MY GREATEST KNIGHT, SIR REGINALD, IN COMBAT, WILL RECEIVE A PLATTER OF THE FINEST FIREBURGERS! SO, WHOEVER BE SO BRAVE--
--RAISE YOUR HAND TO VOLUNTEER... FOR BATTLE!

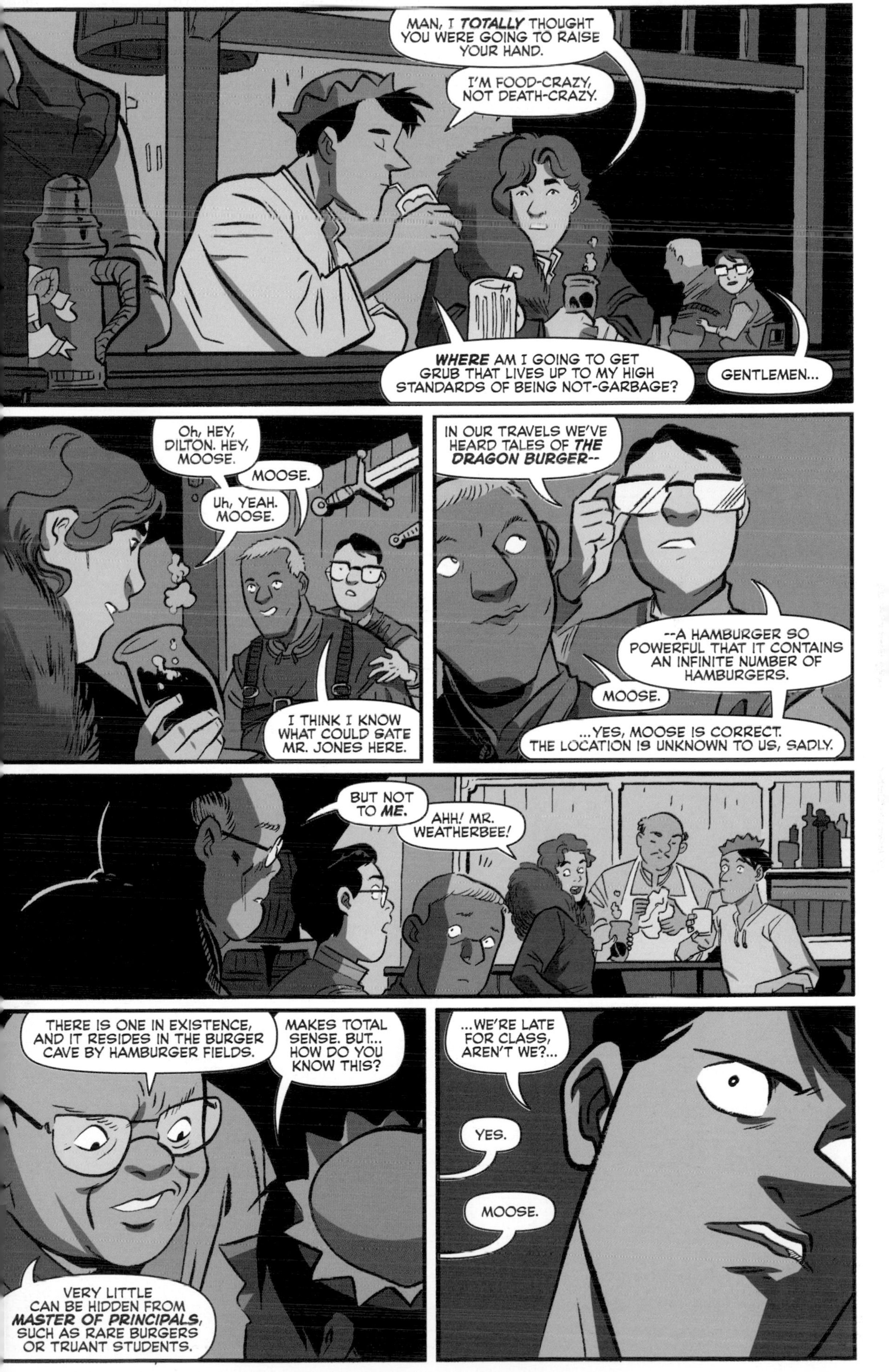
MAN, I **TOTALLY** THOUGHT YOU WERE GOING TO RAISE YOUR HAND.
I'M FOOD-CRAZY, NOT DEATH-CRAZY.
WHERE AM I GOING TO GET GRUB THAT LIVES UP TO MY HIGH STANDARDS OF BEING NOT-GARBAGE?
GENTLEMEN...
Oh, HEY, DILTON. HEY, MOOSE.
MOOSE.
Uh, YEAH. MOOSE.
I THINK I KNOW WHAT COULD SATE MR. JONES HERE.
IN OUR TRAVELS WE'VE HEARD TALES OF ***THE DRAGON BURGER***--
--A HAMBURGER SO POWERFUL THAT IT CONTAINS AN INFINITE NUMBER OF HAMBURGERS.
MOOSE.
...YES, MOOSE IS CORRECT. THE LOCATION IS UNKNOWN TO US, SADLY.
BUT NOT TO **ME**.
AHH! MR. WEATHERBEE!
THERE IS ONE IN EXISTENCE, AND IT RESIDES IN THE BURGER CAVE BY HAMBURGER FIELDS.
MAKES TOTAL SENSE. BUT... HOW DO YOU KNOW THIS?
VERY LITTLE CAN BE HIDDEN FROM ***MASTER OF PRINCIPALS***, SUCH AS RARE BURGERS OR TRUANT STUDENTS.
...WE'RE LATE FOR CLASS, AREN'T WE?...
YES.
MOOSE.

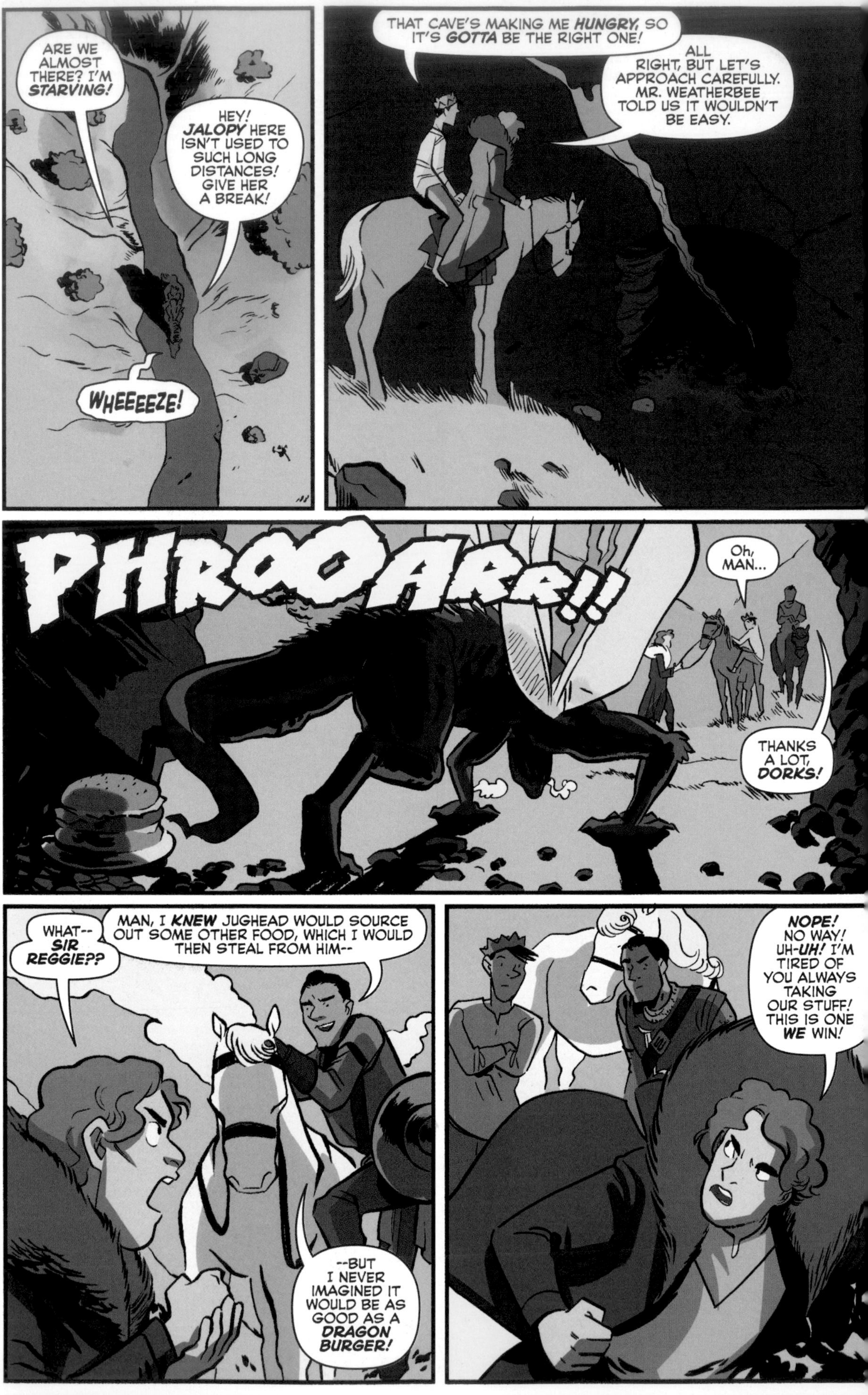
ARE WE ALMOST THERE? I'M STARVING!
HEY! JALOPY HERE ISN'T USED TO SUCH LONG DISTANCES! GIVE HER A BREAK!
WHEEEEZE!
THAT CAVE'S MAKING ME HUNGRY, SO IT'S GOTTA BE THE RIGHT ONE!
ALL RIGHT, BUT LET'S APPROACH CAREFULLY. MR. WEATHERBEE TOLD US IT WOULDN'T BE EASY.
PHROOARR!!
Oh, MAN...
THANKS A LOT, DORKS!
WHAT-- SIR REGGIE??
MAN, I KNEW JUGHEAD WOULD SOURCE OUT SOME OTHER FOOD, WHICH I WOULD THEN STEAL FROM HIM--
--BUT I NEVER IMAGINED IT WOULD BE AS GOOD AS A DRAGON BURGER!
NOPE! NO WAY! UH-UH! I'M TIRED OF YOU ALWAYS TAKING OUR STUFF! THIS IS ONE WE WIN!

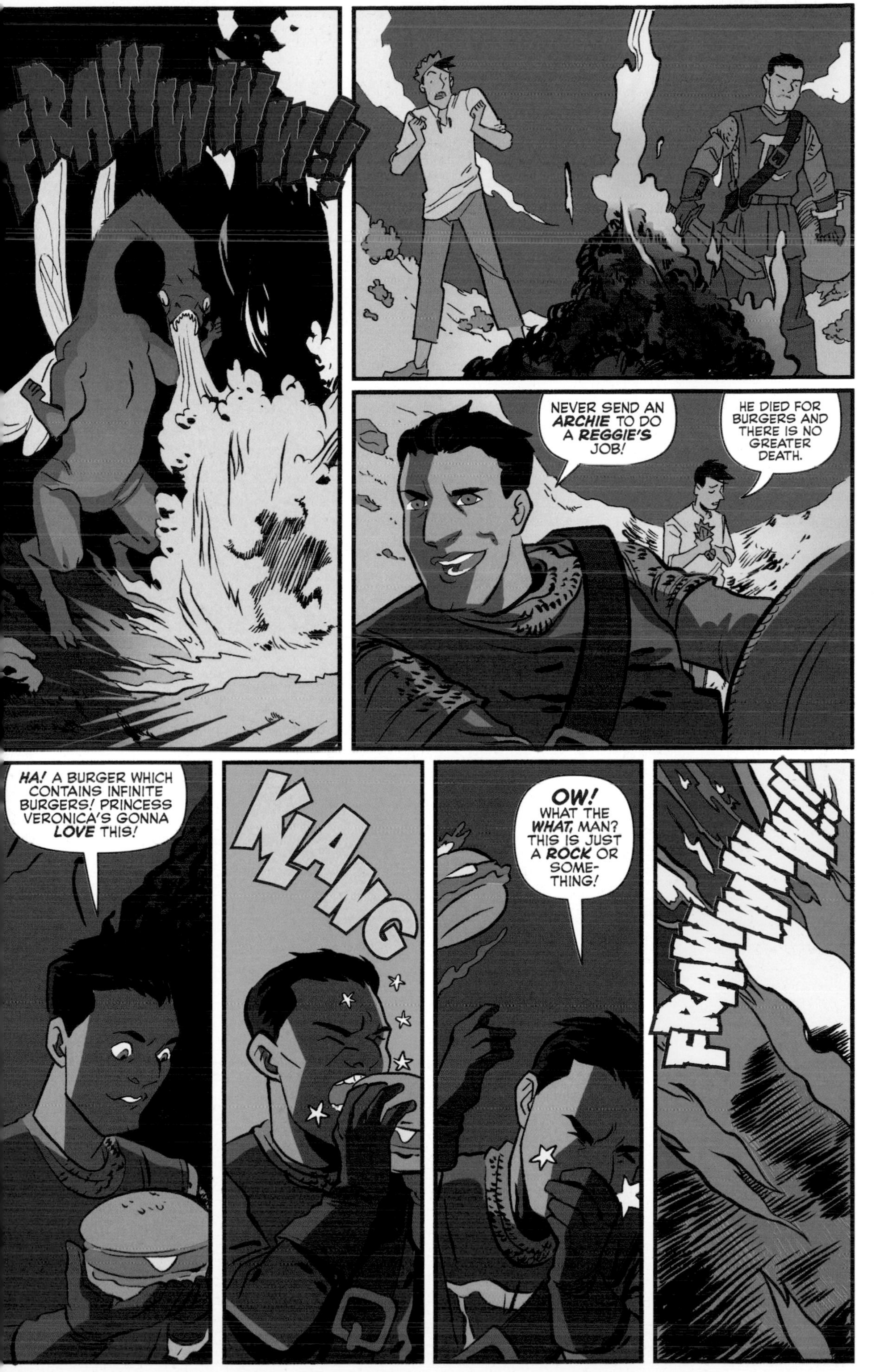

FRAWWWWW!!
NEVER SEND AN ARCHIE TO DO A REGGIE'S JOB!
HE DIED FOR BURGERS AND THERE IS NO GREATER DEATH.
HA! A BURGER WHICH CONTAINS INFINITE BURGERS! PRINCESS VERONICA'S GONNA LOVE THIS!
KLANG
OW! WHAT THE WHAT, MAN? THIS IS JUST A ROCK OR SOME-THING!
FRAWWWWW!!

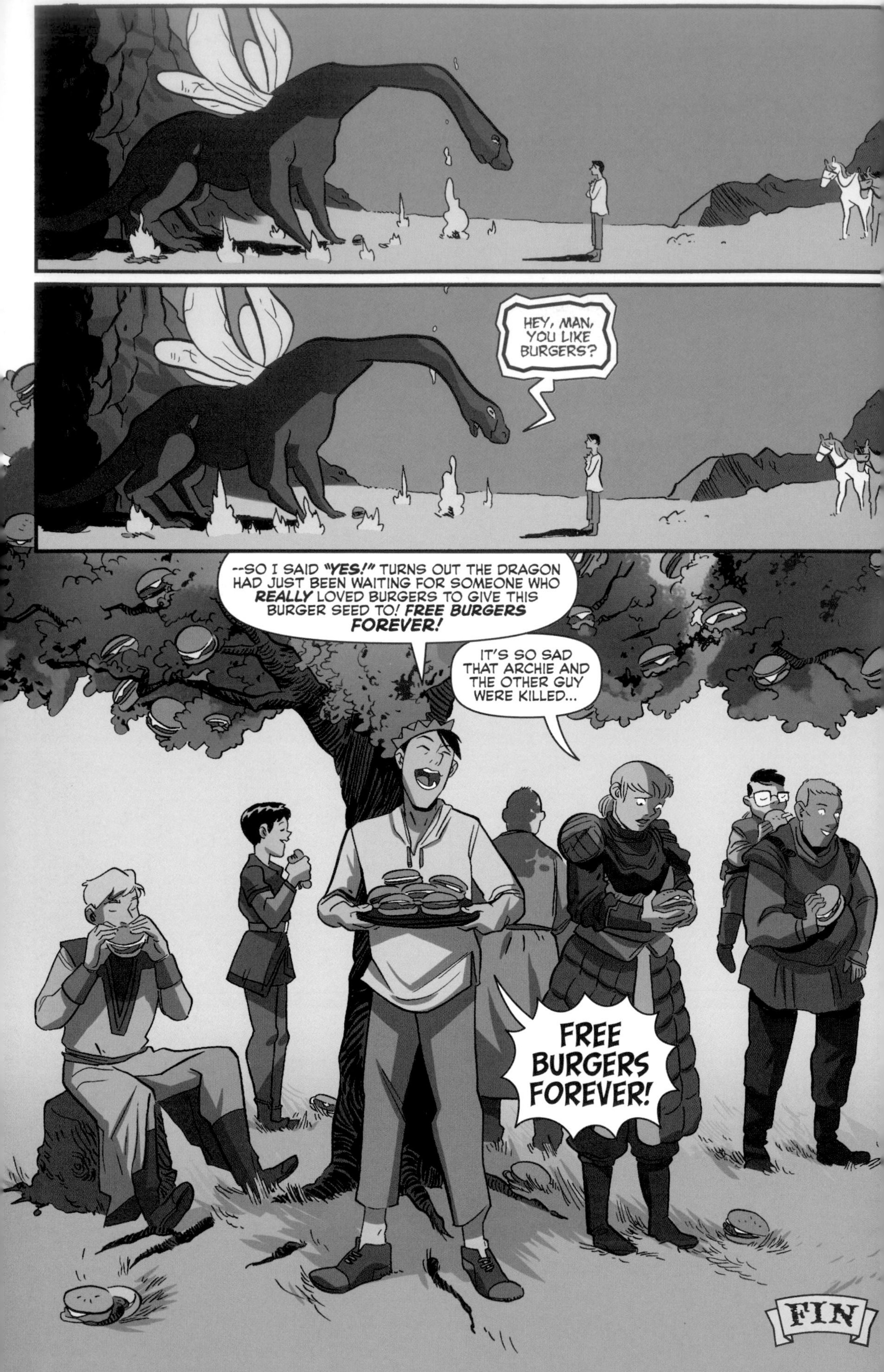
HEY, MAN, YOU LIKE BURGERS?
--SO I SAID "YES!" TURNS OUT THE DRAGON HAD JUST BEEN WAITING FOR SOMEONE WHO REALLY LOVED BURGERS TO GIVE THIS BURGER SEED TO! FREE BURGERS FOREVER!
IT'S SO SAD THAT ARCHIE AND THE OTHER GUY WERE KILLED...
FREE BURGERS FOREVER!
FIN

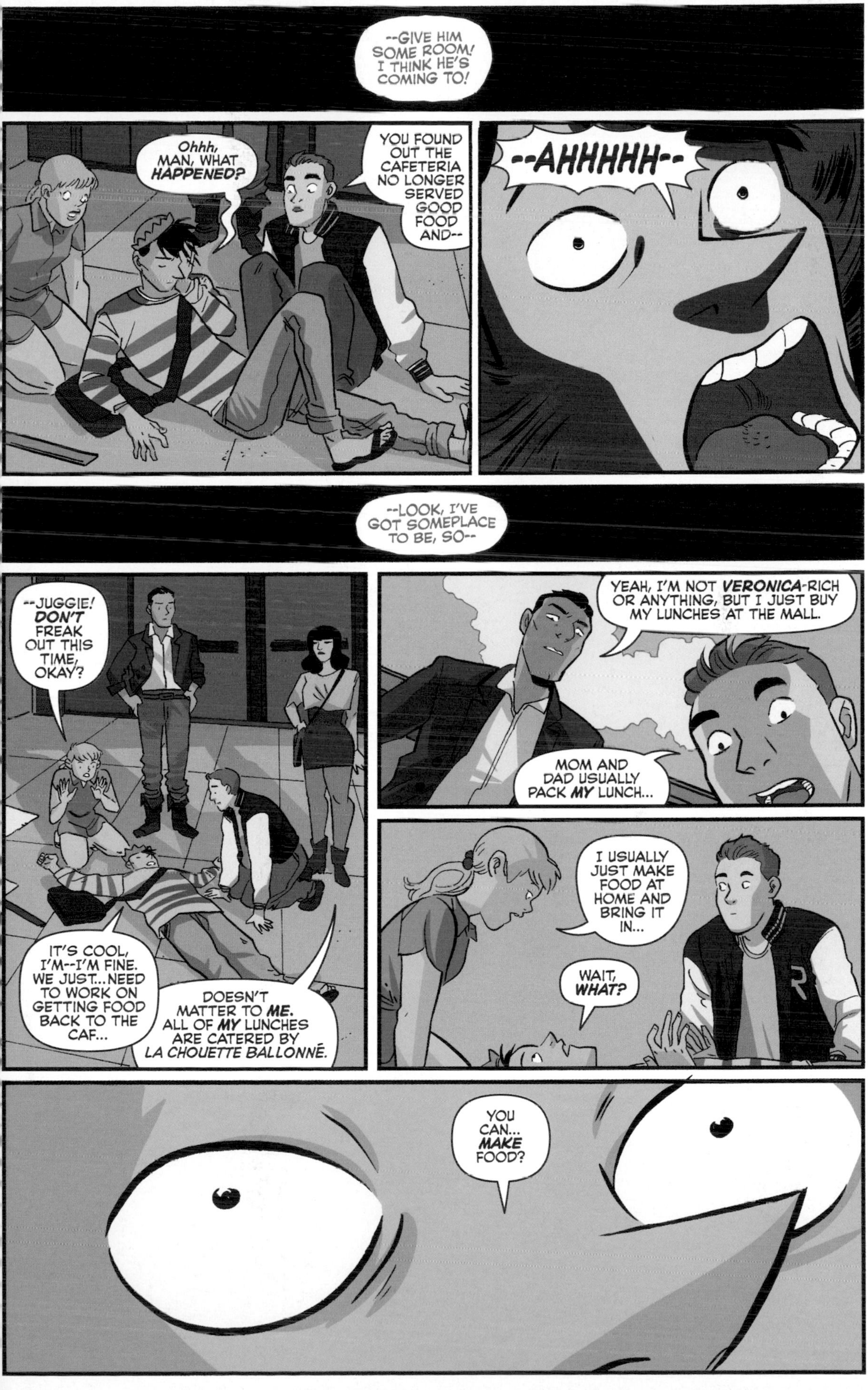
--GIVE HIM SOME ROOM! I THINK HE'S COMING TO!
Ohhh, MAN, WHAT HAPPENED?
YOU FOUND OUT THE CAFETERIA NO LONGER SERVED GOOD FOOD AND--
--AHHHHH--
--LOOK, I'VE GOT SOMEPLACE TO BE, SO--
--JUGGIE! DON'T FREAK OUT THIS TIME, OKAY?
IT'S COOL, I'M--I'M FINE. WE JUST...NEED TO WORK ON GETTING FOOD BACK TO THE CAF...
DOESN'T MATTER TO ME. ALL OF MY LUNCHES ARE CATERED BY LA CHOUETTE BALLONNÉ.
YEAH, I'M NOT VERONICA-RICH OR ANYTHING, BUT I JUST BUY MY LUNCHES AT THE MALL.
MOM AND DAD USUALLY PACK MY LUNCH...
I USUALLY JUST MAKE FOOD AT HOME AND BRING IT IN...
WAIT, WHAT?
YOU CAN... MAKE FOOD?

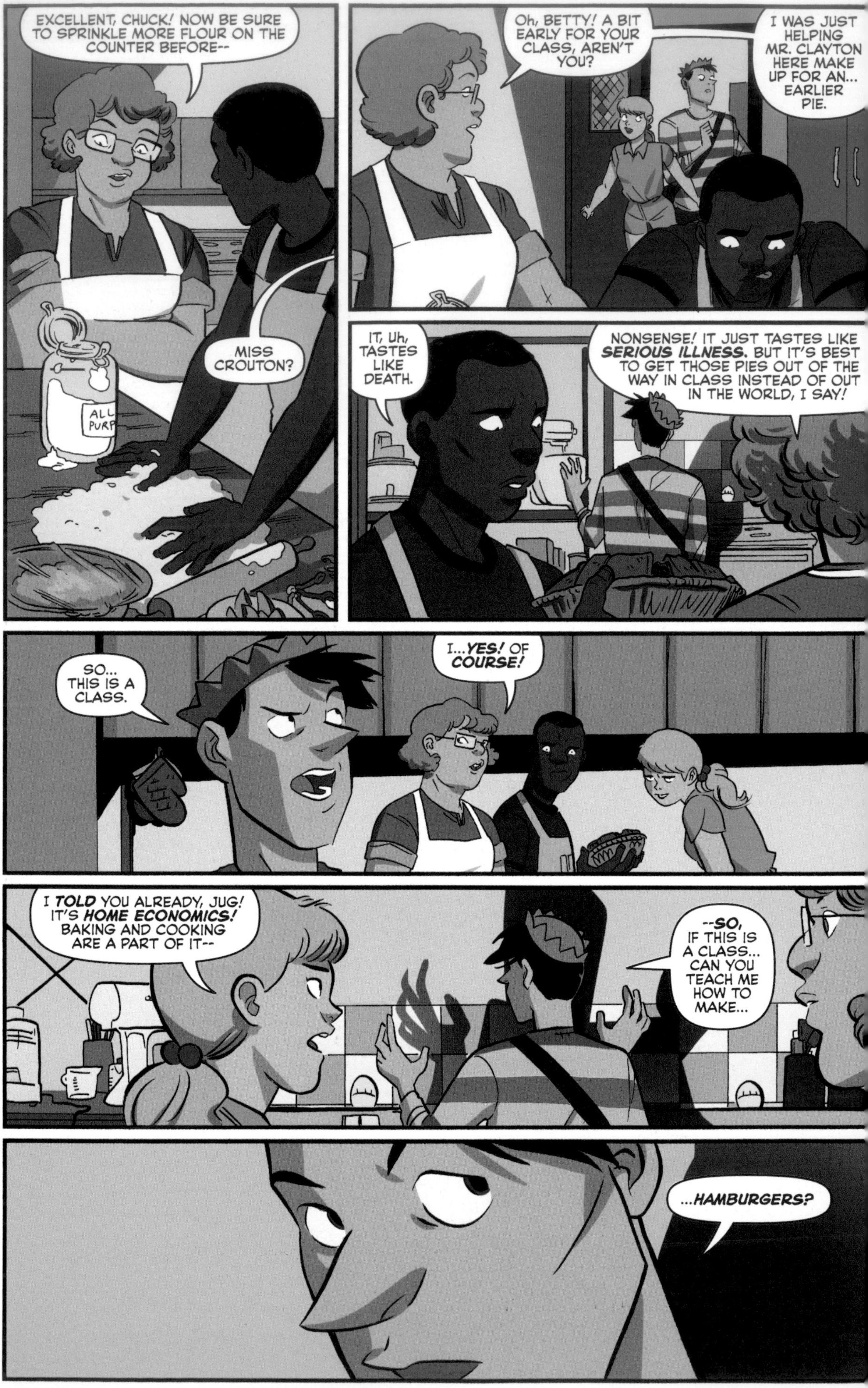

EXCELLENT, CHUCK! NOW BE SURE TO SPRINKLE MORE FLOUR ON THE COUNTER BEFORE--
MISS CROUTON?
ALL PURP
Oh, BETTY! A BIT EARLY FOR YOUR CLASS, AREN'T YOU?
I WAS JUST HELPING MR. CLAYTON HERE MAKE UP FOR AN... EARLIER PIE.
IT, Uh, TASTES LIKE DEATH.
NONSENSE! IT JUST TASTES LIKE SERIOUS ILLNESS. BUT IT'S BEST TO GET THOSE PIES OUT OF THE WAY IN CLASS INSTEAD OF OUT IN THE WORLD, I SAY!
SO... THIS IS A CLASS.
I...YES! OF COURSE!
I TOLD YOU ALREADY, JUG! IT'S HOME ECONOMICS! BAKING AND COOKING ARE A PART OF IT--
--SO, IF THIS IS A CLASS... CAN YOU TEACH ME HOW TO MAKE...
...HAMBURGERS?

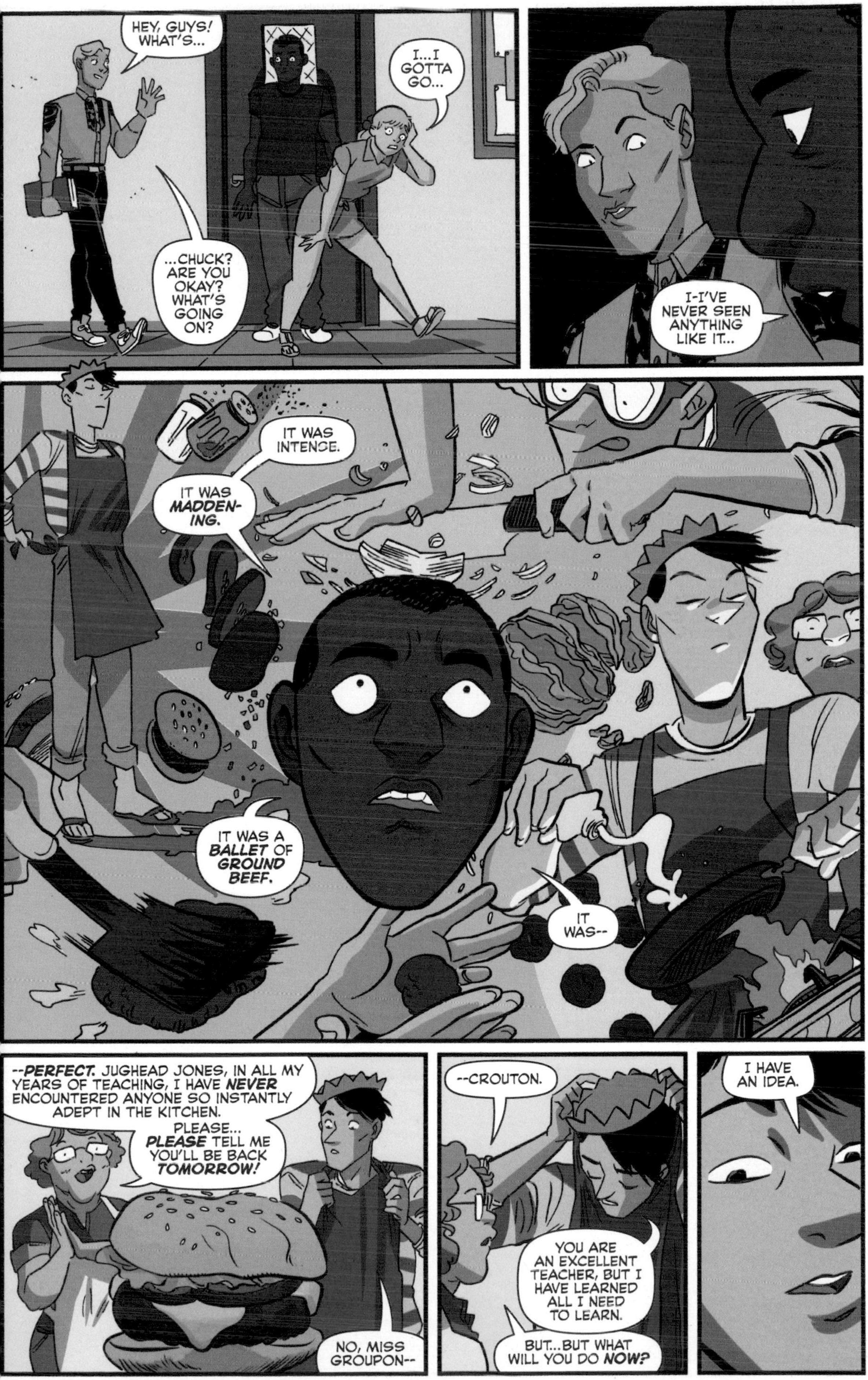
HEY, GUYS! WHAT'S...
I...I GOTTA GO...
...CHUCK? ARE YOU OKAY? WHAT'S GOING ON?
I-I'VE NEVER SEEN ANYTHING LIKE IT...
IT WAS INTENSE.
IT WAS MADDENING.
IT WAS A BALLET OF GROUND BEEF.
IT WAS--
--PERFECT. JUGHEAD JONES, IN ALL MY YEARS OF TEACHING, I HAVE NEVER ENCOUNTERED ANYONE SO INSTANTLY ADEPT IN THE KITCHEN.
PLEASE... PLEASE TELL ME YOU'LL BE BACK TOMORROW!
NO, MISS GROUPON--
--CROUTON.
YOU ARE AN EXCELLENT TEACHER, BUT I HAVE LEARNED ALL I NEED TO LEARN.
BUT...BUT WHAT WILL YOU DO NOW?
I HAVE AN IDEA.

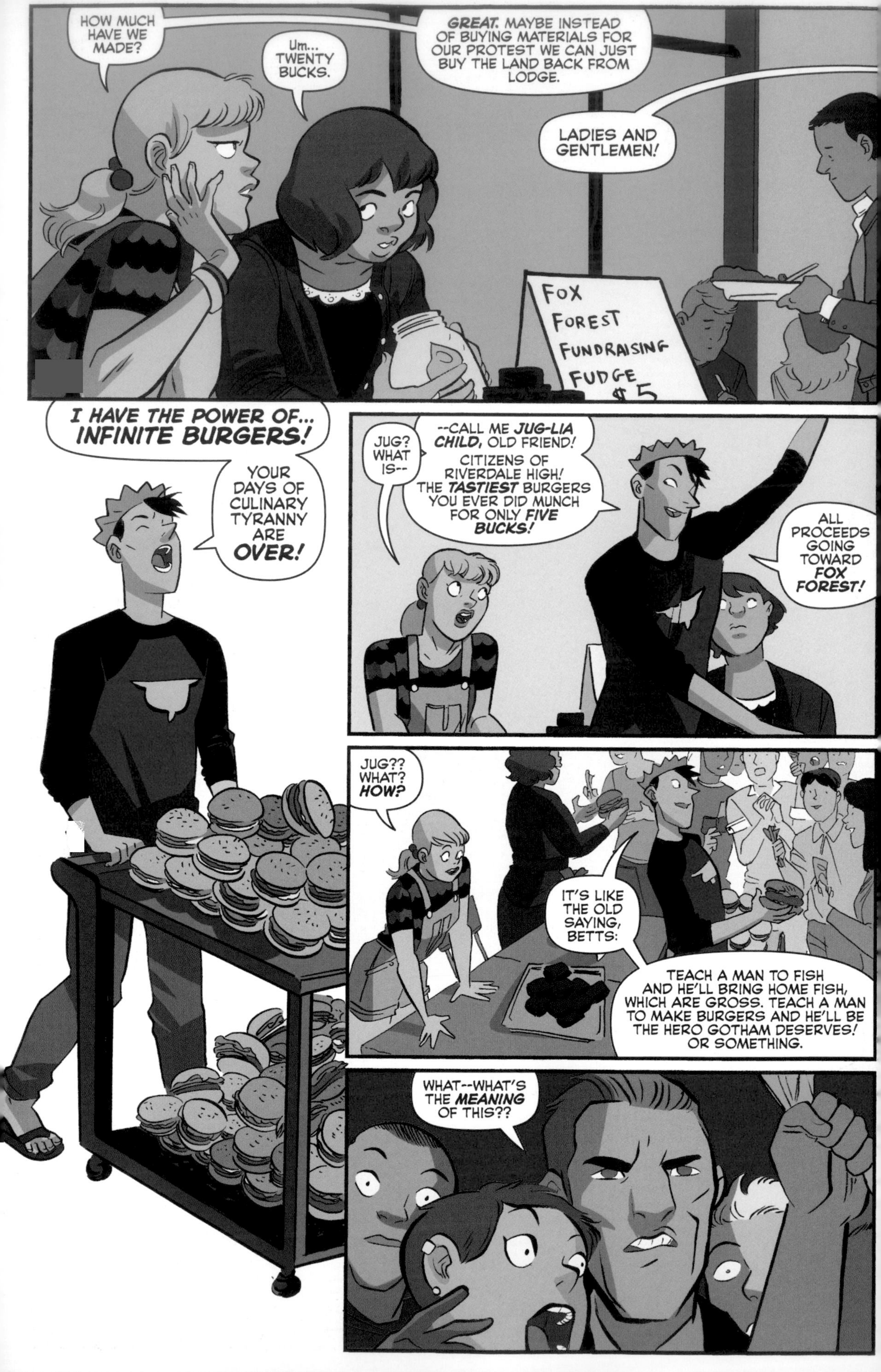
HOW MUCH HAVE WE MADE?
Um... TWENTY BUCKS.
GREAT. MAYBE INSTEAD OF BUYING MATERIALS FOR OUR PROTEST WE CAN JUST BUY THE LAND BACK FROM LODGE.
LADIES AND GENTLEMEN!
FOX FOREST FUNDRAISING FUDGE $5
I HAVE THE POWER OF... INFINITE BURGERS!
YOUR DAYS OF CULINARY TYRANNY ARE OVER!
JUG? WHAT IS--
--CALL ME JUG-LIA CHILD, OLD FRIEND!
CITIZENS OF RIVERDALE HIGH! THE TASTIEST BURGERS YOU EVER DID MUNCH FOR ONLY FIVE BUCKS!
ALL PROCEEDS GOING TOWARD FOX FOREST!
JUG?? WHAT? HOW?
IT'S LIKE THE OLD SAYING, BETTS:
TEACH A MAN TO FISH AND HE'LL BRING HOME FISH, WHICH ARE GROSS. TEACH A MAN TO MAKE BURGERS AND HE'LL BE THE HERO GOTHAM DESERVES! OR SOMETHING.
WHAT--WHAT'S THE MEANING OF THIS??

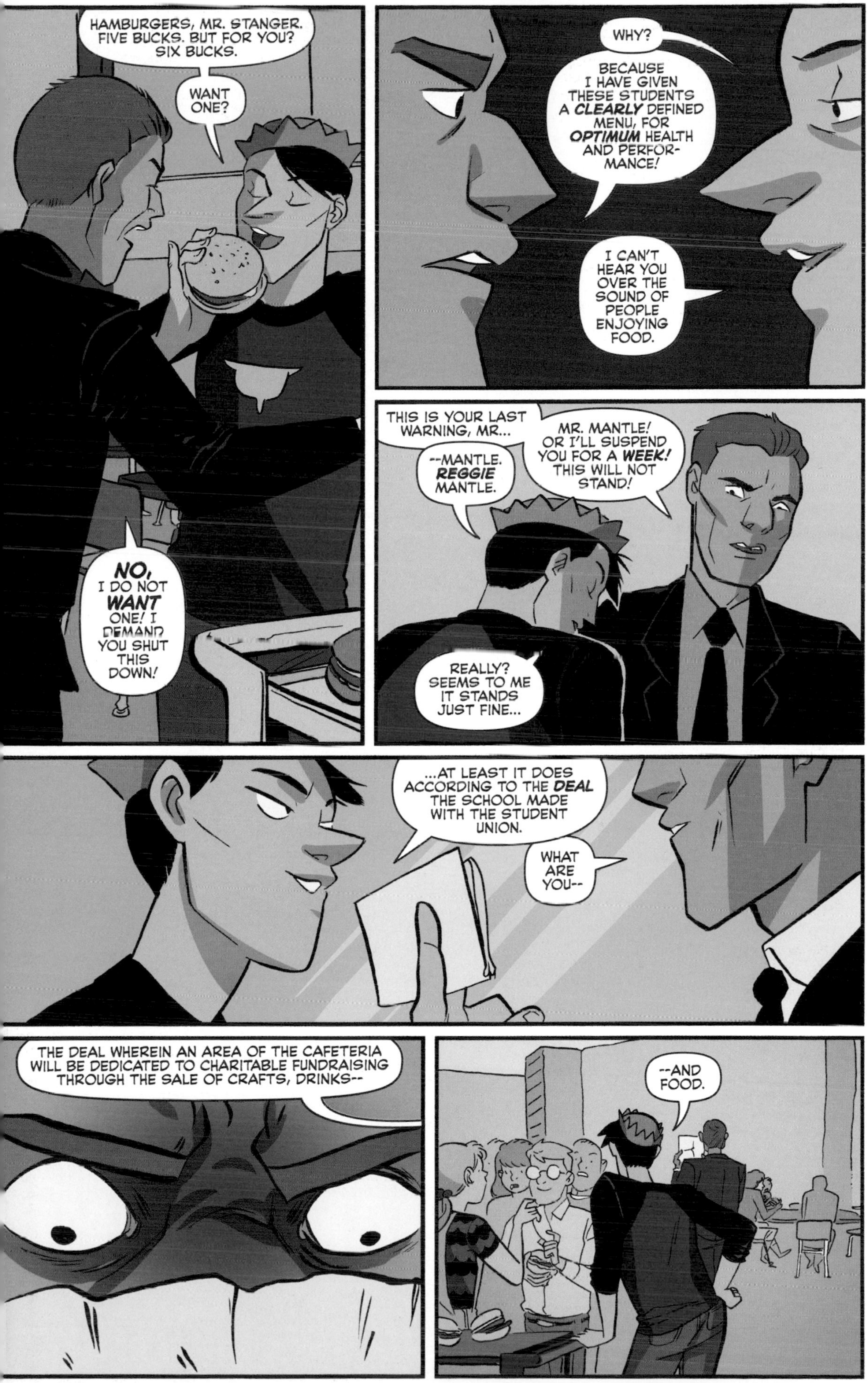
HAMBURGERS, MR. STANGER. FIVE BUCKS. BUT FOR YOU? SIX BUCKS.
WANT ONE?
NO, I DO NOT WANT ONE! I DEMAND YOU SHUT THIS DOWN!
WHY?
BECAUSE I HAVE GIVEN THESE STUDENTS A CLEARLY DEFINED MENU, FOR OPTIMUM HEALTH AND PERFORMANCE!
I CAN'T HEAR YOU OVER THE SOUND OF PEOPLE ENJOYING FOOD.
THIS IS YOUR LAST WARNING, MR...
--MANTLE. REGGIE MANTLE.
MR. MANTLE! OR I'LL SUSPEND YOU FOR A WEEK! THIS WILL NOT STAND!
REALLY? SEEMS TO ME IT STANDS JUST FINE...
...AT LEAST IT DOES ACCORDING TO THE DEAL THE SCHOOL MADE WITH THE STUDENT UNION.
WHAT ARE YOU--
THE DEAL WHEREIN AN AREA OF THE CAFETERIA WILL BE DEDICATED TO CHARITABLE FUNDRAISING THROUGH THE SALE OF CRAFTS, DRINKS--
--AND FOOD.

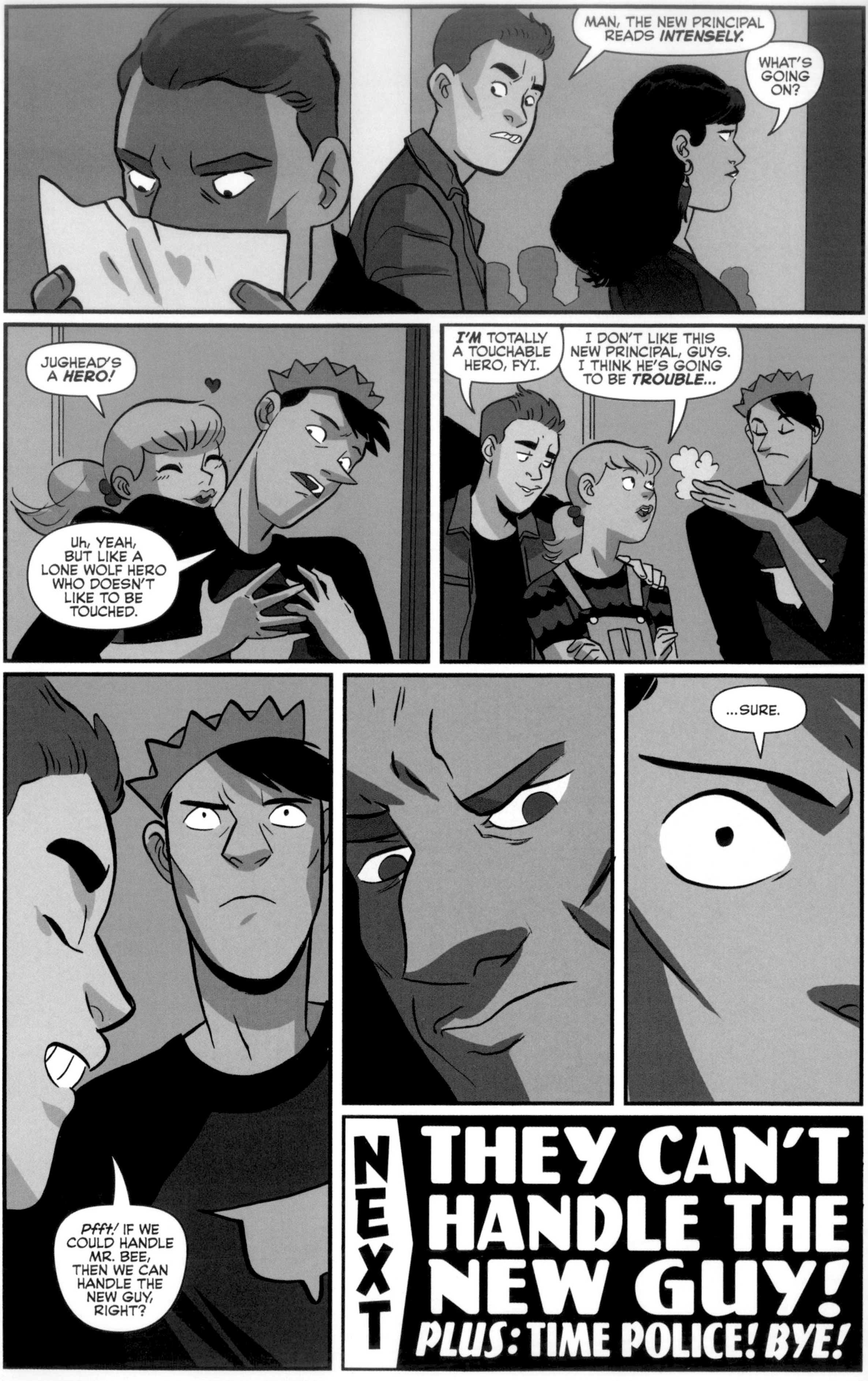
MAN, THE NEW PRINCIPAL READS *INTENSELY.*
WHAT'S GOING ON?
JUGHEAD'S A *HERO!*
Uh, YEAH, BUT LIKE A LONE WOLF HERO WHO DOESN'T LIKE TO BE TOUCHED.
I'M TOTALLY A TOUCHABLE HERO, FYI.
I DON'T LIKE THIS NEW PRINCIPAL, GUYS. I THINK HE'S GOING TO BE *TROUBLE...*
Pfft! IF WE COULD HANDLE MR. BEE, THEN WE CAN HANDLE THE NEW GUY, RIGHT?
...SURE.
NEXT
THEY CAN'T HANDLE THE NEW GUY!
PLUS: TIME POLICE! *BYE!*

It only made sense that Riverdale's famous frenemies would be next to get their chance to shine!

While Betty and Veronica both play integral roles in the main Archie series, the opportunity was still needed to expand upon their friendship and lives *outside* of their relationship with Archie. Betty and Veronica are more than two polar opposites who happen to love the same teenage boy—they're worldly, interesting and thoughtful young women.

Legendary comic artist Adam Hughes took up the task of crafting the world of *Betty and Veronica* in a way that is intelligent and alluring while still being humorous.

STORY & ART BY
ADAM HUGHES

COLORING BY
JOSÉ VILLARRUBIA

LETTERING BY
JACK MORELLI

ROAD TO RIVERDALE®

BETTY & VERONICA

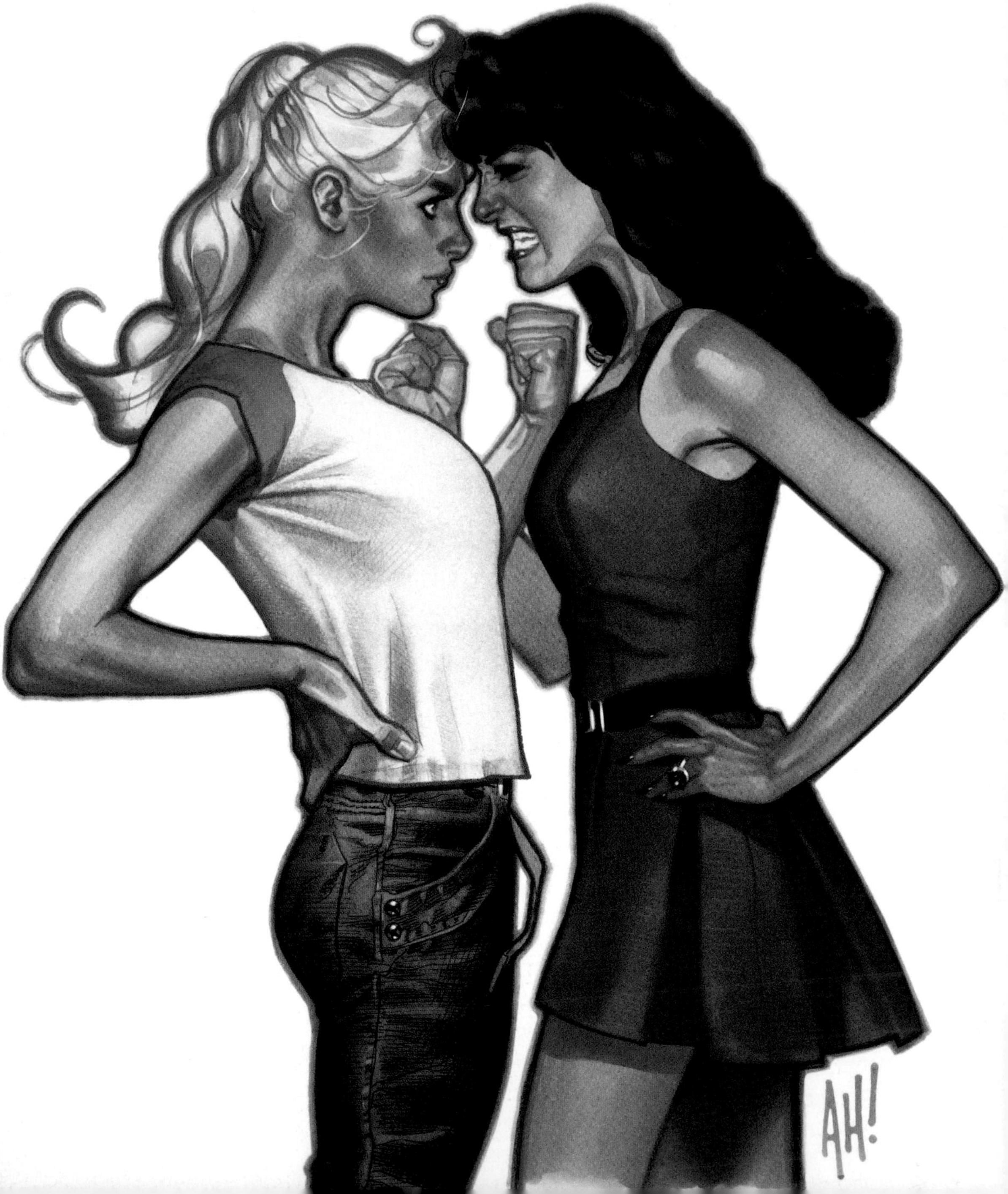
AH!

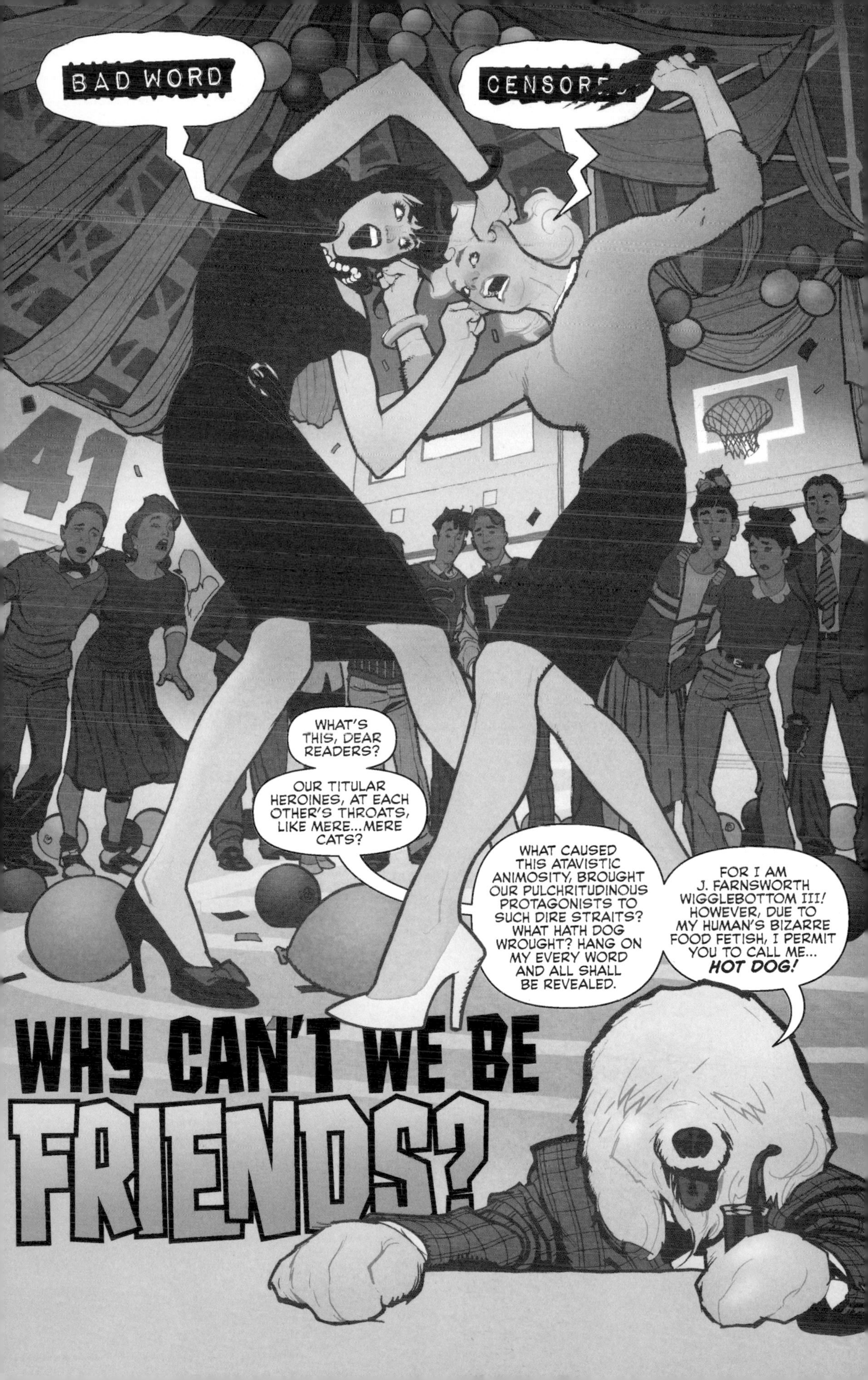
BAD WORD
CENSORE
WHAT'S THIS, DEAR READERS?
OUR TITULAR HEROINES, AT EACH OTHER'S THROATS, LIKE MERE...MERE CATS?
WHAT CAUSED THIS ATAVISTIC ANIMOSITY, BROUGHT OUR PULCHRITUDINOUS PROTAGONISTS TO SUCH DIRE STRAITS? WHAT HATH DOG WROUGHT? HANG ON MY EVERY WORD AND ALL SHALL BE REVEALED.
FOR I AM J. FARNSWORTH WIGGLEBOTTOM III! HOWEVER, DUE TO MY HUMAN'S BIZARRE FOOD FETISH, I PERMIT YOU TO CALL ME... ***HOT DOG!***
WHY CAN'T WE BE FRIENDS?

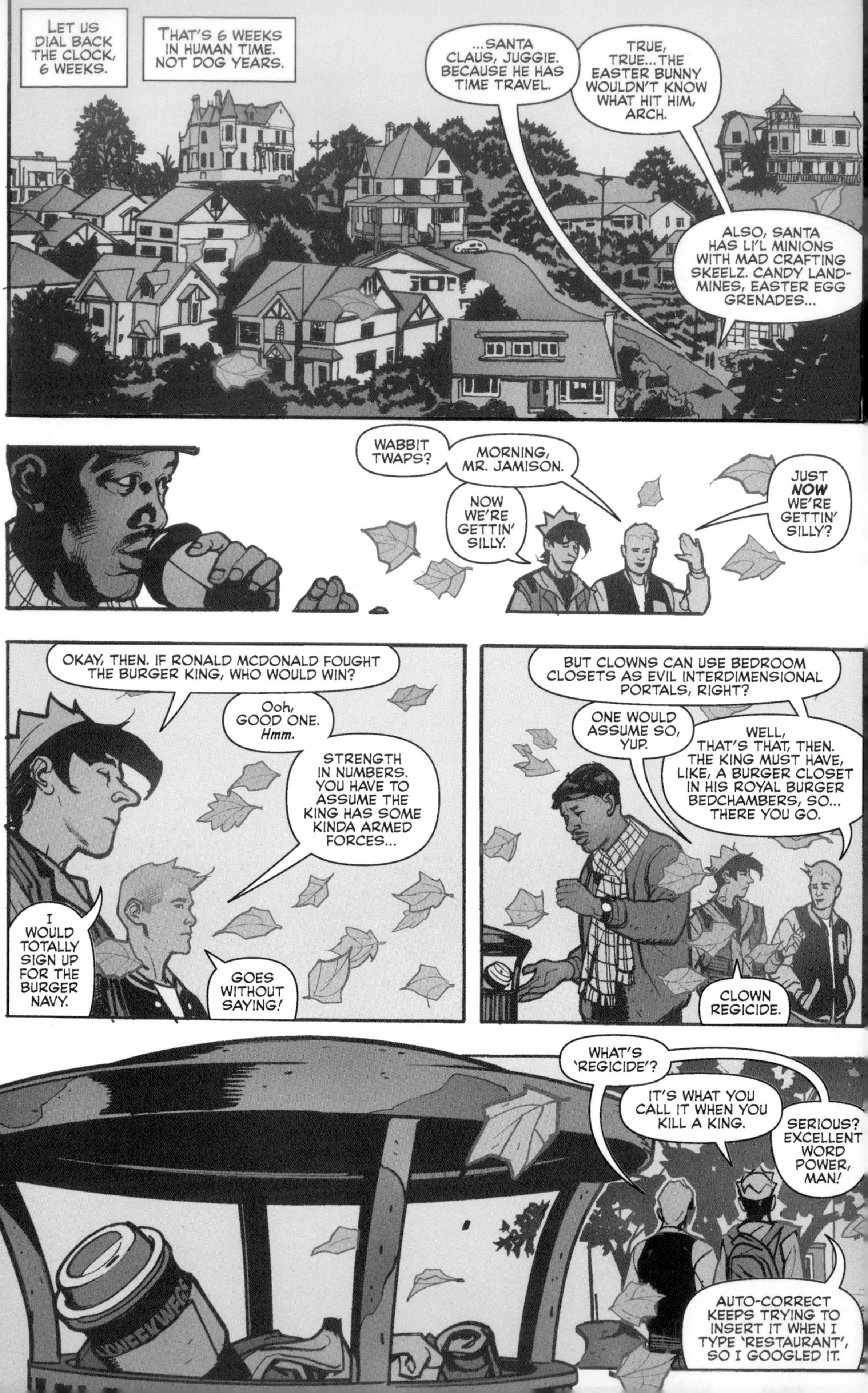

LET US DIAL BACK THE CLOCK, 6 WEEKS.
THAT'S 6 WEEKS IN HUMAN TIME. NOT DOG YEARS.
...SANTA CLAUS, JUGGIE. BECAUSE HE HAS TIME TRAVEL.
TRUE, TRUE... THE EASTER BUNNY WOULDN'T KNOW WHAT HIT HIM, ARCH.
ALSO, SANTA HAS LI'L MINIONS WITH MAD CRAFTING SKEELZ. CANDY LAND-MINES, EASTER EGG GRENADES...
WABBIT TWAPS?
MORNING, MR. JAMISON.
NOW WE'RE GETTIN' SILLY.
JUST NOW WE'RE GETTIN' SILLY?
OKAY, THEN. IF RONALD MCDONALD FOUGHT THE BURGER KING, WHO WOULD WIN?
Ooh, GOOD ONE. Hmm.
STRENGTH IN NUMBERS. YOU HAVE TO ASSUME THE KING HAS SOME KINDA ARMED FORCES...
I WOULD TOTALLY SIGN UP FOR THE BURGER NAVY.
GOES WITHOUT SAYING!
BUT CLOWNS CAN USE BEDROOM CLOSETS AS EVIL INTERDIMENSIONAL PORTALS, RIGHT?
ONE WOULD ASSUME SO, YUP.
WELL, THAT'S THAT, THEN. THE KING MUST HAVE, LIKE, A BURGER CLOSET IN HIS ROYAL BURGER BEDCHAMBERS, SO... THERE YOU GO.
CLOWN REGICIDE.
WHAT'S 'REGICIDE'?
IT'S WHAT YOU CALL IT WHEN YOU KILL A KING.
SERIOUS? EXCELLENT WORD POWER, MAN!
AUTO-CORRECT KEEPS TRYING TO INSERT IT WHEN I TYPE 'RESTAURANT', SO I GOOGLED IT.

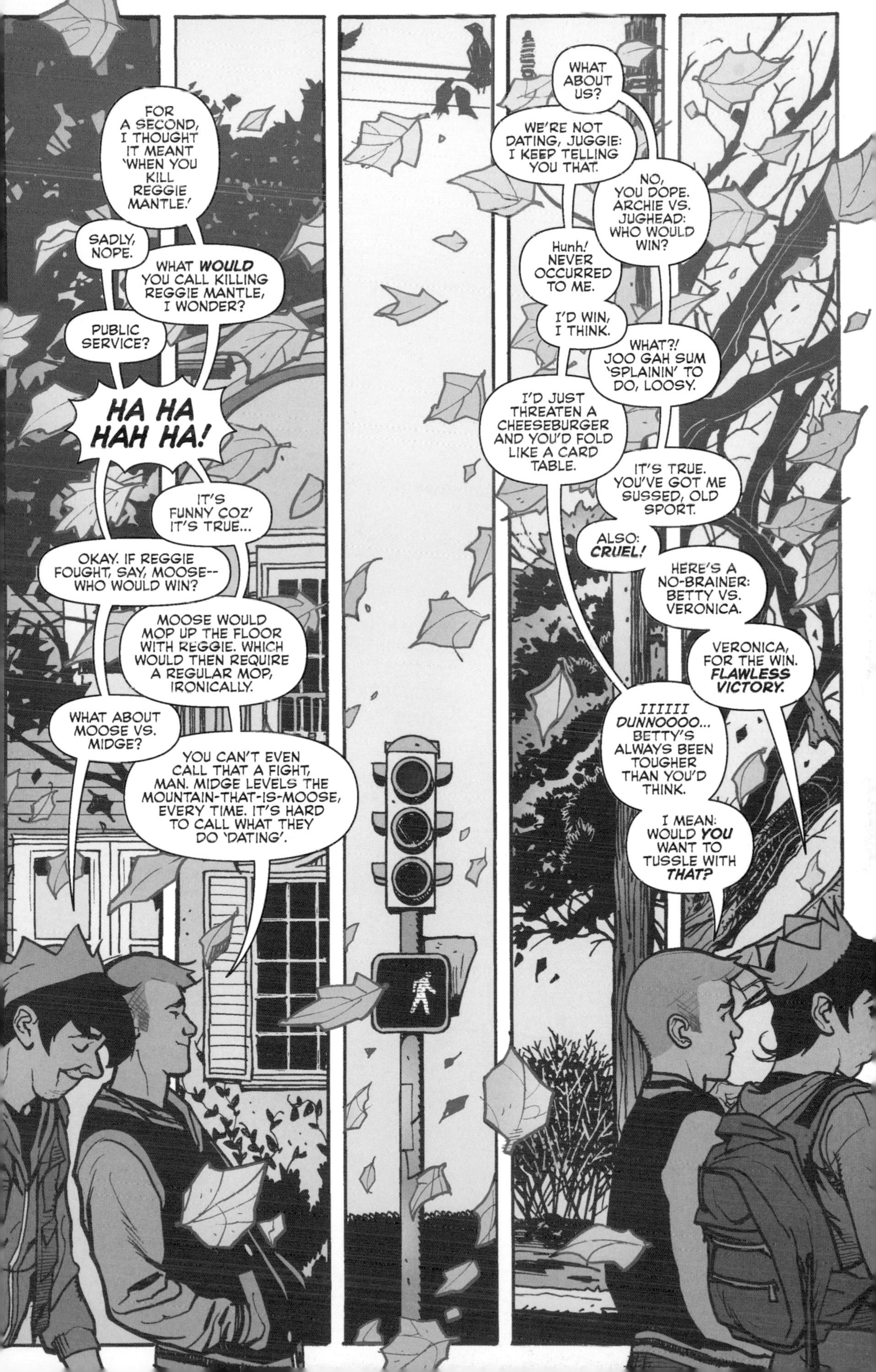

FOR A SECOND, I THOUGHT IT MEANT 'WHEN YOU KILL REGGIE MANTLE.'
SADLY, NOPE.
WHAT **WOULD** YOU CALL KILLING REGGIE MANTLE, I WONDER?
PUBLIC SERVICE?
HA HA HAH HA!
IT'S FUNNY COZ' IT'S TRUE...
OKAY. IF REGGIE FOUGHT, SAY, MOOSE-- WHO WOULD WIN?
MOOSE WOULD MOP UP THE FLOOR WITH REGGIE. WHICH WOULD THEN REQUIRE A REGULAR MOP, IRONICALLY.
WHAT ABOUT MOOSE VS. MIDGE?
YOU CAN'T EVEN CALL THAT A FIGHT, MAN. MIDGE LEVELS THE MOUNTAIN-THAT-IS-MOOSE, EVERY TIME. IT'S HARD TO CALL WHAT THEY DO 'DATING'.
WHAT ABOUT US?
WE'RE NOT DATING, JUGGIE: I KEEP TELLING YOU THAT.
NO, YOU DOPE. ARCHIE VS. JUGHEAD: WHO WOULD WIN?
Hunh! NEVER OCCURRED TO ME.
I'D WIN, I THINK.
WHAT?! JOO GAH SUM 'SPLAININ' TO DO, LOOSY.
I'D JUST THREATEN A CHEESEBURGER AND YOU'D FOLD LIKE A CARD TABLE.
IT'S TRUE. YOU'VE GOT ME SUSSED, OLD SPORT.
ALSO: **CRUEL!**
HERE'S A NO-BRAINER: BETTY VS. VERONICA.
VERONICA, FOR THE WIN. **FLAWLESS VICTORY.**
IIIIII **DUNNOOOO**... BETTY'S ALWAYS BEEN TOUGHER THAN YOU'D THINK.
I MEAN: WOULD **YOU** WANT TO TUSSLE WITH **THAT?**

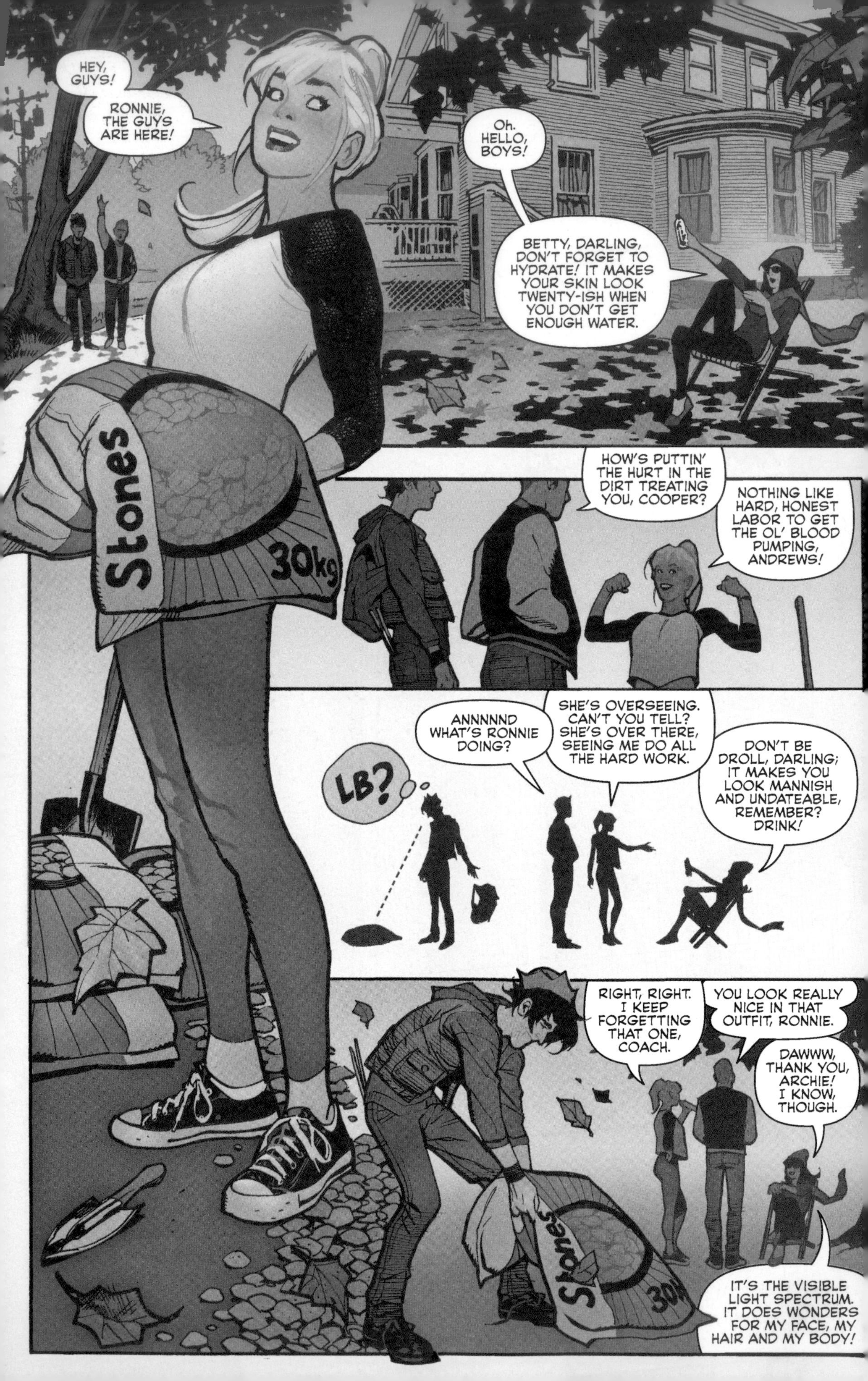
HEY, GUYS!
RONNIE, THE GUYS ARE HERE!
Oh. HELLO, BOYS!
BETTY, DARLING, DON'T FORGET TO HYDRATE! IT MAKES YOUR SKIN LOOK TWENTY-ISH WHEN YOU DON'T GET ENOUGH WATER.
Stones
30kg
HOW'S PUTTIN' THE HURT IN THE DIRT TREATING YOU, COOPER?
NOTHING LIKE HARD, HONEST LABOR TO GET THE OL' BLOOD PUMPING, ANDREWS!
ANNNNND WHAT'S RONNIE DOING?
SHE'S OVERSEEING. CAN'T YOU TELL? SHE'S OVER THERE, SEEING ME DO ALL THE HARD WORK.
LB?
DON'T BE DROLL, DARLING; IT MAKES YOU LOOK MANNISH AND UNDATEABLE, REMEMBER? DRINK!
RIGHT, RIGHT. I KEEP FORGETTING THAT ONE, COACH.
YOU LOOK REALLY NICE IN THAT OUTFIT, RONNIE.
DAWWW, THANK YOU, ARCHIE! I KNOW, THOUGH.
IT'S THE VISIBLE LIGHT SPECTRUM. IT DOES WONDERS FOR MY FACE, MY HAIR AND MY BODY!

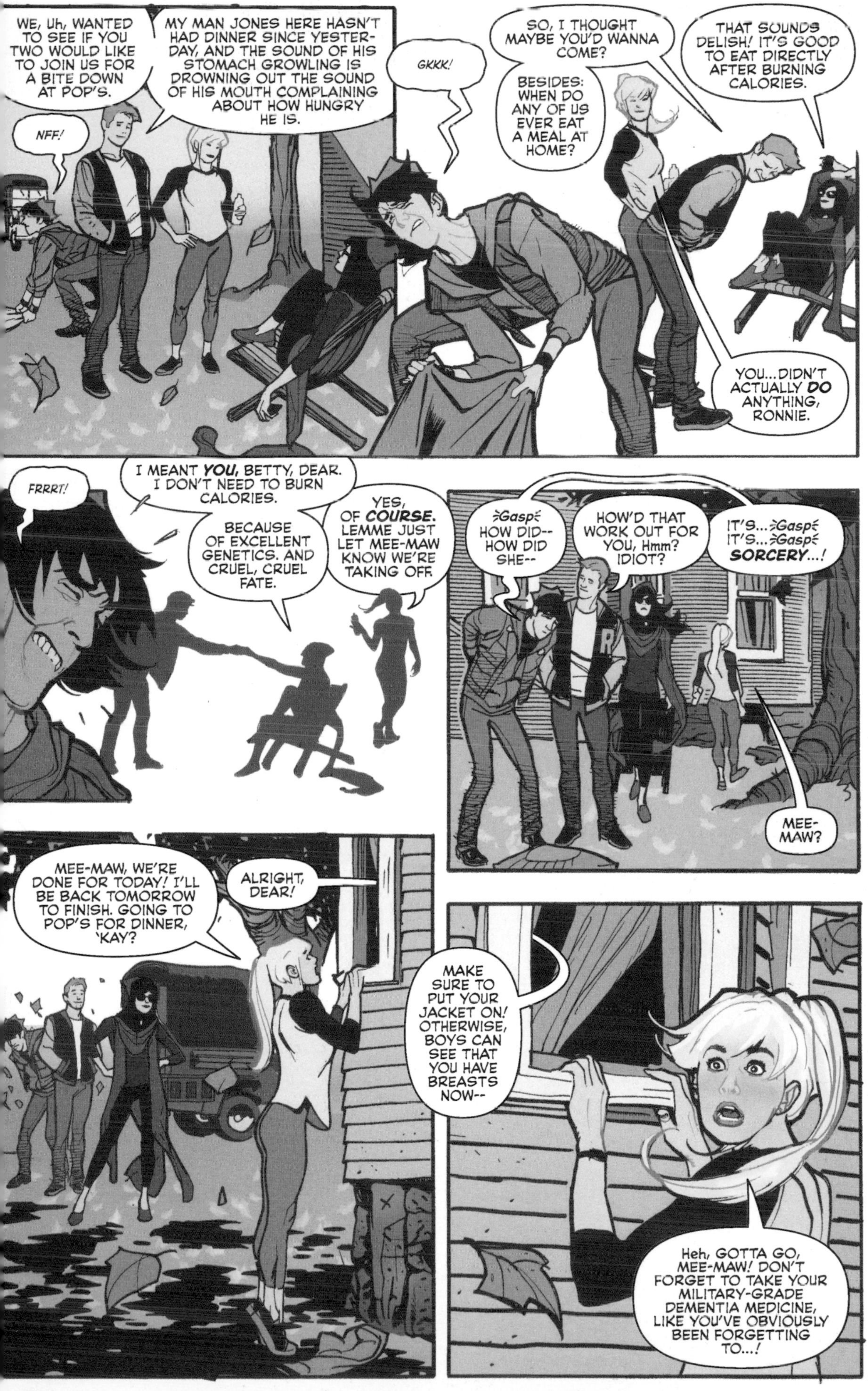
WE, Uh, WANTED TO SEE IF YOU TWO WOULD LIKE TO JOIN US FOR A BITE DOWN AT POP'S.
MY MAN JONES HERE HASN'T HAD DINNER SINCE YESTERDAY, AND THE SOUND OF HIS STOMACH GROWLING IS DROWNING OUT THE SOUND OF HIS MOUTH COMPLAINING ABOUT HOW HUNGRY HE IS.
NFF!
GKKK!
SO, I THOUGHT MAYBE YOU'D WANNA COME?
BESIDES: WHEN DO ANY OF US EVER EAT A MEAL AT HOME?
THAT SOUNDS DELISH! IT'S GOOD TO EAT DIRECTLY AFTER BURNING CALORIES.
YOU...DIDN'T ACTUALLY DO ANYTHING, RONNIE.
FRRRT!
I MEANT YOU, BETTY, DEAR. I DON'T NEED TO BURN CALORIES.
BECAUSE OF EXCELLENT GENETICS. AND CRUEL, CRUEL FATE.
YES, OF COURSE. LEMME JUST LET MEE-MAW KNOW WE'RE TAKING OFF.
Gasp HOW DID-- HOW DID SHE--
HOW'D THAT WORK OUT FOR YOU, Hmm? IDIOT?
IT'S... Gasp IT'S... Gasp SORCERY...!
MEE-MAW?
MEE-MAW, WE'RE DONE FOR TODAY! I'LL BE BACK TOMORROW TO FINISH. GOING TO POP'S FOR DINNER, 'KAY?
ALRIGHT, DEAR!
MAKE SURE TO PUT YOUR JACKET ON! OTHERWISE, BOYS CAN SEE THAT YOU HAVE BREASTS NOW--
Heh, GOTTA GO, MEE-MAW! DON'T FORGET TO TAKE YOUR MILITARY-GRADE DEMENTIA MEDICINE, LIKE YOU'VE OBVIOUSLY BEEN FORGETTING TO...!

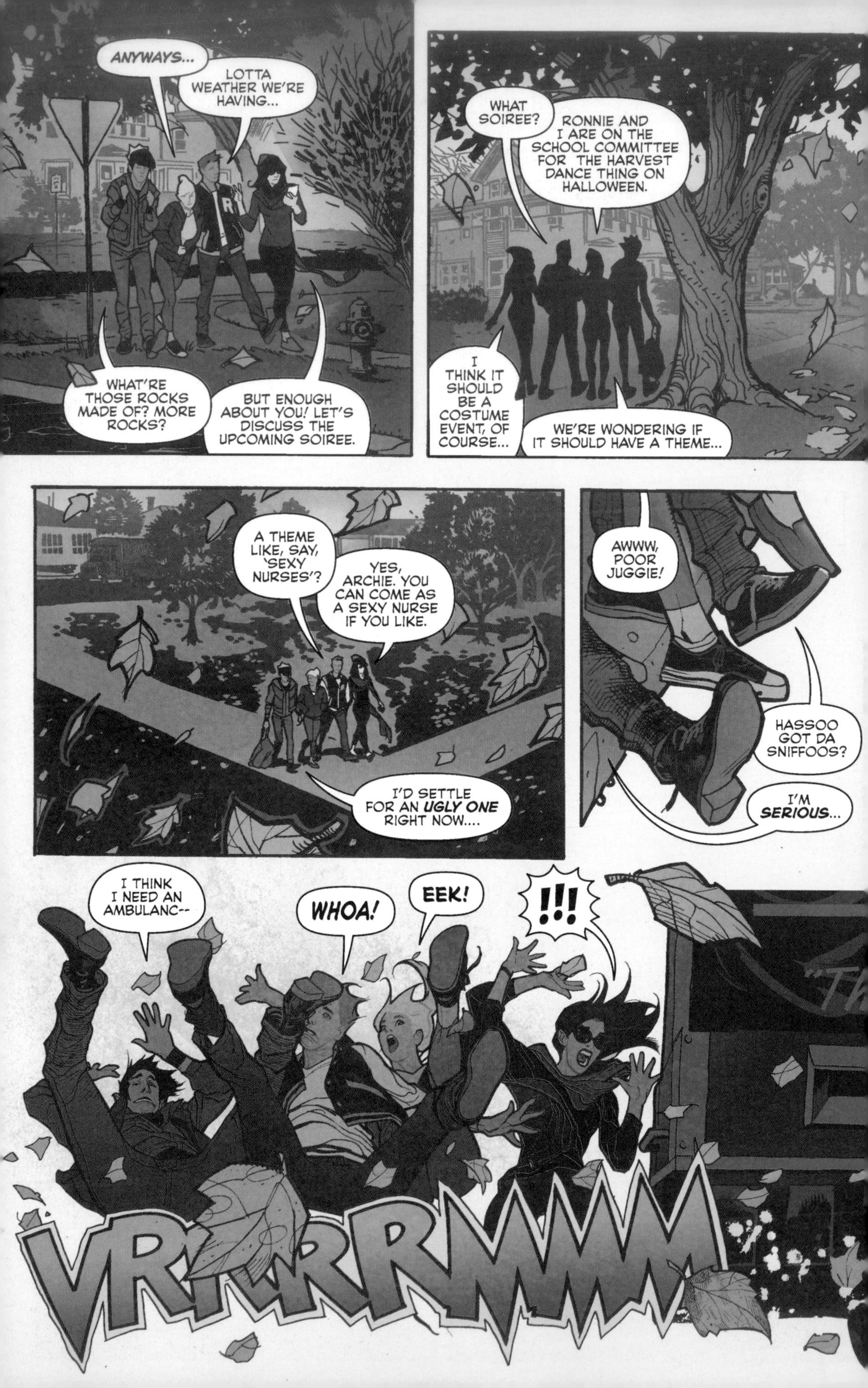
ANYWAYS...
LOTTA WEATHER WE'RE HAVING...
WHAT'RE THOSE ROCKS MADE OF? MORE ROCKS?
BUT ENOUGH ABOUT YOU! LET'S DISCUSS THE UPCOMING SOIREE.
WHAT SOIREE?
RONNIE AND I ARE ON THE SCHOOL COMMITTEE FOR THE HARVEST DANCE THING ON HALLOWEEN.
I THINK IT SHOULD BE A COSTUME EVENT, OF COURSE...
WE'RE WONDERING IF IT SHOULD HAVE A THEME...
A THEME LIKE, SAY, 'SEXY NURSES'?
YES, ARCHIE. YOU CAN COME AS A SEXY NURSE IF YOU LIKE.
I'D SETTLE FOR AN UGLY ONE RIGHT NOW....
AWWW, POOR JUGGIE!
HASSOO GOT DA SNIFFOOS?
I'M SERIOUS...
I THINK I NEED AN AMBULANC--
WHOA!
EEK!
!!!
VRRRMMM

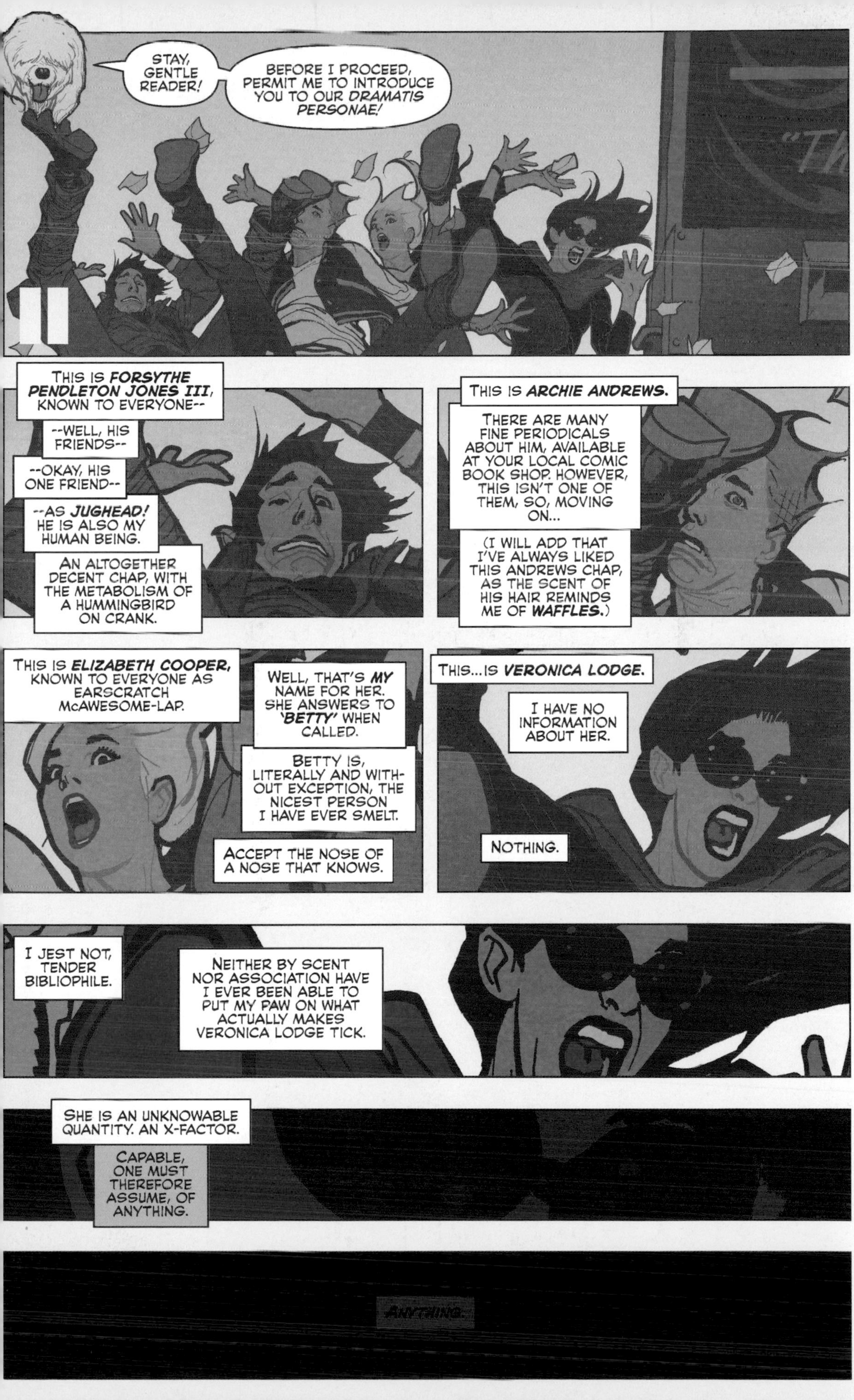
STAY, GENTLE READER!
BEFORE I PROCEED, PERMIT ME TO INTRODUCE YOU TO OUR *DRAMATIS PERSONAE!*
THIS IS ***FORSYTHE PENDLETON JONES III***, KNOWN TO EVERYONE--
--WELL, HIS FRIENDS--
--OKAY, HIS ONE FRIEND--
--AS ***JUGHEAD!*** HE IS ALSO MY HUMAN BEING.
AN ALTOGETHER DECENT CHAP, WITH THE METABOLISM OF A HUMMINGBIRD ON CRANK.
THIS IS ***ARCHIE ANDREWS.***
THERE ARE MANY FINE PERIODICALS ABOUT HIM, AVAILABLE AT YOUR LOCAL COMIC BOOK SHOP. HOWEVER, THIS ISN'T ONE OF THEM, SO, MOVING ON...
(I WILL ADD THAT I'VE ALWAYS LIKED THIS ANDREWS CHAP, AS THE SCENT OF HIS HAIR REMINDS ME OF ***WAFFLES.***)
THIS IS ***ELIZABETH COOPER,*** KNOWN TO EVERYONE AS EARSCRATCH McAWESOME-LAP.
WELL, THAT'S ***MY*** NAME FOR HER. SHE ANSWERS TO ***'BETTY'*** WHEN CALLED.
BETTY IS, LITERALLY AND WITHOUT EXCEPTION, THE NICEST PERSON I HAVE EVER SMELT.
ACCEPT THE NOSE OF A NOSE THAT KNOWS.
THIS...IS ***VERONICA LODGE.***
I HAVE NO INFORMATION ABOUT HER.
NOTHING.
I JEST NOT, TENDER BIBLIOPHILE.
NEITHER BY SCENT NOR ASSOCIATION HAVE I EVER BEEN ABLE TO PUT MY PAW ON WHAT ACTUALLY MAKES VERONICA LODGE TICK.
SHE IS AN UNKNOWABLE QUANTITY. AN X-FACTOR.
CAPABLE, ONE MUST THEREFORE ASSUME, OF ANYTHING.
ANYTHING.

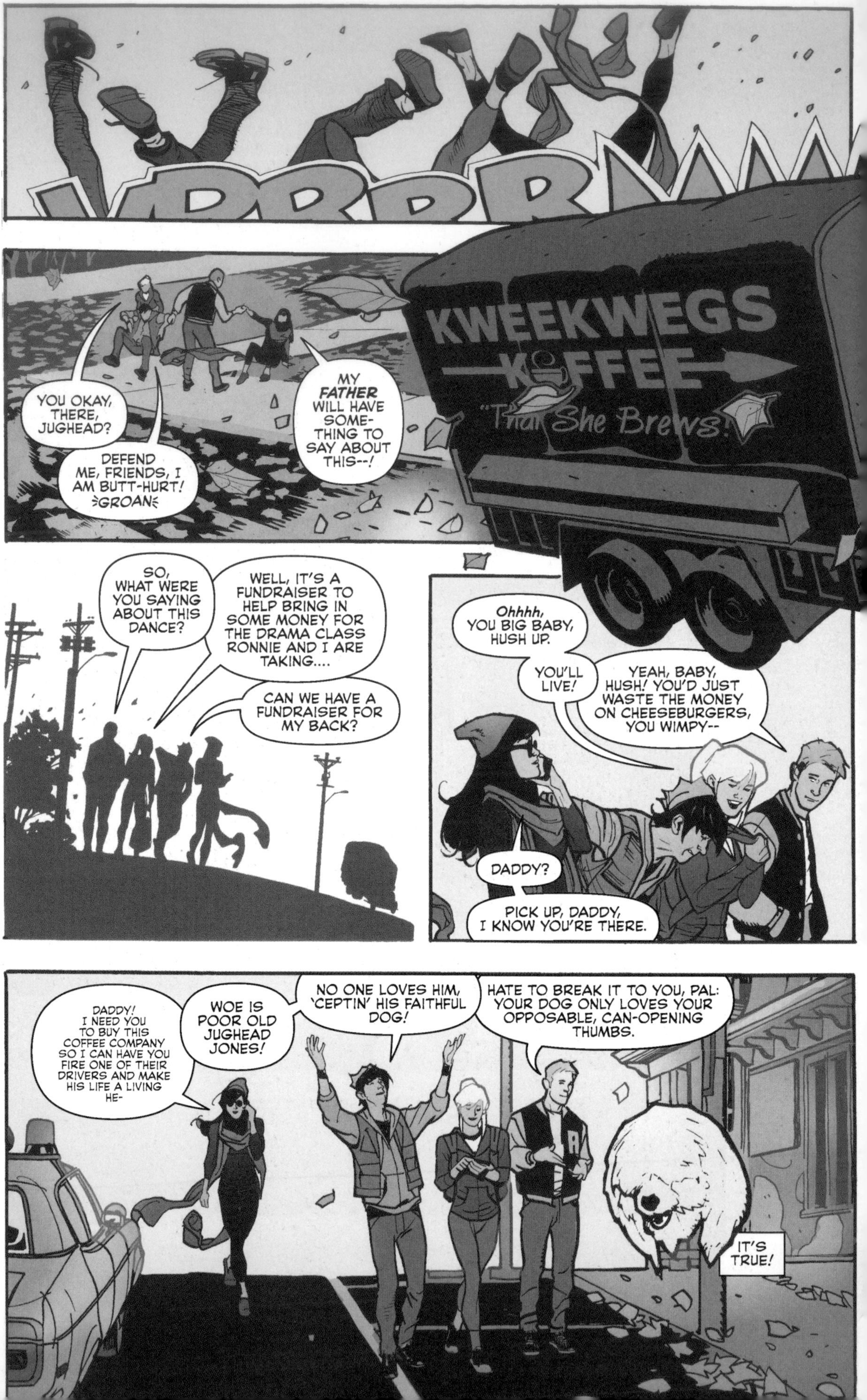
VRRRRAAAAAAA
KWEEKWEGS KOFFEE "That She Brews!"
YOU OKAY, THERE, JUGHEAD?
DEFEND ME, FRIENDS, I AM BUTT-HURT! ≥GROAN≤
MY *FATHER* WILL HAVE SOME-THING TO SAY ABOUT THIS--!
SO, WHAT WERE YOU SAYING ABOUT THIS DANCE?
WELL, IT'S A FUNDRAISER TO HELP BRING IN SOME MONEY FOR THE DRAMA CLASS RONNIE AND I ARE TAKING....
CAN WE HAVE A FUNDRAISER FOR MY BACK?
Ohhhh, YOU BIG BABY, HUSH UP.
YOU'LL LIVE!
YEAH, BABY, HUSH! YOU'D JUST WASTE THE MONEY ON CHEESEBURGERS, YOU WIMPY--
DADDY?
PICK UP, DADDY, I KNOW YOU'RE THERE.
DADDY! I NEED YOU TO BUY THIS COFFEE COMPANY SO I CAN HAVE YOU FIRE ONE OF THEIR DRIVERS AND MAKE HIS LIFE A LIVING HE-
WOE IS POOR OLD JUGHEAD JONES!
NO ONE LOVES HIM, 'CEPTIN' HIS FAITHFUL DOG!
HATE TO BREAK IT TO YOU, PAL: YOUR DOG ONLY LOVES YOUR OPPOSABLE, CAN-OPENING THUMBS.
IT'S TRUE!

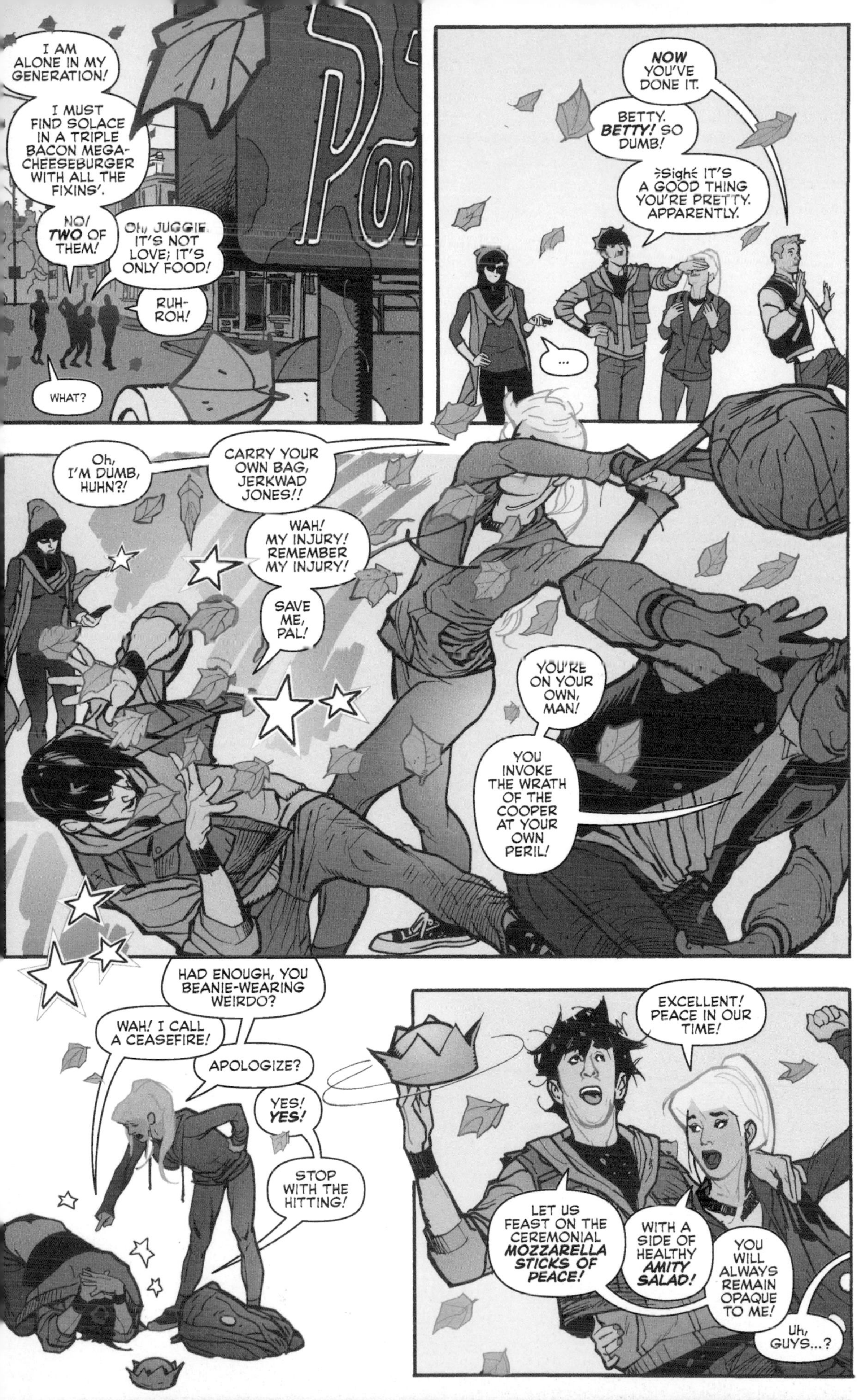

I AM ALONE IN MY GENERATION!
I MUST FIND SOLACE IN A TRIPLE BACON MEGA-CHEESEBURGER WITH ALL THE FIXINS'.
NO! TWO OF THEM!
OH, JUGGIE. IT'S NOT LOVE; IT'S ONLY FOOD!
RUH-ROH!
WHAT?
NOW YOU'VE DONE IT.
BETTY. BETTY! SO DUMB!
≈Sigh≈ IT'S A GOOD THING YOU'RE PRETTY. APPARENTLY.
...
Oh, I'M DUMB, HUHN?!
CARRY YOUR OWN BAG, JERKWAD JONES!!
WAH! MY INJURY! REMEMBER MY INJURY!
SAVE ME, PAL!
YOU'RE ON YOUR OWN, MAN!
YOU INVOKE THE WRATH OF THE COOPER AT YOUR OWN PERIL!
HAD ENOUGH, YOU BEANIE-WEARING WEIRDO?
WAH! I CALL A CEASEFIRE!
APOLOGIZE?
YES! YES!
STOP WITH THE HITTING!
EXCELLENT! PEACE IN OUR TIME!
LET US FEAST ON THE CEREMONIAL MOZZARELLA STICKS OF PEACE!
WITH A SIDE OF HEALTHY AMITY SALAD!
YOU WILL ALWAYS REMAIN OPAQUE TO ME!
Uh, GUYS...?

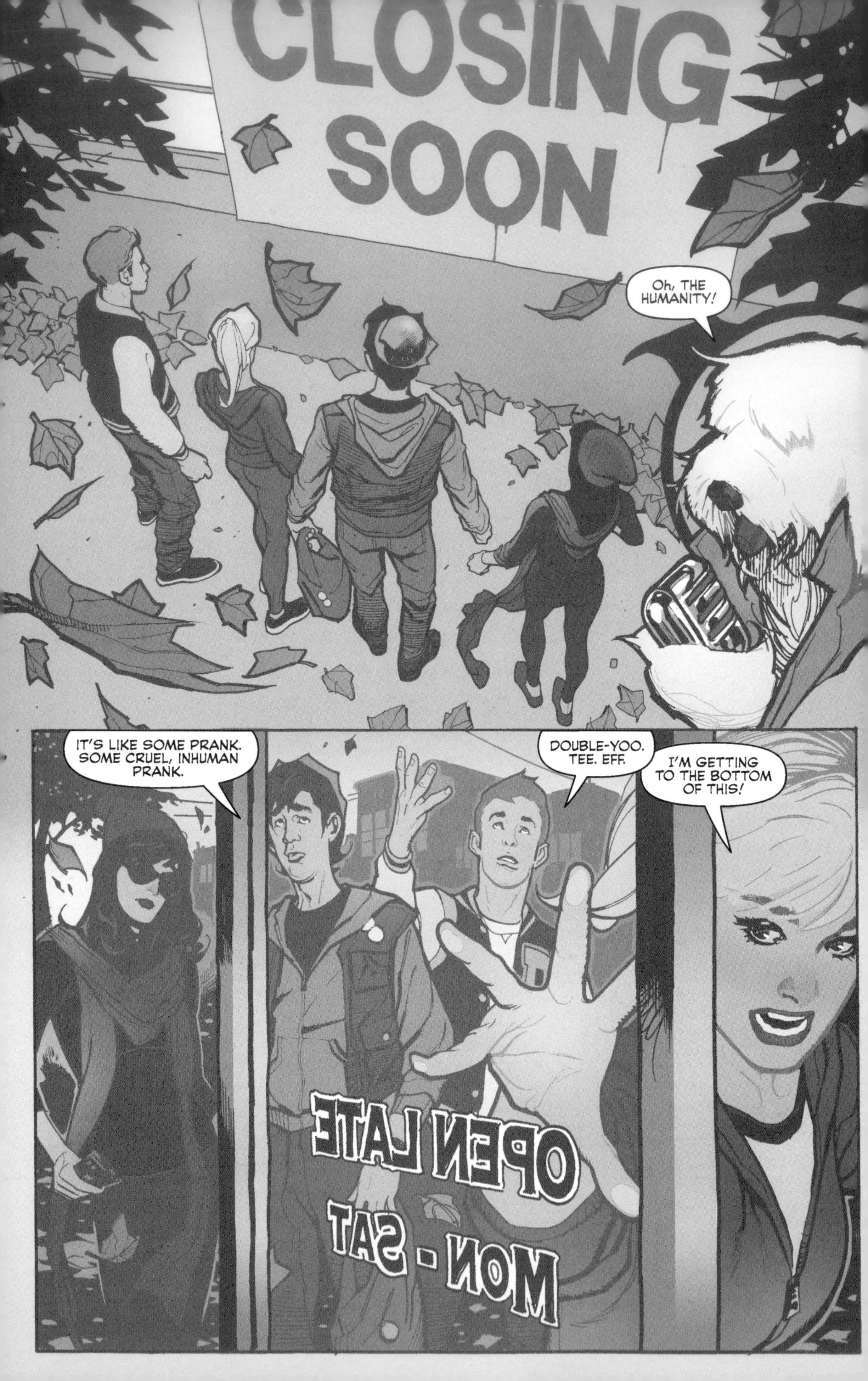
CLOSING SOON
Oh, THE HUMANITY!
IT'S LIKE SOME PRANK. SOME CRUEL, INHUMAN PRANK.
DOUBLE-YOO. TEE. EFF.
I'M GETTING TO THE BOTTOM OF THIS!

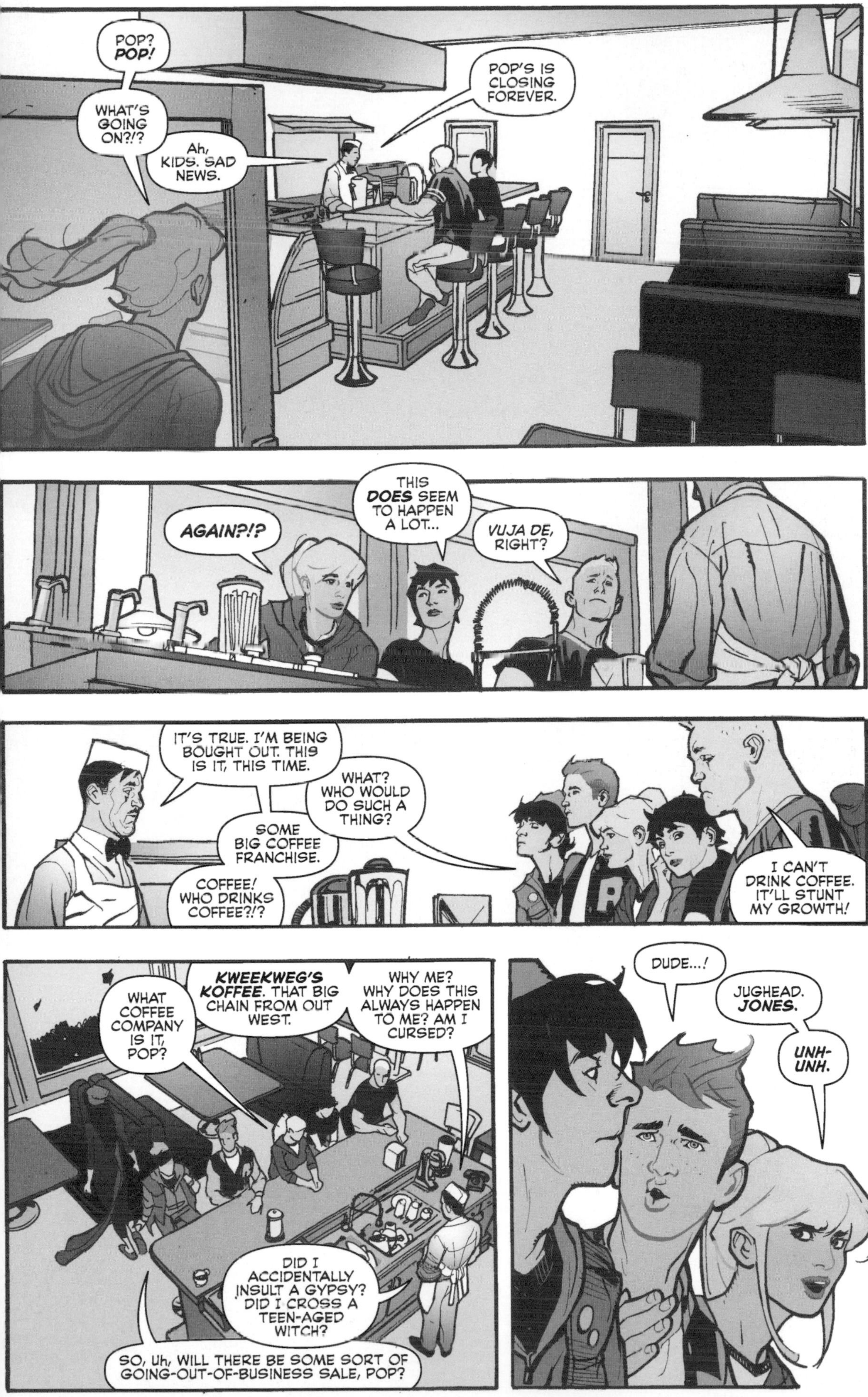
POP? POP!
WHAT'S GOING ON?!?
Ah, KIDS. SAD NEWS.
POP'S IS CLOSING FOREVER.
AGAIN?!?
THIS DOES SEEM TO HAPPEN A LOT...
VUJA DE, RIGHT?
IT'S TRUE. I'M BEING BOUGHT OUT. THIS IS IT, THIS TIME.
WHAT? WHO WOULD DO SUCH A THING?
SOME BIG COFFEE FRANCHISE.
COFFEE! WHO DRINKS COFFEE?!?
I CAN'T DRINK COFFEE. IT'LL STUNT MY GROWTH!
WHAT COFFEE COMPANY IS IT, POP?
KWEEKWEG'S KOFFEE. THAT BIG CHAIN FROM OUT WEST.
WHY ME? WHY DOES THIS ALWAYS HAPPEN TO ME? AM I CURSED?
DID I ACCIDENTALLY INSULT A GYPSY? DID I CROSS A TEEN-AGED WITCH?
SO, Uh, WILL THERE BE SOME SORT OF GOING-OUT-OF-BUSINESS SALE, POP?
DUDE...!
JUGHEAD. JONES.
UNH-UNH.

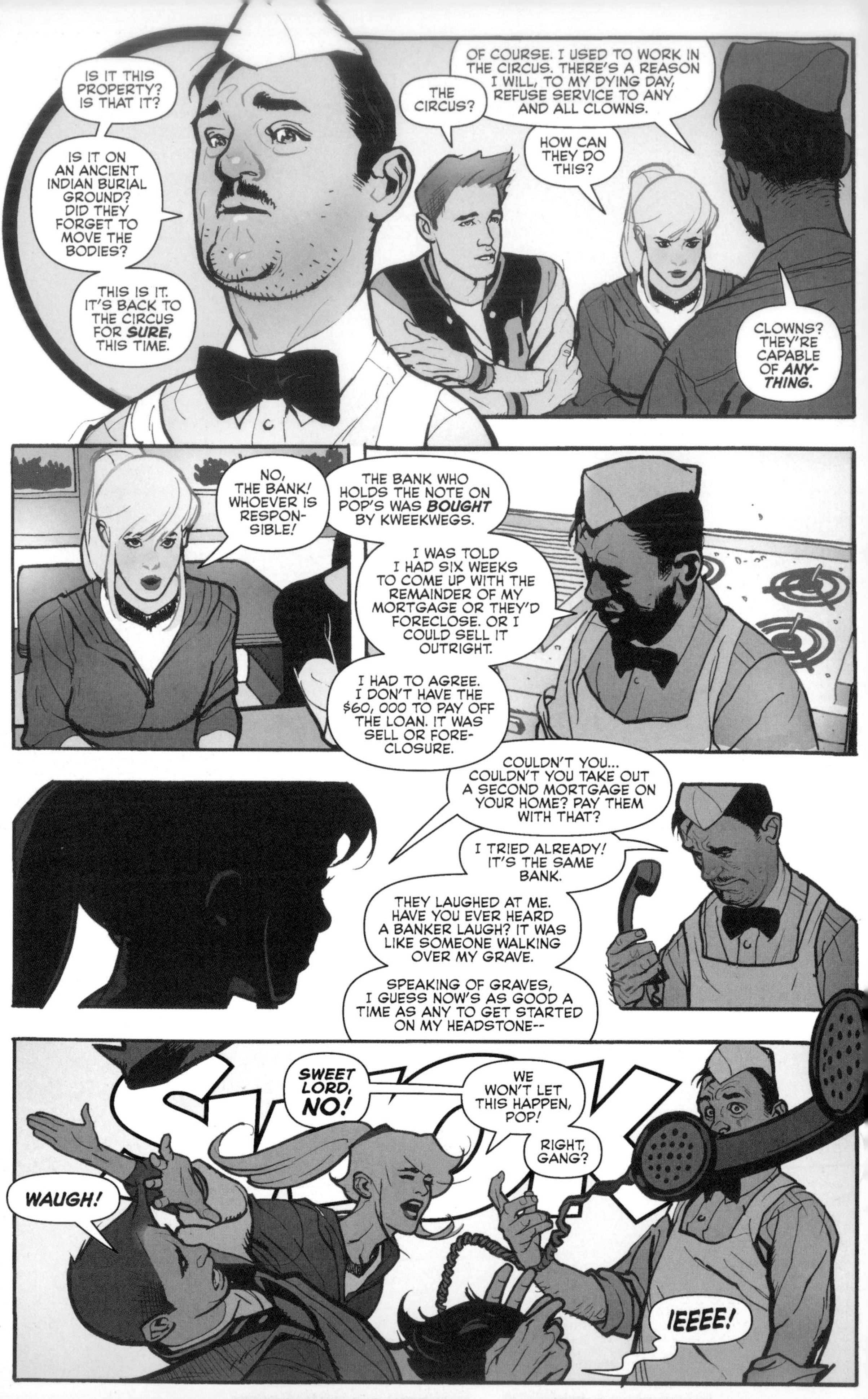
IS IT THIS PROPERTY? IS THAT IT?
IS IT ON AN ANCIENT INDIAN BURIAL GROUND? DID THEY FORGET TO MOVE THE BODIES?
THIS IS IT. IT'S BACK TO THE CIRCUS FOR SURE, THIS TIME.
THE CIRCUS?
OF COURSE. I USED TO WORK IN THE CIRCUS. THERE'S A REASON I WILL, TO MY DYING DAY, REFUSE SERVICE TO ANY AND ALL CLOWNS.
HOW CAN THEY DO THIS?
CLOWNS? THEY'RE CAPABLE OF ANYTHING.
NO, THE BANK! WHOEVER IS RESPONSIBLE!
THE BANK WHO HOLDS THE NOTE ON POP'S WAS BOUGHT BY KWEEKWEGS.
I WAS TOLD I HAD SIX WEEKS TO COME UP WITH THE REMAINDER OF MY MORTGAGE OR THEY'D FORECLOSE. OR I COULD SELL IT OUTRIGHT.
I HAD TO AGREE. I DON'T HAVE THE $60, 000 TO PAY OFF THE LOAN. IT WAS SELL OR FORECLOSURE.
COULDN'T YOU... COULDN'T YOU TAKE OUT A SECOND MORTGAGE ON YOUR HOME? PAY THEM WITH THAT?
I TRIED ALREADY! IT'S THE SAME BANK.
THEY LAUGHED AT ME. HAVE YOU EVER HEARD A BANKER LAUGH? IT WAS LIKE SOMEONE WALKING OVER MY GRAVE.
SPEAKING OF GRAVES, I GUESS NOW'S AS GOOD A TIME AS ANY TO GET STARTED ON MY HEADSTONE--
SWEET LORD, NO!
WE WON'T LET THIS HAPPEN, POP!
RIGHT, GANG?
WAUGH!
IEEEE!

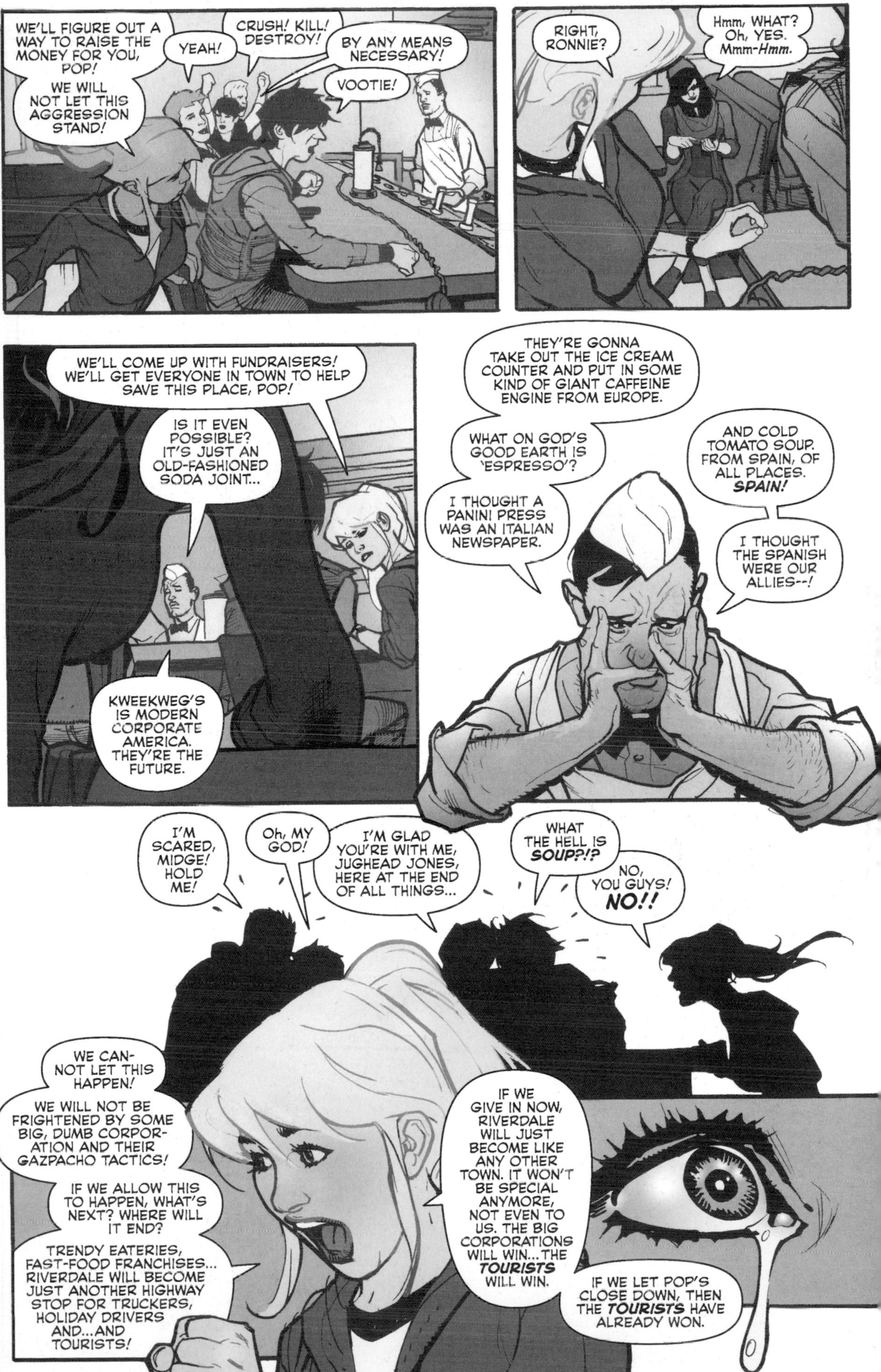

WE'LL FIGURE OUT A WAY TO RAISE THE MONEY FOR YOU, POP!
WE WILL NOT LET THIS AGGRESSION STAND!
YEAH!
CRUSH! KILL! DESTROY!
BY ANY MEANS NECESSARY!
VOOTIE!
RIGHT, RONNIE?
Hmm, WHAT? Oh, YES. Mmm-Hmm.
WE'LL COME UP WITH FUNDRAISERS! WE'LL GET EVERYONE IN TOWN TO HELP SAVE THIS PLACE, POP!
IS IT EVEN POSSIBLE? IT'S JUST AN OLD-FASHIONED SODA JOINT...
KWEEKWEG'S IS MODERN CORPORATE AMERICA. THEY'RE THE FUTURE.
THEY'RE GONNA TAKE OUT THE ICE CREAM COUNTER AND PUT IN SOME KIND OF GIANT CAFFEINE ENGINE FROM EUROPE.
WHAT ON GOD'S GOOD EARTH IS 'ESPRESSO'?
I THOUGHT A PANINI PRESS WAS AN ITALIAN NEWSPAPER.
AND COLD TOMATO SOUP. FROM SPAIN, OF ALL PLACES. SPAIN!
I THOUGHT THE SPANISH WERE OUR ALLIES--!
I'M SCARED, MIDGE! HOLD ME!
Oh, MY GOD!
I'M GLAD YOU'RE WITH ME, JUGHEAD JONES, HERE AT THE END OF ALL THINGS...
WHAT THE HELL IS SOUP?!?
NO, YOU GUYS! NO!!
WE CAN-NOT LET THIS HAPPEN!
WE WILL NOT BE FRIGHTENED BY SOME BIG, DUMB CORPOR-ATION AND THEIR GAZPACHO TACTICS!
IF WE ALLOW THIS TO HAPPEN, WHAT'S NEXT? WHERE WILL IT END?
TRENDY EATERIES, FAST-FOOD FRANCHISES... RIVERDALE WILL BECOME JUST ANOTHER HIGHWAY STOP FOR TRUCKERS, HOLIDAY DRIVERS AND...AND TOURISTS!
IF WE GIVE IN NOW, RIVERDALE WILL JUST BECOME LIKE ANY OTHER TOWN. IT WON'T BE SPECIAL ANYMORE, NOT EVEN TO US. THE BIG CORPORATIONS WILL WIN...THE TOURISTS WILL WIN.
IF WE LET POP'S CLOSE DOWN, THEN THE TOURISTS HAVE ALREADY WON.

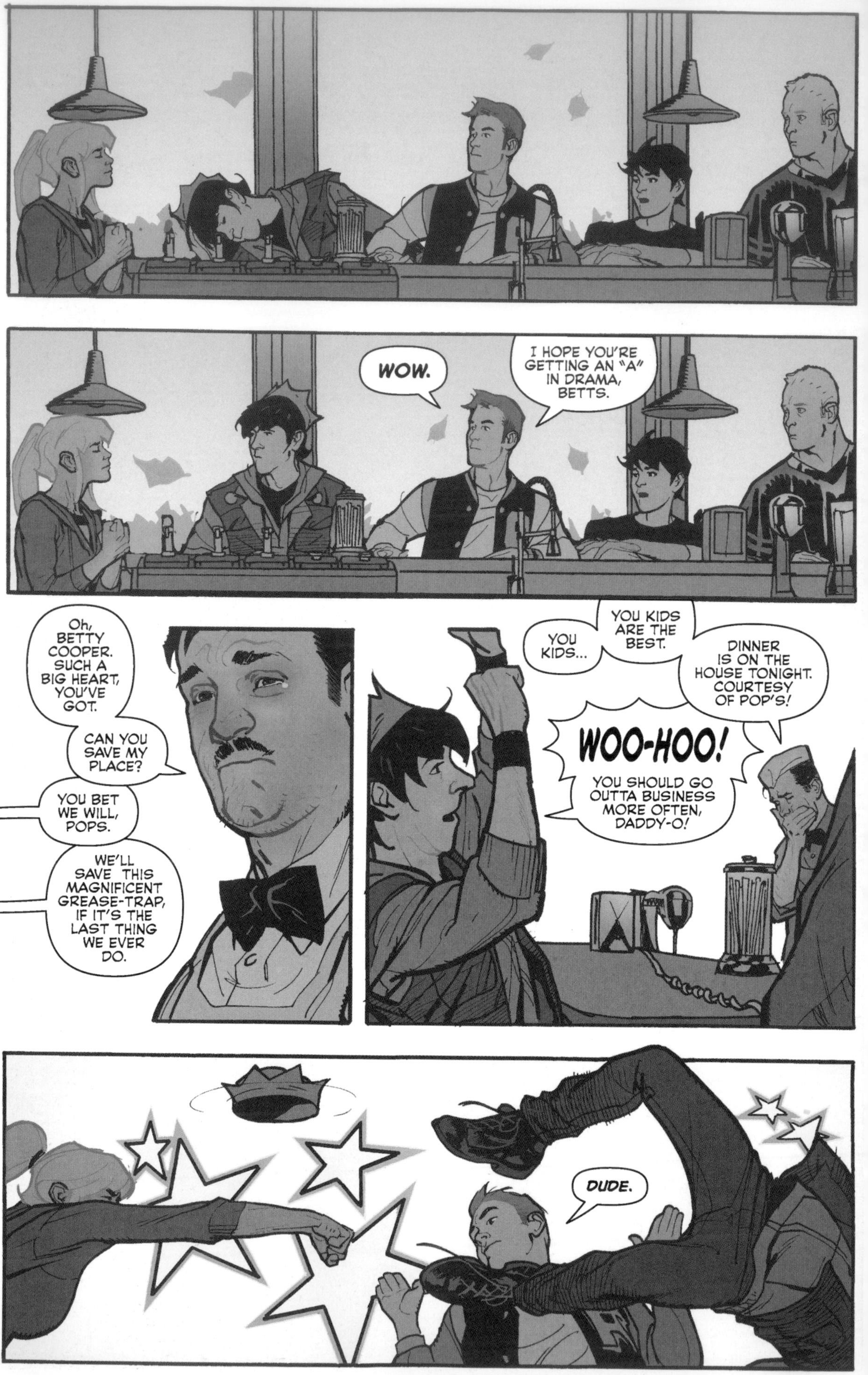
WOW.
I HOPE YOU'RE GETTING AN "A" IN DRAMA, BETTS.
Oh, BETTY COOPER. SUCH A BIG HEART, YOU'VE GOT.
CAN YOU SAVE MY PLACE?
YOU BET WE WILL, POPS.
WE'LL SAVE THIS MAGNIFICENT GREASE-TRAP, IF IT'S THE LAST THING WE EVER DO.
YOU KIDS...
YOU KIDS ARE THE BEST.
DINNER IS ON THE HOUSE TONIGHT. COURTESY OF POP'S!
WOO-HOO!
YOU SHOULD GO OUTTA BUSINESS MORE OFTEN, DADDY-O!
DUDE.

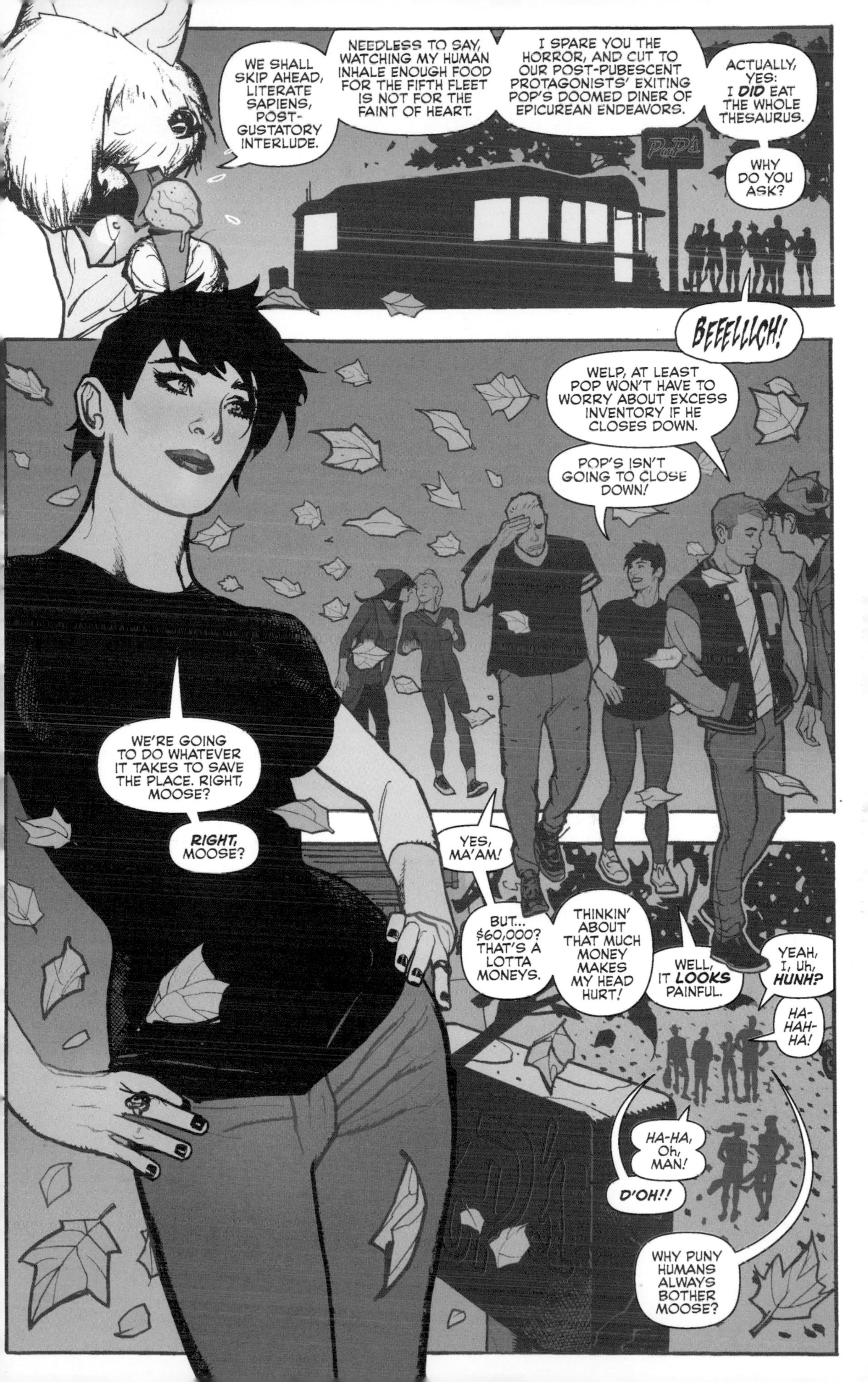

WE SHALL SKIP AHEAD, LITERATE SAPIENS, POST-GUSTATORY INTERLUDE.
NEEDLESS TO SAY, WATCHING MY HUMAN INHALE ENOUGH FOOD FOR THE FIFTH FLEET IS NOT FOR THE FAINT OF HEART.
I SPARE YOU THE HORROR, AND CUT TO OUR POST-PUBESCENT PROTAGONISTS' EXITING POP'S DOOMED DINER OF EPICUREAN ENDEAVORS.
ACTUALLY, YES: I **DID** EAT THE WHOLE THESAURUS.
WHY DO YOU ASK?
POP'S
BEEELLLCH!
WELP, AT LEAST POP WON'T HAVE TO WORRY ABOUT EXCESS INVENTORY IF HE CLOSES DOWN.
POP'S ISN'T GOING TO CLOSE DOWN!
WE'RE GOING TO DO WHATEVER IT TAKES TO SAVE THE PLACE. RIGHT, MOOSE?
RIGHT, MOOSE?
YES, MA'AM!
BUT... $60,000? THAT'S A LOTTA MONEYS.
THINKIN' ABOUT THAT MUCH MONEY MAKES MY HEAD HURT!
WELL, IT **LOOKS** PAINFUL.
YEAH, I, Uh, **HUNH?**
HA-HAH-HA!
HA-HA, Oh, MAN!
D'OH!!
WHY PUNY HUMANS ALWAYS BOTHER MOOSE?

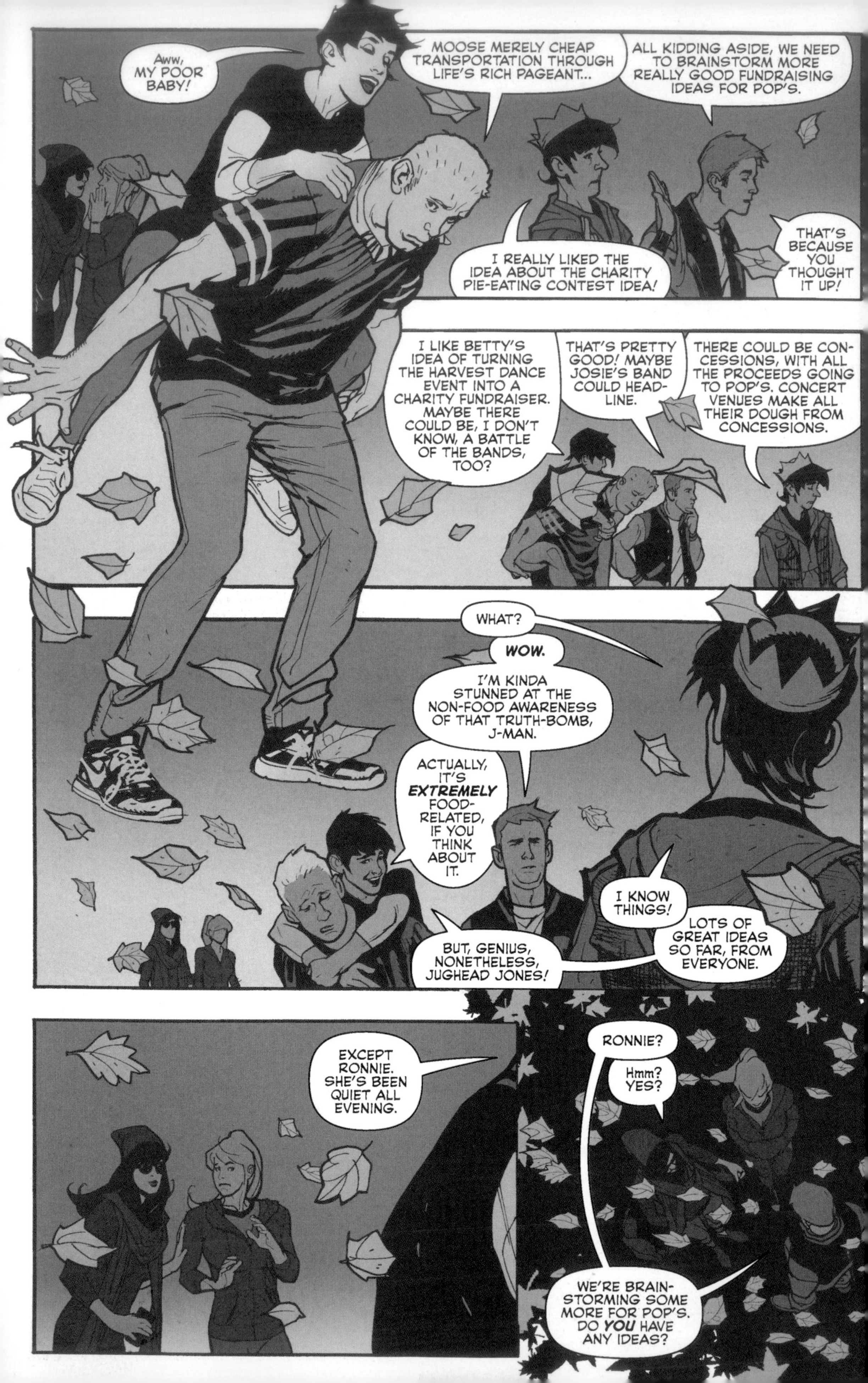
Aww, MY POOR BABY!
MOOSE MERELY CHEAP TRANSPORTATION THROUGH LIFE'S RICH PAGEANT...
ALL KIDDING ASIDE, WE NEED TO BRAINSTORM MORE REALLY GOOD FUNDRAISING IDEAS FOR POP'S.
I REALLY LIKED THE IDEA ABOUT THE CHARITY PIE-EATING CONTEST IDEA!
THAT'S BECAUSE YOU THOUGHT IT UP!
I LIKE BETTY'S IDEA OF TURNING THE HARVEST DANCE EVENT INTO A CHARITY FUNDRAISER. MAYBE THERE COULD BE, I DON'T KNOW, A BATTLE OF THE BANDS, TOO?
THAT'S PRETTY GOOD! MAYBE JOSIE'S BAND COULD HEAD-LINE.
THERE COULD BE CON-CESSIONS, WITH ALL THE PROCEEDS GOING TO POP'S. CONCERT VENUES MAKE ALL THEIR DOUGH FROM CONCESSIONS.
WHAT?
WOW.
I'M KINDA STUNNED AT THE NON-FOOD AWARENESS OF THAT TRUTH-BOMB, J-MAN.
ACTUALLY, IT'S ***EXTREMELY*** FOOD-RELATED, IF YOU THINK ABOUT IT.
I KNOW THINGS!
BUT, GENIUS, NONETHELESS, JUGHEAD JONES!
LOTS OF GREAT IDEAS SO FAR, FROM EVERYONE.
EXCEPT RONNIE. SHE'S BEEN QUIET ALL EVENING.
RONNIE?
Hmm? YES?
WE'RE BRAIN-STORMING SOME MORE FOR POP'S. DO ***YOU*** HAVE ANY IDEAS?

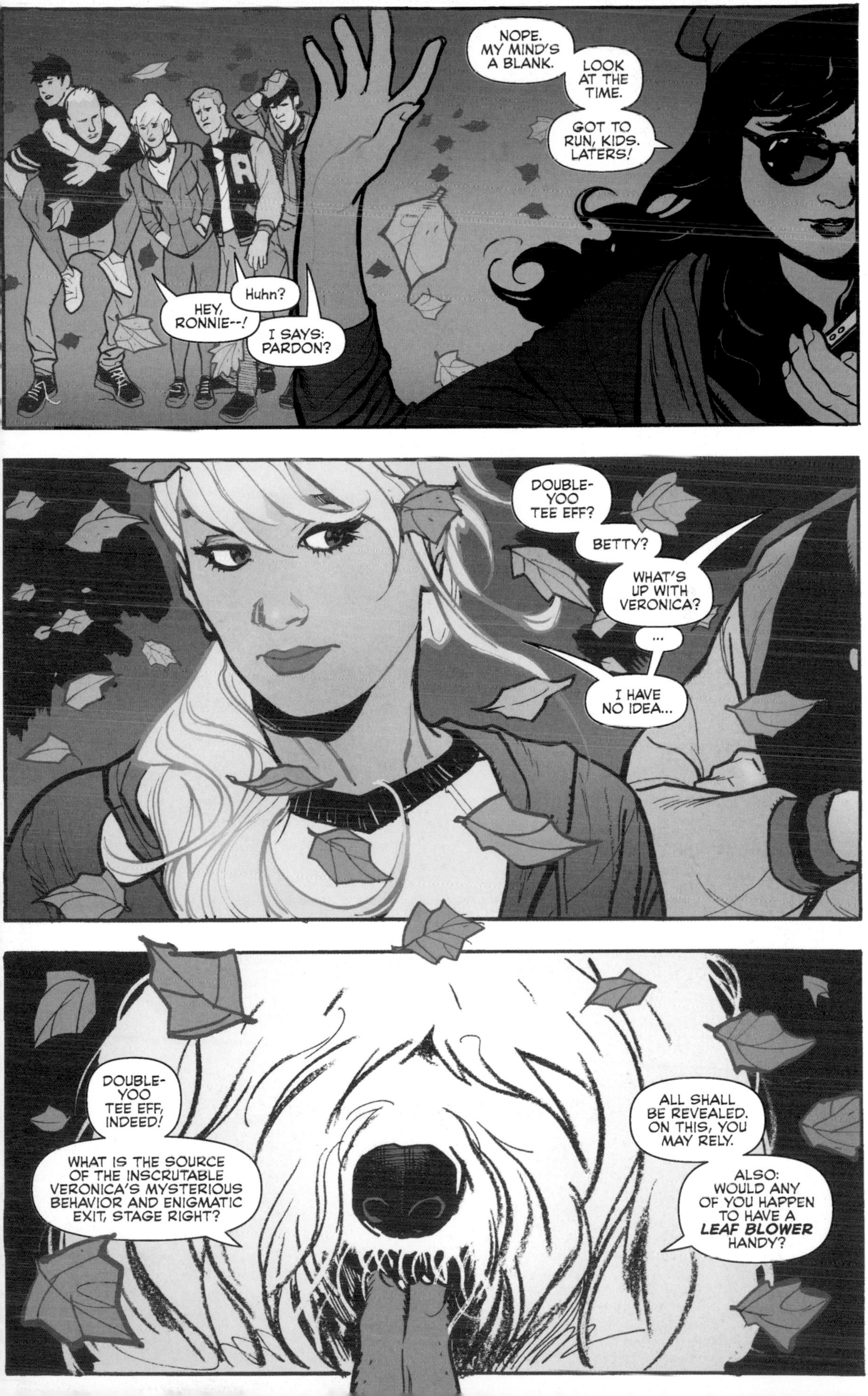
NOPE. MY MIND'S A BLANK.
LOOK AT THE TIME.
GOT TO RUN, KIDS. LATERS!
HEY, RONNIE--!
Huhn?
I SAYS: PARDON?
DOUBLE-YOO TEE EFF?
BETTY?
WHAT'S UP WITH VERONICA?
...
I HAVE NO IDEA...
DOUBLE-YOO TEE EFF, INDEED!
WHAT IS THE SOURCE OF THE INSCRUTABLE VERONICA'S MYSTERIOUS BEHAVIOR AND ENIGMATIC EXIT, STAGE RIGHT?
ALL SHALL BE REVEALED. ON THIS, YOU MAY RELY.
ALSO: WOULD ANY OF YOU HAPPEN TO HAVE A **LEAF BLOWER** HANDY?

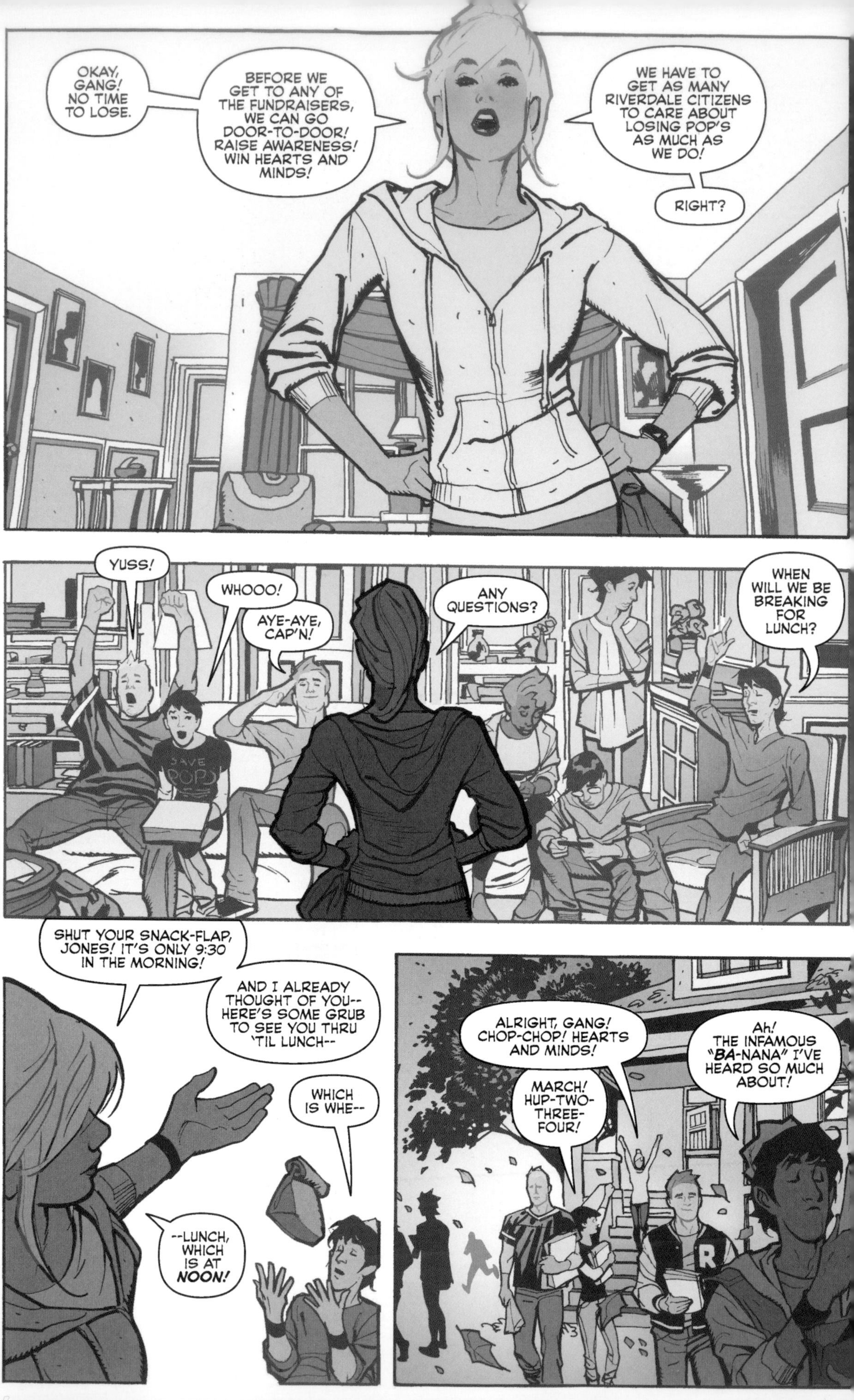
OKAY, GANG! NO TIME TO LOSE.
BEFORE WE GET TO ANY OF THE FUNDRAISERS, WE CAN GO DOOR-TO-DOOR! RAISE AWARENESS! WIN HEARTS AND MINDS!
WE HAVE TO GET AS MANY RIVERDALE CITIZENS TO CARE ABOUT LOSING POP'S AS MUCH AS WE DO!
RIGHT?
YUSS!
WHOOO!
AYE-AYE, CAP'N!
ANY QUESTIONS?
WHEN WILL WE BE BREAKING FOR LUNCH?
SAVE POP'S
SHUT YOUR SNACK-FLAP, JONES! IT'S ONLY 9:30 IN THE MORNING!
AND I ALREADY THOUGHT OF YOU-- HERE'S SOME GRUB TO SEE YOU THRU 'TIL LUNCH--
WHICH IS WHE--
--LUNCH, WHICH IS AT NOON!
ALRIGHT, GANG! CHOP-CHOP! HEARTS AND MINDS!
MARCH! HUP-TWO-THREE-FOUR!
Ah! THE INFAMOUS "BA-NANA" I'VE HEARD SO MUCH ABOUT!
R

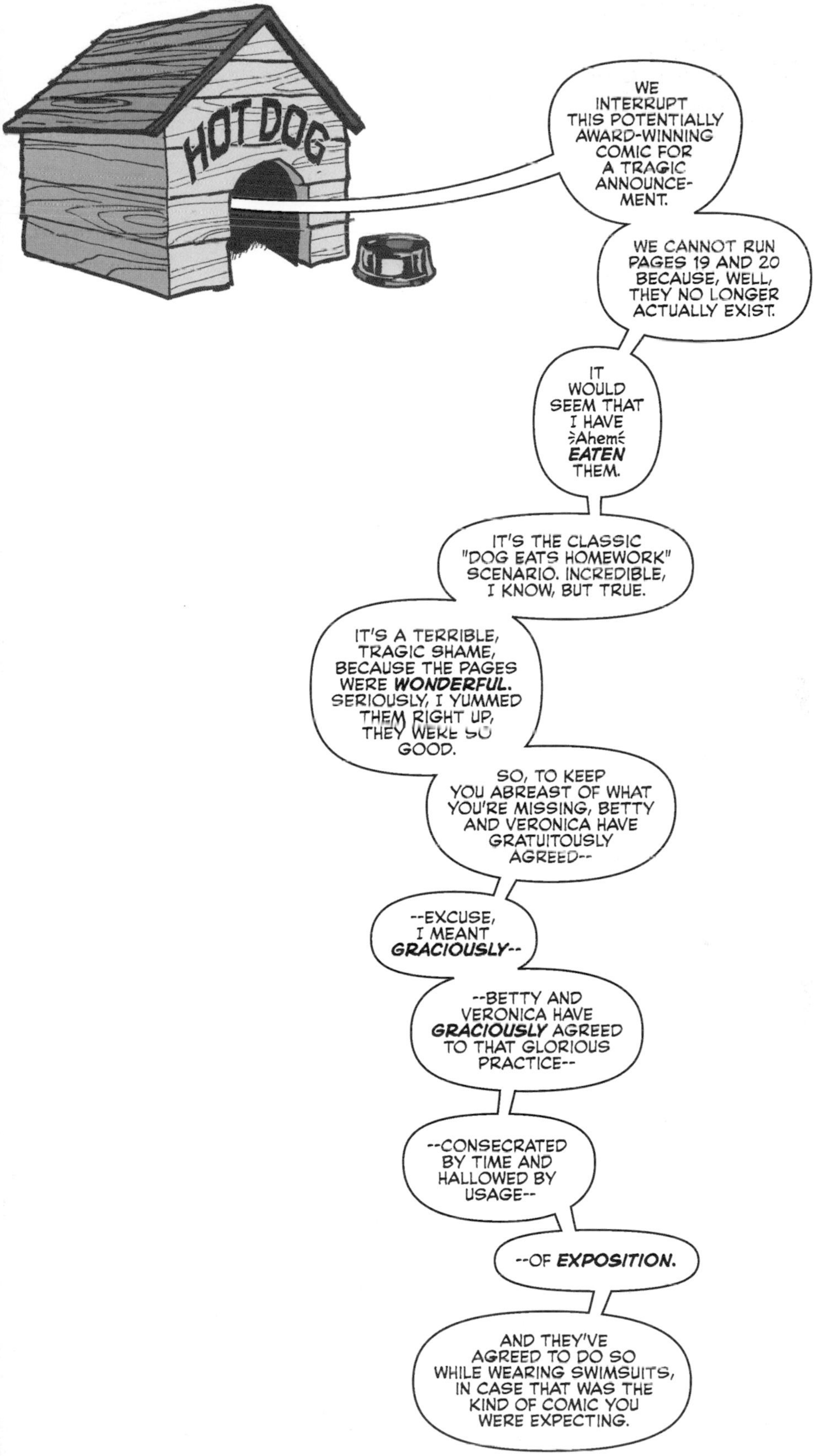
HOT DOG
WE INTERRUPT THIS POTENTIALLY AWARD-WINNING COMIC FOR A TRAGIC ANNOUNCE-MENT.
WE CANNOT RUN PAGES 19 AND 20 BECAUSE, WELL, THEY NO LONGER ACTUALLY EXIST.
IT WOULD SEEM THAT I HAVE Ahem EATEN THEM.
IT'S THE CLASSIC "DOG EATS HOMEWORK" SCENARIO. INCREDIBLE, I KNOW, BUT TRUE.
IT'S A TERRIBLE, TRAGIC SHAME, BECAUSE THE PAGES WERE WONDERFUL. SERIOUSLY, I YUMMED THEM RIGHT UP, THEY WERE SO GOOD.
SO, TO KEEP YOU ABREAST OF WHAT YOU'RE MISSING, BETTY AND VERONICA HAVE GRATUITOUSLY AGREED--
--EXCUSE, I MEANT GRACIOUSLY--
--BETTY AND VERONICA HAVE GRACIOUSLY AGREED TO THAT GLORIOUS PRACTICE--
--CONSECRATED BY TIME AND HALLOWED BY USAGE--
--OF EXPOSITION.
AND THEY'VE AGREED TO DO SO WHILE WEARING SWIMSUITS, IN CASE THAT WAS THE KIND OF COMIC YOU WERE EXPECTING.

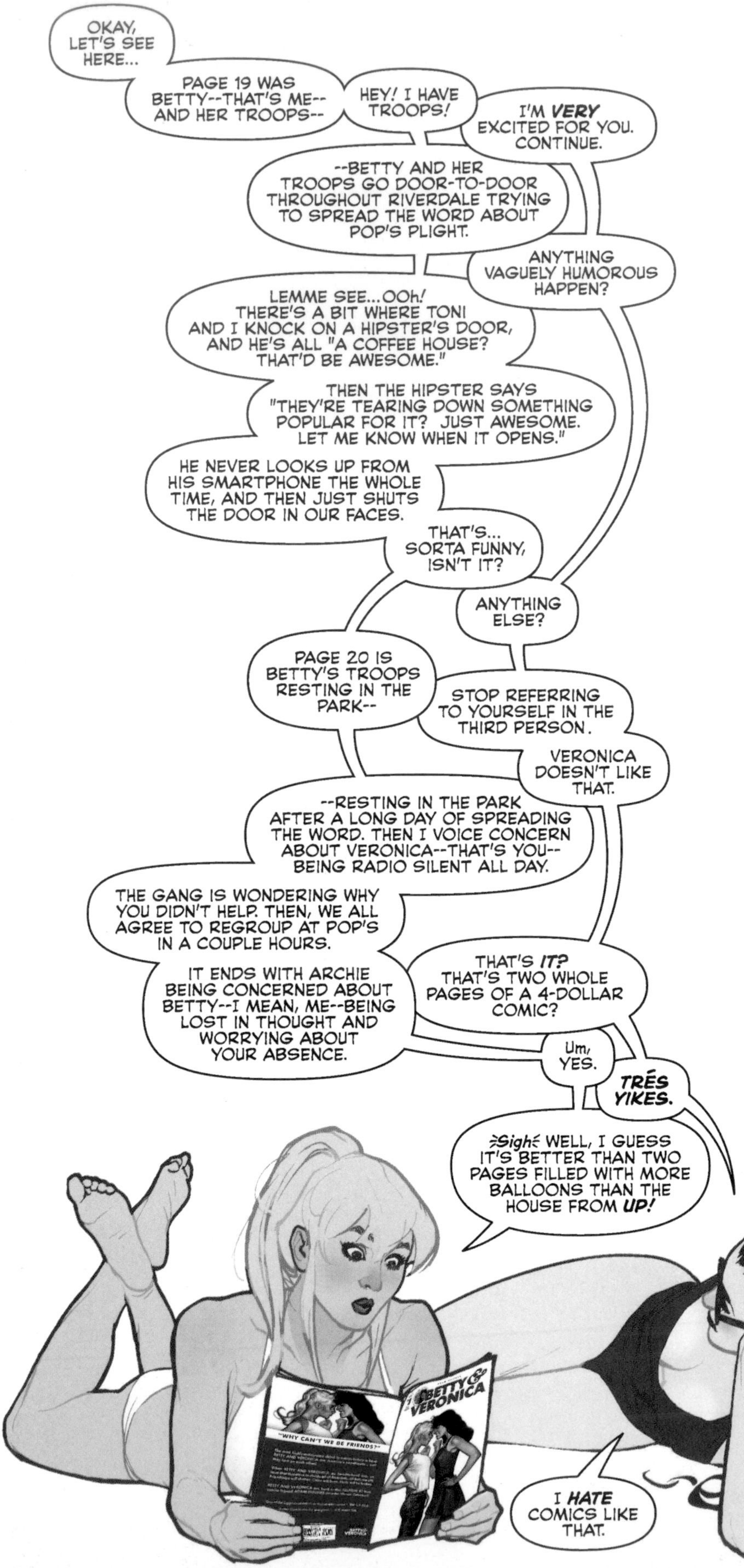
OKAY, LET'S SEE HERE...
PAGE 19 WAS BETTY--THAT'S ME--AND HER TROOPS--
HEY! I HAVE TROOPS!
I'M VERY EXCITED FOR YOU. CONTINUE.
--BETTY AND HER TROOPS GO DOOR-TO-DOOR THROUGHOUT RIVERDALE TRYING TO SPREAD THE WORD ABOUT POP'S PLIGHT.
ANYTHING VAGUELY HUMOROUS HAPPEN?
LEMME SEE...OOh! THERE'S A BIT WHERE TONI AND I KNOCK ON A HIPSTER'S DOOR, AND HE'S ALL "A COFFEE HOUSE? THAT'D BE AWESOME."
THEN THE HIPSTER SAYS "THEY'RE TEARING DOWN SOMETHING POPULAR FOR IT? JUST AWESOME. LET ME KNOW WHEN IT OPENS."
HE NEVER LOOKS UP FROM HIS SMARTPHONE THE WHOLE TIME, AND THEN JUST SHUTS THE DOOR IN OUR FACES.
THAT'S... SORTA FUNNY, ISN'T IT?
ANYTHING ELSE?
PAGE 20 IS BETTY'S TROOPS RESTING IN THE PARK--
STOP REFERRING TO YOURSELF IN THE THIRD PERSON.
VERONICA DOESN'T LIKE THAT.
--RESTING IN THE PARK AFTER A LONG DAY OF SPREADING THE WORD. THEN I VOICE CONCERN ABOUT VERONICA--THAT'S YOU--BEING RADIO SILENT ALL DAY.
THE GANG IS WONDERING WHY YOU DIDN'T HELP. THEN, WE ALL AGREE TO REGROUP AT POP'S IN A COUPLE HOURS.
IT ENDS WITH ARCHIE BEING CONCERNED ABOUT BETTY--I MEAN, ME--BEING LOST IN THOUGHT AND WORRYING ABOUT YOUR ABSENCE.
THAT'S IT? THAT'S TWO WHOLE PAGES OF A 4-DOLLAR COMIC?
Um, YES.
TRÉS YIKES.
Sigh WELL, I GUESS IT'S BETTER THAN TWO PAGES FILLED WITH MORE BALLOONS THAN THE HOUSE FROM UP!
BETTY & VERONICA
"WHY CAN'T WE BE FRIENDS?"
I HATE COMICS LIKE THAT.

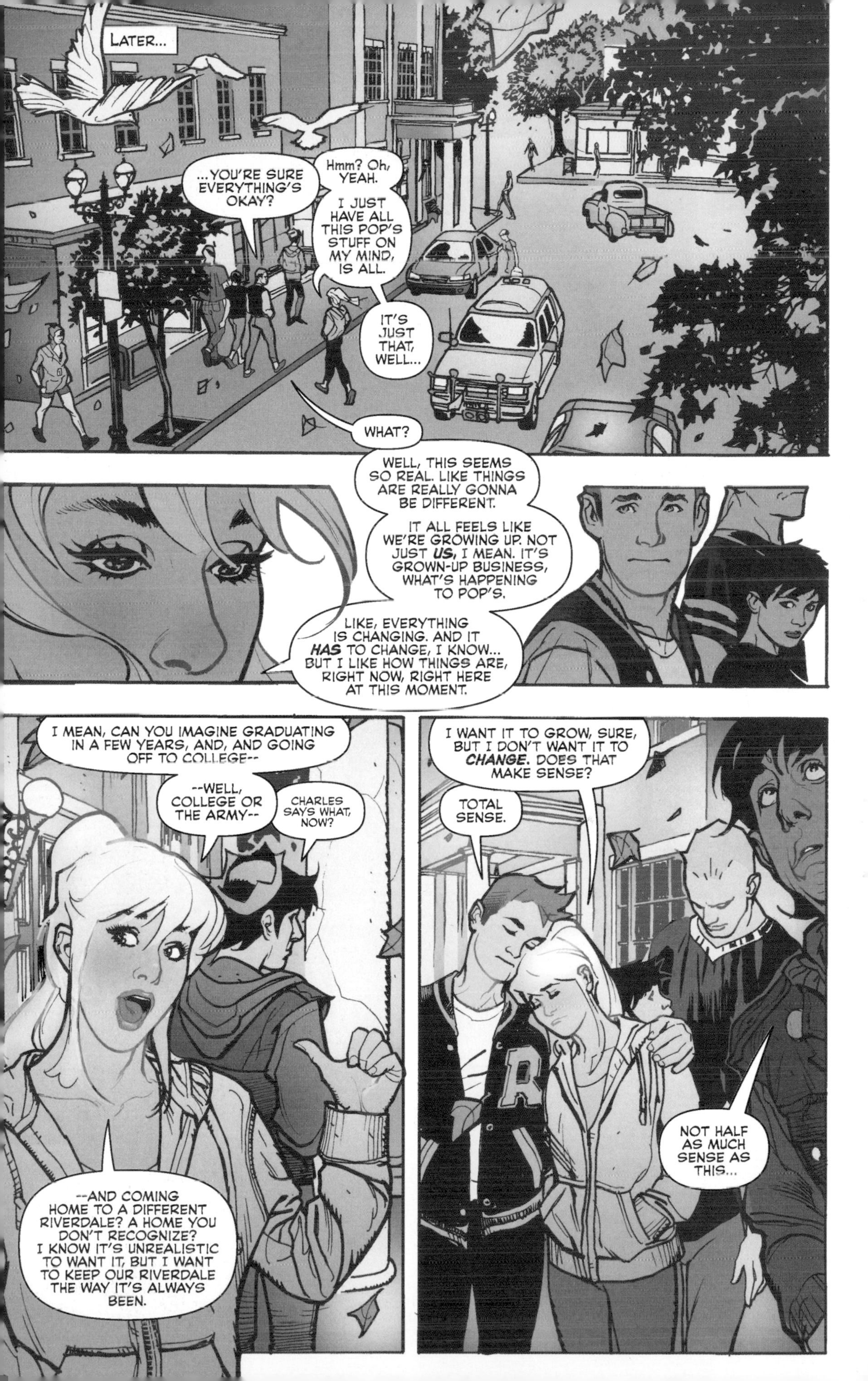
LATER...
...YOU'RE SURE EVERYTHING'S OKAY?
Hmm? Oh, YEAH.
I JUST HAVE ALL THIS POP'S STUFF ON MY MIND, IS ALL.
IT'S JUST THAT, WELL...
WHAT?
WELL, THIS SEEMS SO REAL. LIKE THINGS ARE REALLY GONNA BE DIFFERENT.
IT ALL FEELS LIKE WE'RE GROWING UP. NOT JUST US, I MEAN. IT'S GROWN-UP BUSINESS, WHAT'S HAPPENING TO POP'S.
LIKE, EVERYTHING IS CHANGING. AND IT HAS TO CHANGE, I KNOW... BUT I LIKE HOW THINGS ARE, RIGHT NOW, RIGHT HERE AT THIS MOMENT.
I MEAN, CAN YOU IMAGINE GRADUATING IN A FEW YEARS, AND, AND GOING OFF TO COLLEGE--
--WELL, COLLEGE OR THE ARMY--
CHARLES SAYS WHAT, NOW?
--AND COMING HOME TO A DIFFERENT RIVERDALE? A HOME YOU DON'T RECOGNIZE? I KNOW IT'S UNREALISTIC TO WANT IT, BUT I WANT TO KEEP OUR RIVERDALE THE WAY IT'S ALWAYS BEEN.
I WANT IT TO GROW, SURE, BUT I DON'T WANT IT TO CHANGE. DOES THAT MAKE SENSE?
TOTAL SENSE.
NOT HALF AS MUCH SENSE AS THIS...

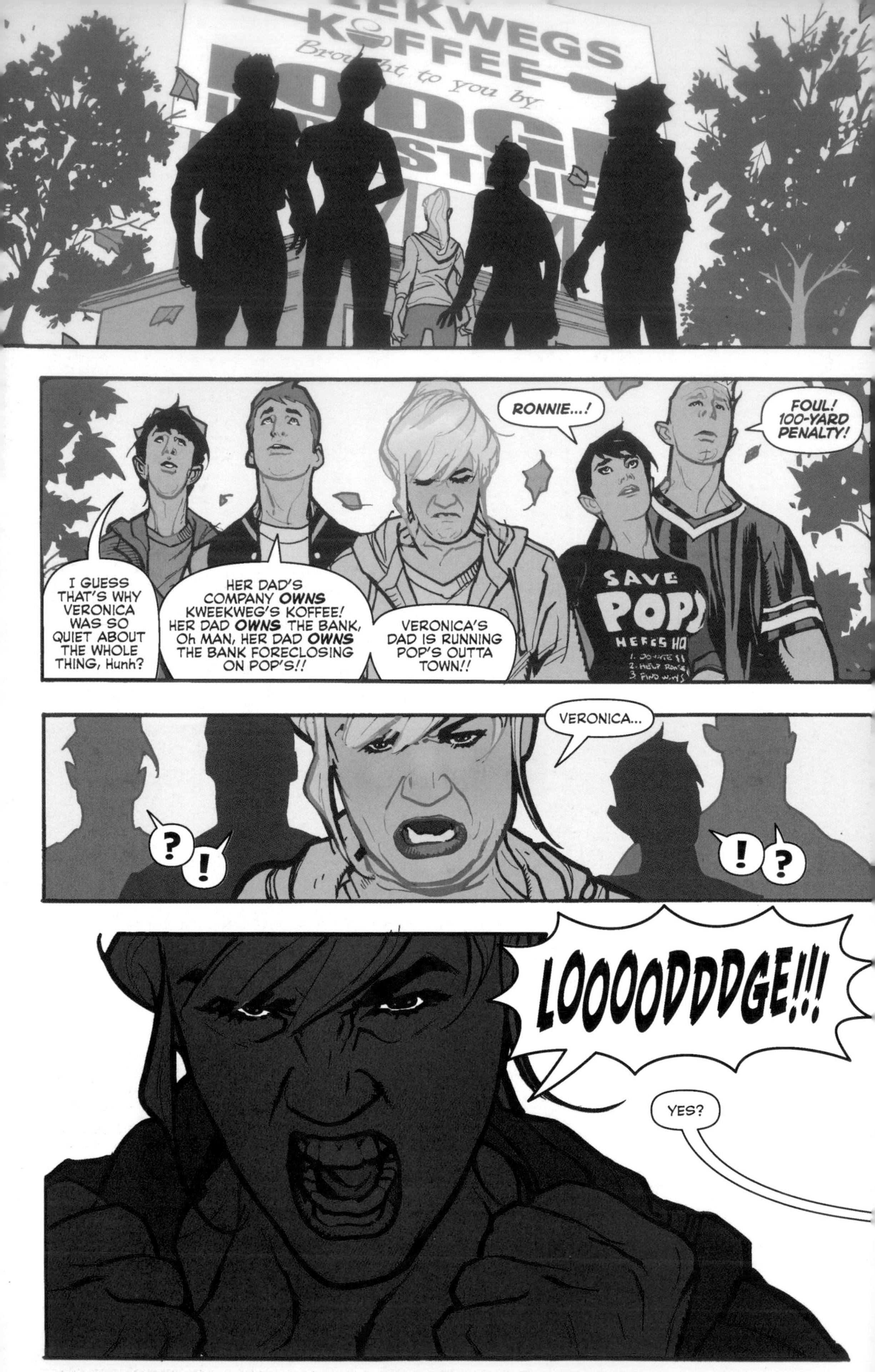
EKWEGS KOFFEE
Brought to you by
LODGE INDUSTRIES
RONNIE...!
FOUL! 100-YARD PENALTY!
I GUESS THAT'S WHY VERONICA WAS SO QUIET ABOUT THE WHOLE THING, Hunh?
HER DAD'S COMPANY OWNS KWEEKWEG'S KOFFEE! HER DAD OWNS THE BANK, Oh MAN, HER DAD OWNS THE BANK FORECLOSING ON POP'S!!
VERONICA'S DAD IS RUNNING POP'S OUTTA TOWN!!
SAVE POP'S
VERONICA...
?!
!?
LOOOODDDGE!!!
YES?

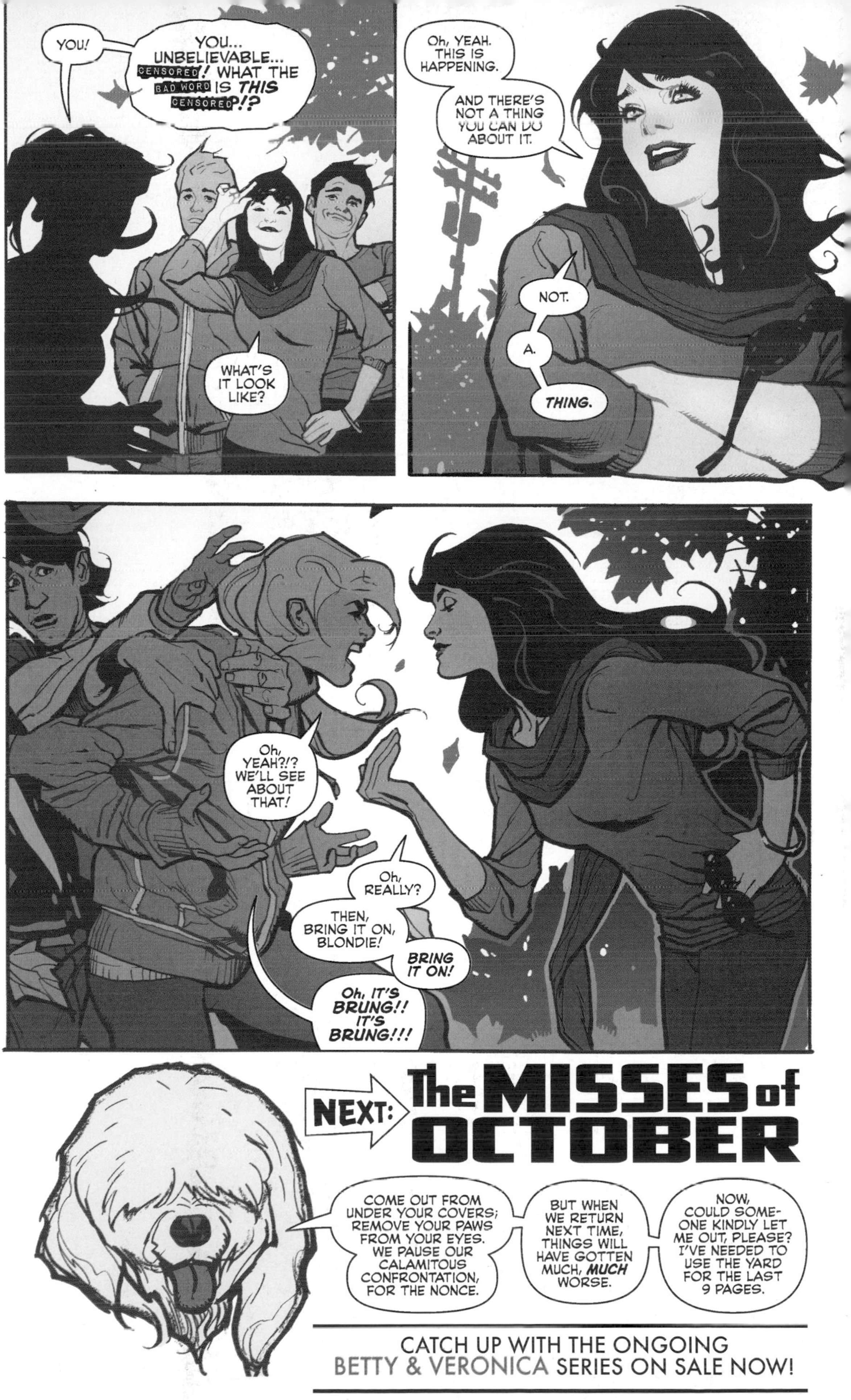
YOU!
YOU... UNBELIEVABLE... CENSORED! WHAT THE BAD WORD IS THIS CENSORED?!?
WHAT'S IT LOOK LIKE?
Oh, YEAH. THIS IS HAPPENING.
AND THERE'S NOT A THING YOU CAN DO ABOUT IT.
NOT.
A.
THING.
Oh, YEAH?!? WE'LL SEE ABOUT THAT!
Oh, REALLY?
THEN, BRING IT ON, BLONDIE!
BRING IT ON!
Oh, IT'S BRUNG!! IT'S BRUNG!!!
NEXT: The MISSES of OCTOBER
COME OUT FROM UNDER YOUR COVERS; REMOVE YOUR PAWS FROM YOUR EYES. WE PAUSE OUR CALAMITOUS CONFRONTATION, FOR THE NONCE.
BUT WHEN WE RETURN NEXT TIME, THINGS WILL HAVE GOTTEN MUCH, MUCH WORSE.
NOW, COULD SOME-ONE KINDLY LET ME OUT, PLEASE? I'VE NEEDED TO USE THE YARD FOR THE LAST 9 PAGES.
CATCH UP WITH THE ONGOING BETTY & VERONICA SERIES ON SALE NOW!

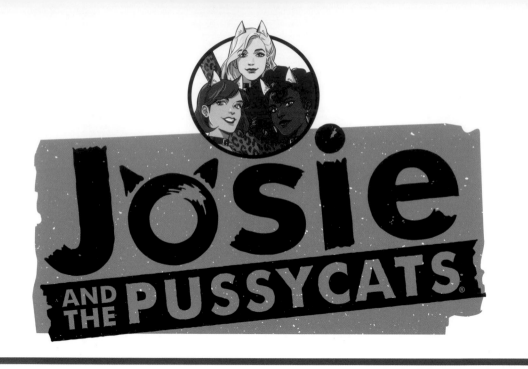

JOSIE AND THE PUSSYCATS®

Josie and the Pussycats are arguably the world's most famous fictitious rock band—yet it's been over a decade since they've starred in their own comic series.

Sure, the girls have made some noteworthy appearances in the classic *Archie* series but the time has finally come for them to headline their very own tour.

The unstoppable comics writing duo of Marguerite Bennett and Cameron DeOrdio along with the hugely talented up-and-coming artist Audrey Mok have presented a new history to how the band came to be, but it's not just long tails and ears for hats, there's a lot of heart, humor and hijinks that drives this series forward!

STORY BY
MARGUERITE BENNETT
&CAMERON DeORDIO

ART BY
AUDREY MOK

COLORING BY
ANDRE SZYMANOWICZ

LETTERING BY
JACK MORELLI

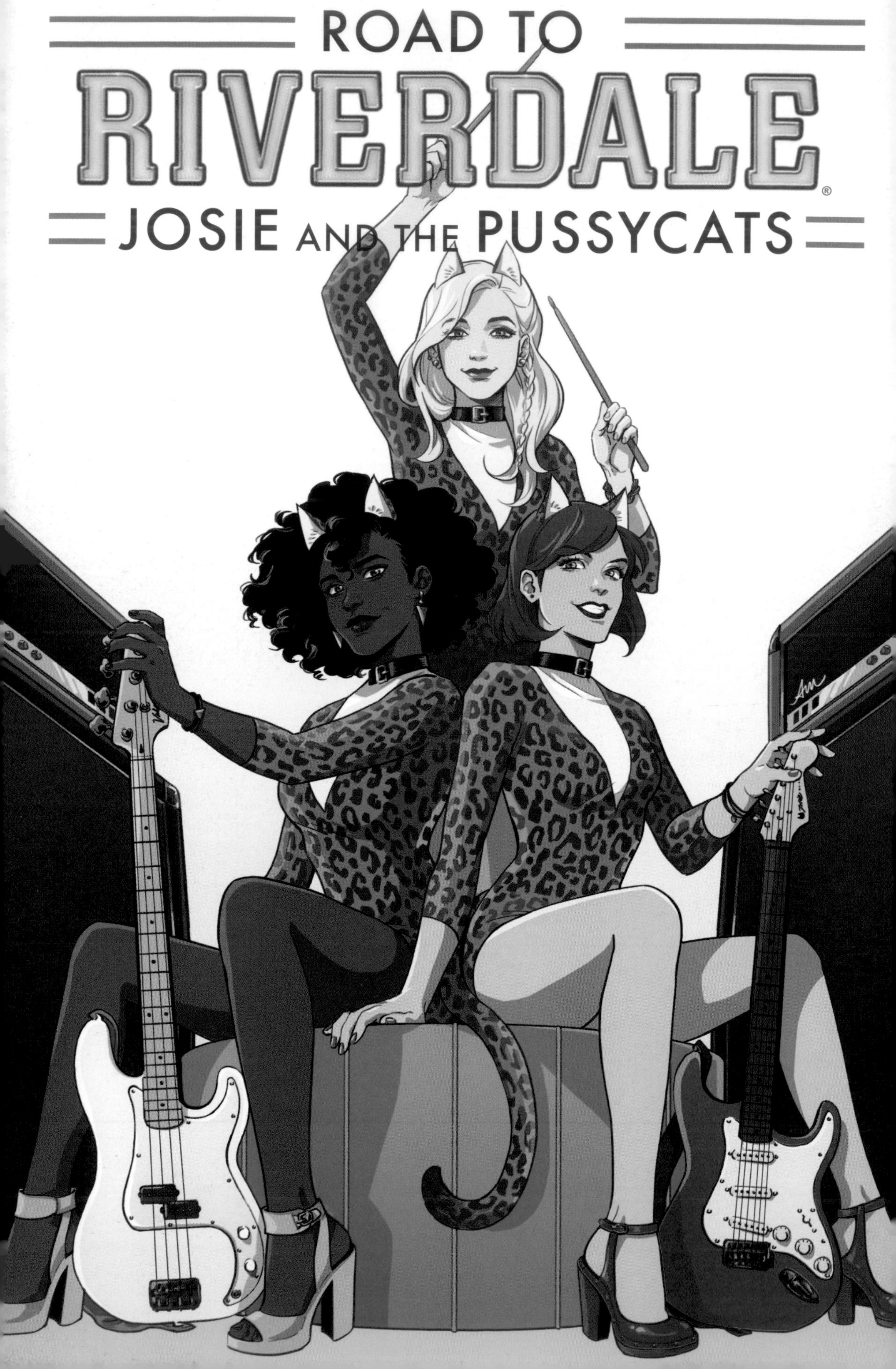
ROAD TO
RIVERDALE®
JOSIE AND THE PUSSYCATS

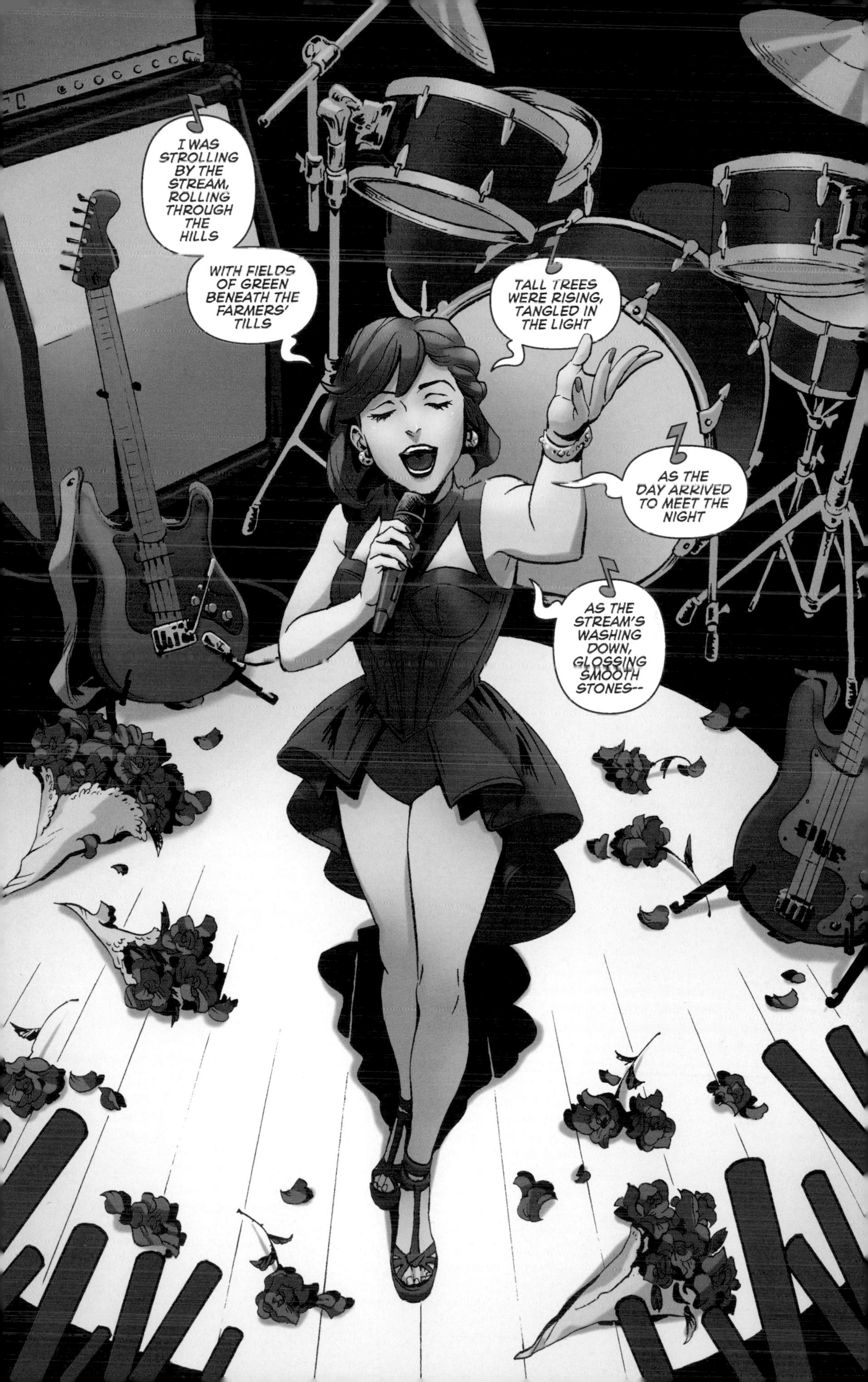
I WAS STROLLING BY THE STREAM, ROLLING THROUGH THE HILLS
WITH FIELDS OF GREEN BENEATH THE FARMERS' TILLS
TALL TREES WERE RISING, TANGLED IN THE LIGHT
AS THE DAY ARRIVED TO MEET THE NIGHT
AS THE STREAM'S WASHING DOWN, GLOSSING SMOOTH STONES--

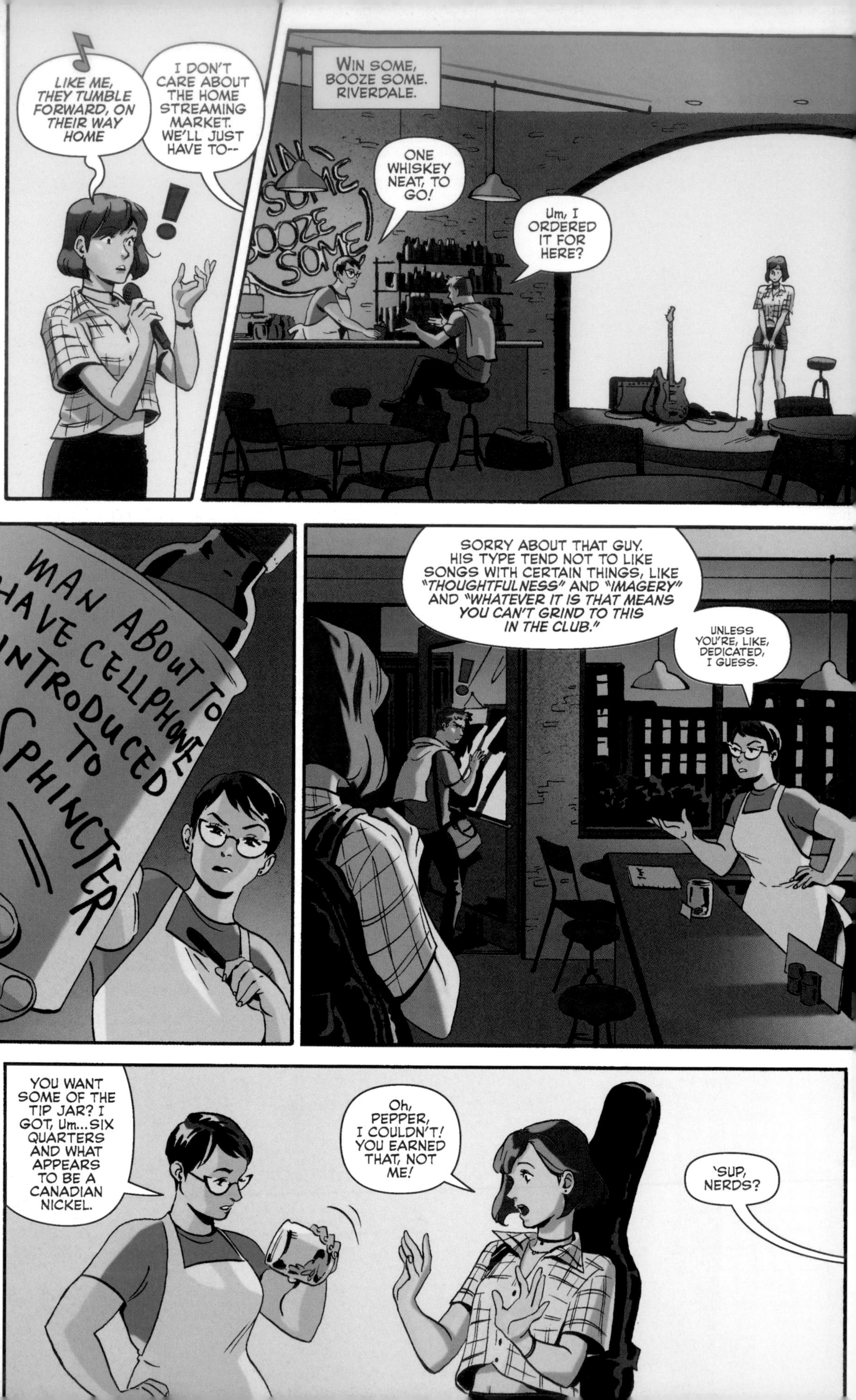
LIKE ME, THEY TUMBLE FORWARD, ON THEIR WAY HOME
I DON'T CARE ABOUT THE HOME STREAMING MARKET. WE'LL JUST HAVE TO--
!
WIN SOME, BOOZE SOME. RIVERDALE.
ONE WHISKEY NEAT, TO GO!
Um, I ORDERED IT FOR HERE?
MAN ABOUT TO HAVE CELLPHONE INTRODUCED TO SPHINCTER
SORRY ABOUT THAT GUY. HIS TYPE TEND NOT TO LIKE SONGS WITH CERTAIN THINGS, LIKE "THOUGHTFULNESS" AND "IMAGERY" AND "WHATEVER IT IS THAT MEANS YOU CAN'T GRIND TO THIS IN THE CLUB."
UNLESS YOU'RE, LIKE, DEDICATED, I GUESS.
YOU WANT SOME OF THE TIP JAR? I GOT, Um...SIX QUARTERS AND WHAT APPEARS TO BE A CANADIAN NICKEL.
Oh, PEPPER, I COULDN'T! YOU EARNED THAT, NOT ME!
'SUP, NERDS?

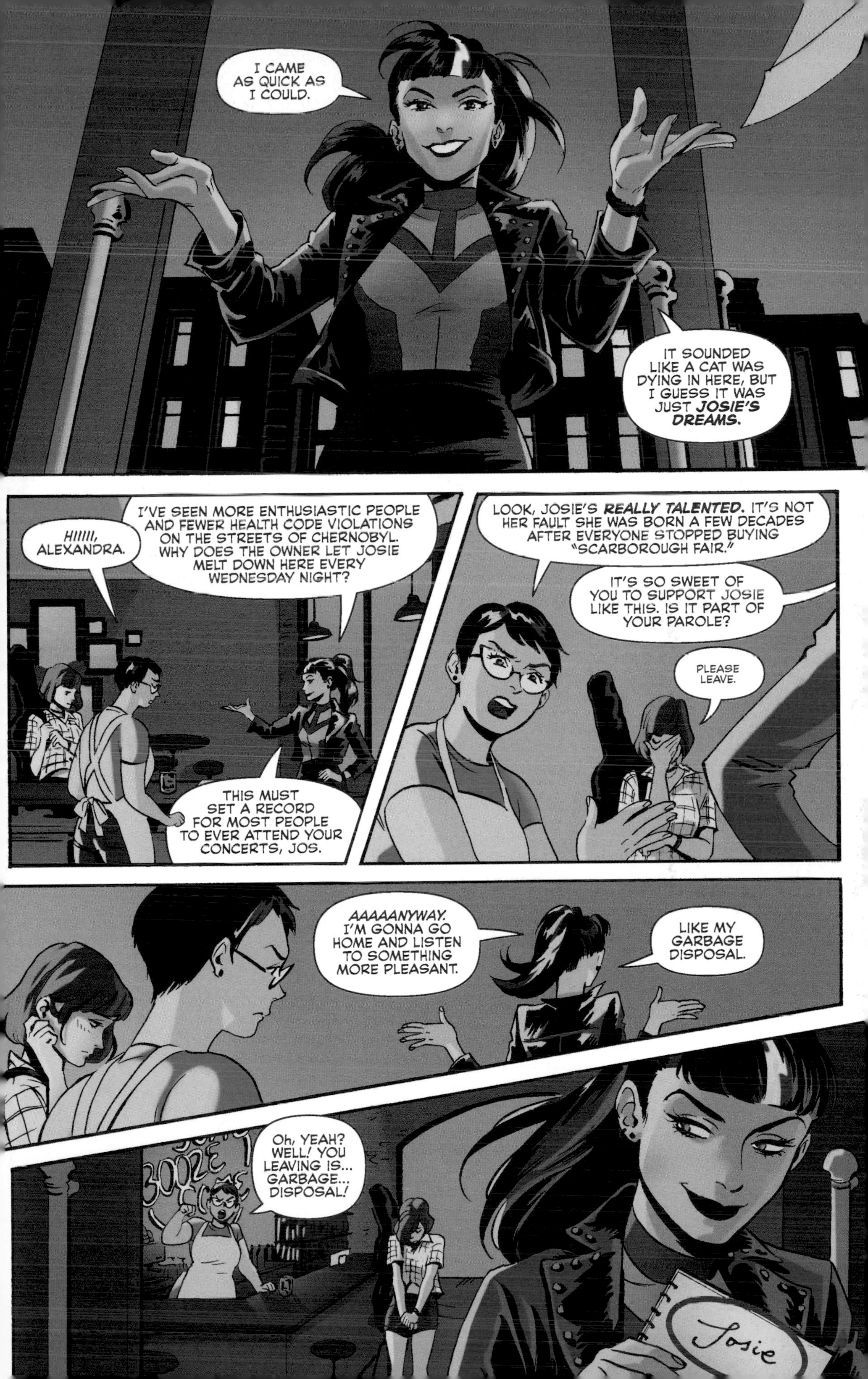

I CAME AS QUICK AS I COULD.
IT SOUNDED LIKE A CAT WAS DYING IN HERE, BUT I GUESS IT WAS JUST ***JOSIE'S DREAMS.***
HIIIII, ALEXANDRA.
I'VE SEEN MORE ENTHUSIASTIC PEOPLE AND FEWER HEALTH CODE VIOLATIONS ON THE STREETS OF CHERNOBYL. WHY DOES THE OWNER LET JOSIE MELT DOWN HERE EVERY WEDNESDAY NIGHT?
THIS MUST SET A RECORD FOR MOST PEOPLE TO EVER ATTEND YOUR CONCERTS, JOS.
LOOK, JOSIE'S ***REALLY TALENTED.*** IT'S NOT HER FAULT SHE WAS BORN A FEW DECADES AFTER EVERYONE STOPPED BUYING "SCARBOROUGH FAIR."
IT'S SO SWEET OF YOU TO SUPPORT JOSIE LIKE THIS. IS IT PART OF YOUR PAROLE?
PLEASE LEAVE.
AAAAANYWAY. I'M GONNA GO HOME AND LISTEN TO SOMETHING MORE PLEASANT.
LIKE MY GARBAGE DISPOSAL.
Oh, YEAH? WELL! YOU LEAVING IS... GARBAGE... DISPOSAL!
Josie

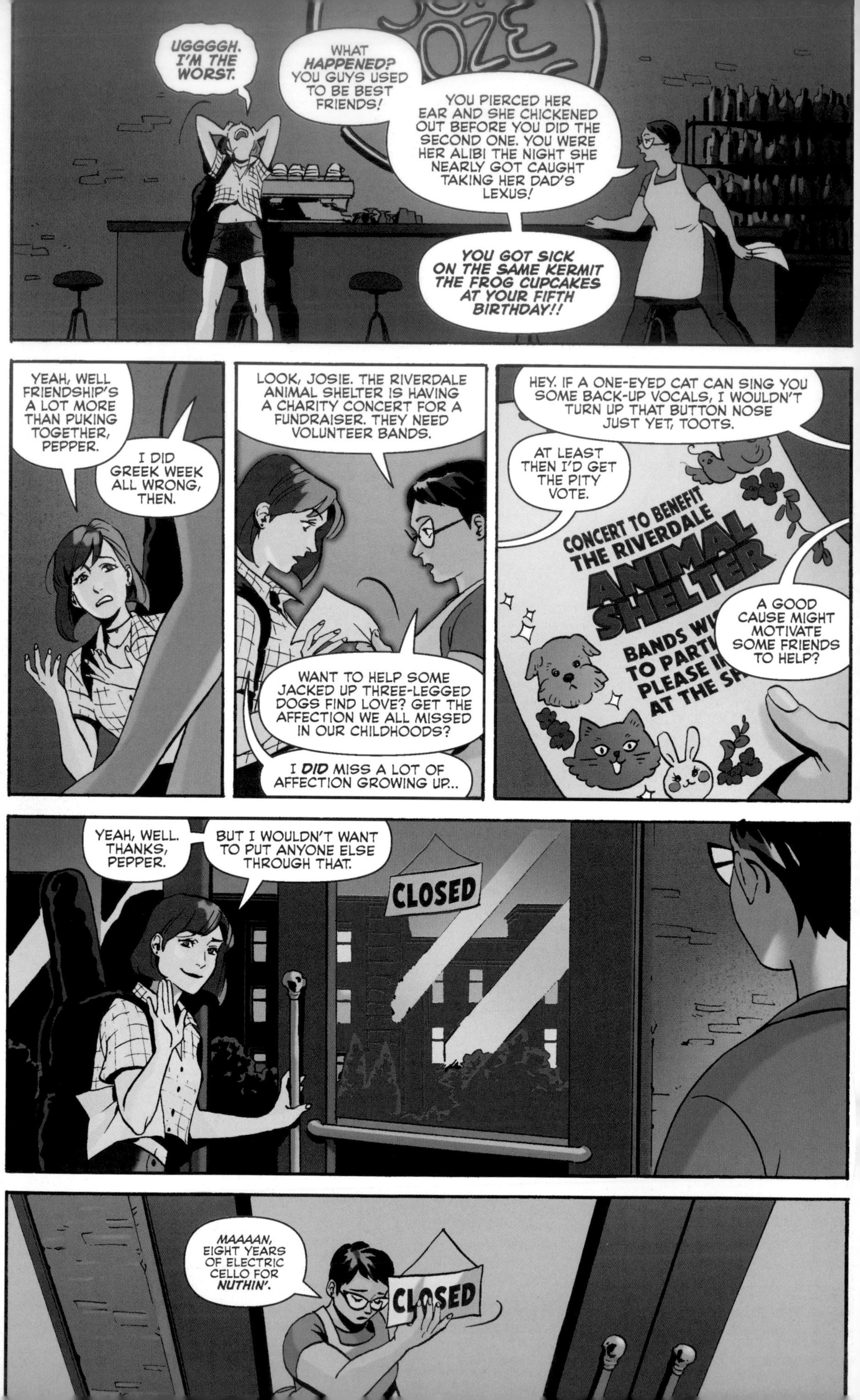

UGGGGH. I'M THE WORST.
WHAT HAPPENED? YOU GUYS USED TO BE BEST FRIENDS!
YOU PIERCED HER EAR AND SHE CHICKENED OUT BEFORE YOU DID THE SECOND ONE. YOU WERE HER ALIBI THE NIGHT SHE NEARLY GOT CAUGHT TAKING HER DAD'S LEXUS!
YOU GOT SICK ON THE SAME KERMIT THE FROG CUPCAKES AT YOUR FIFTH BIRTHDAY!!
YEAH, WELL FRIENDSHIP'S A LOT MORE THAN PUKING TOGETHER, PEPPER.
I DID GREEK WEEK ALL WRONG, THEN.
LOOK, JOSIE. THE RIVERDALE ANIMAL SHELTER IS HAVING A CHARITY CONCERT FOR A FUNDRAISER. THEY NEED VOLUNTEER BANDS.
WANT TO HELP SOME JACKED UP THREE-LEGGED DOGS FIND LOVE? GET THE AFFECTION WE ALL MISSED IN OUR CHILDHOODS?
I DID MISS A LOT OF AFFECTION GROWING UP...
HEY. IF A ONE-EYED CAT CAN SING YOU SOME BACK-UP VOCALS, I WOULDN'T TURN UP THAT BUTTON NOSE JUST YET, TOOTS.
AT LEAST THEN I'D GET THE PITY VOTE.
CONCERT TO BENEFIT THE RIVERDALE ANIMAL SHELTER
A GOOD CAUSE MIGHT MOTIVATE SOME FRIENDS TO HELP?
YEAH, WELL. THANKS, PEPPER.
BUT I WOULDN'T WANT TO PUT ANYONE ELSE THROUGH THAT.
CLOSED
MAAAAN, EIGHT YEARS OF ELECTRIC CELLO FOR NUTHIN'.
CLOSED

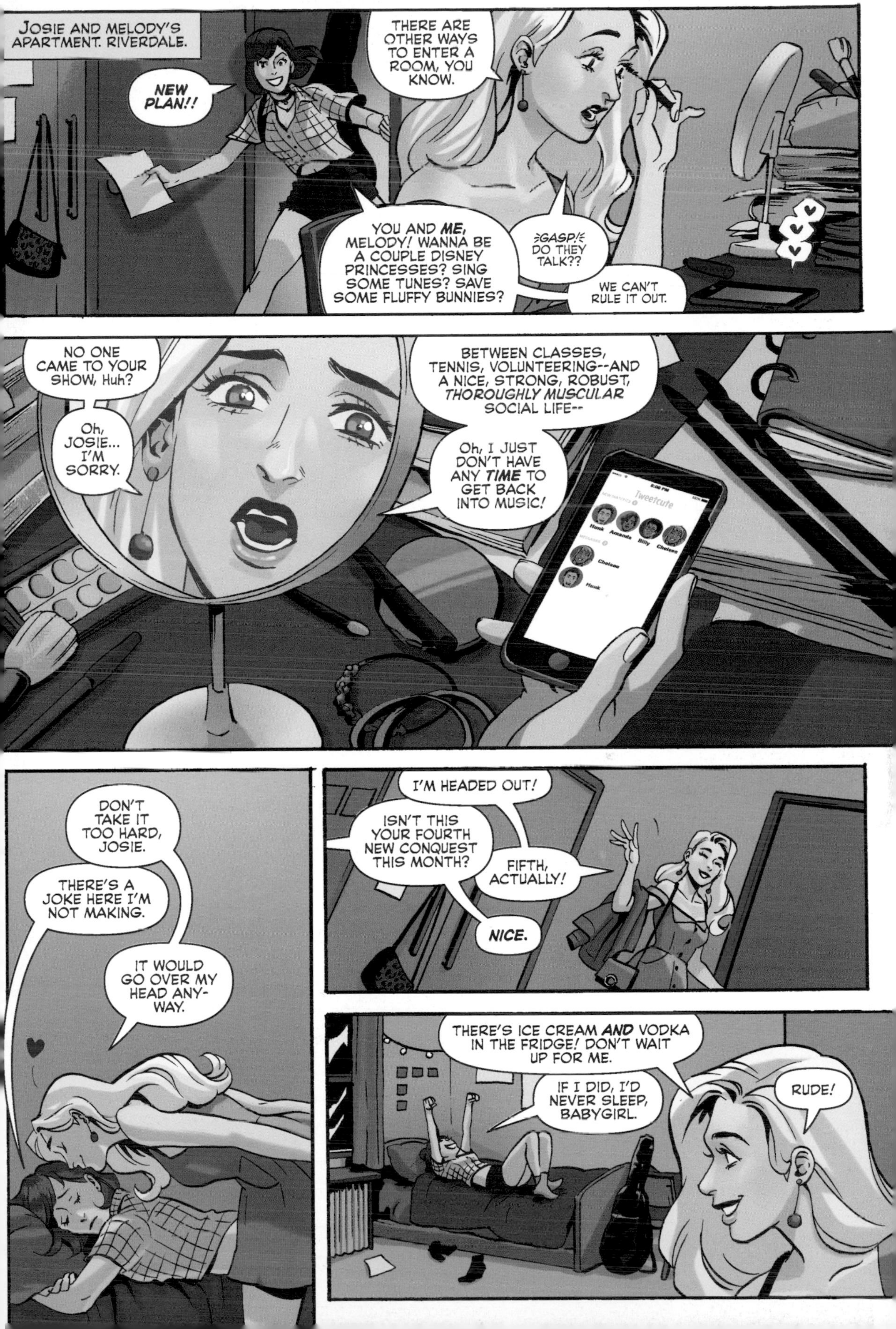
JOSIE AND MELODY'S APARTMENT. RIVERDALE.
NEW PLAN!!
THERE ARE OTHER WAYS TO ENTER A ROOM, YOU KNOW.
YOU AND ME, MELODY! WANNA BE A COUPLE DISNEY PRINCESSES? SING SOME TUNES? SAVE SOME FLUFFY BUNNIES?
GASP! DO THEY TALK??
WE CAN'T RULE IT OUT.
NO ONE CAME TO YOUR SHOW, Huh?
Oh, JOSIE... I'M SORRY.
BETWEEN CLASSES, TENNIS, VOLUNTEERING--AND A NICE, STRONG, ROBUST, THOROUGHLY MUSCULAR SOCIAL LIFE--
Oh, I JUST DON'T HAVE ANY TIME TO GET BACK INTO MUSIC!
Tweetcute
Honk
Amanda
Billy
Chelsea
Chelsea
Honk
DON'T TAKE IT TOO HARD, JOSIE.
THERE'S A JOKE HERE I'M NOT MAKING.
IT WOULD GO OVER MY HEAD ANYWAY.
I'M HEADED OUT!
ISN'T THIS YOUR FOURTH NEW CONQUEST THIS MONTH?
FIFTH, ACTUALLY!
NICE.
THERE'S ICE CREAM AND VODKA IN THE FRIDGE! DON'T WAIT UP FOR ME.
IF I DID, I'D NEVER SLEEP, BABYGIRL.
RUDE!

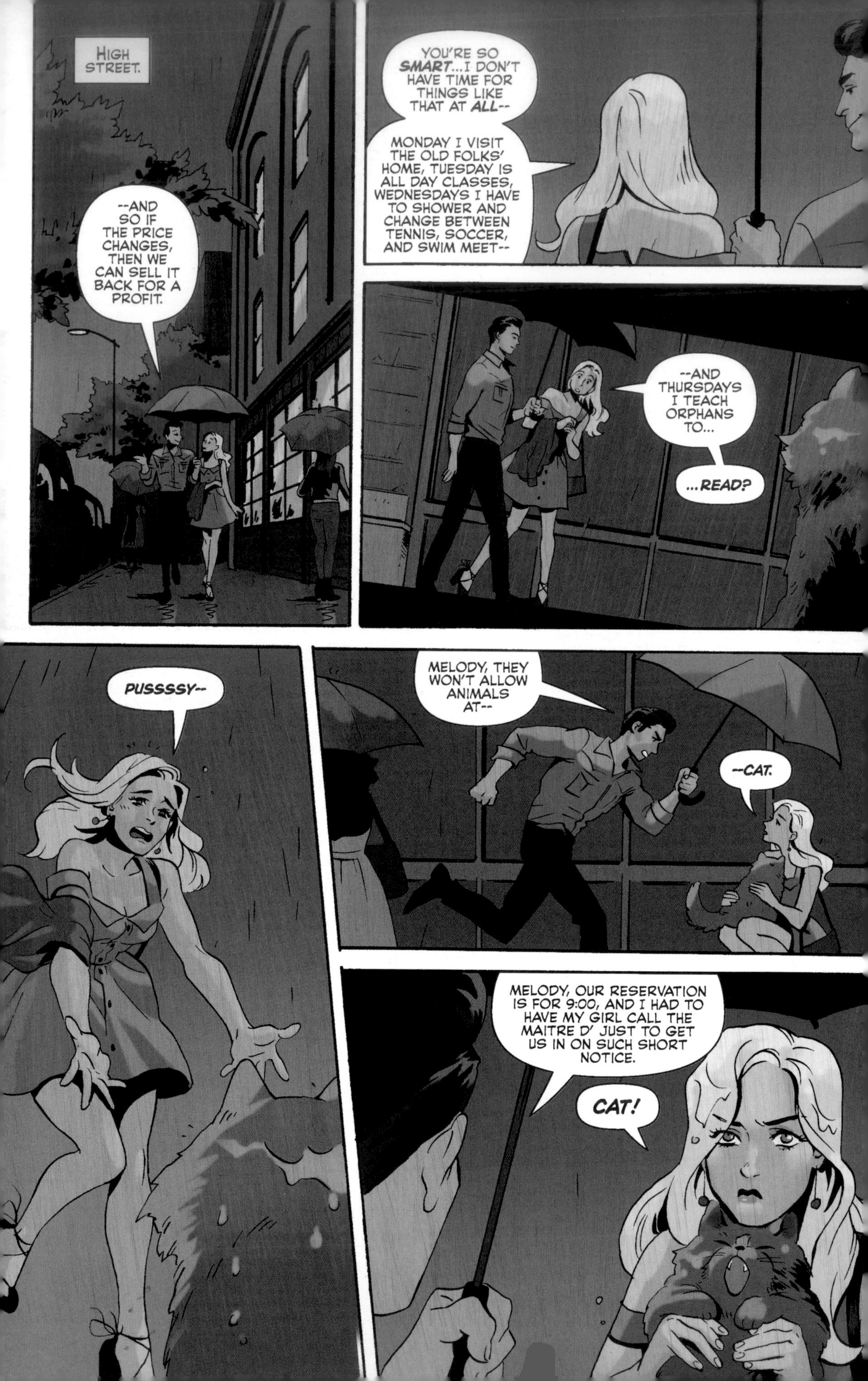
HIGH STREET.
--AND SO IF THE PRICE CHANGES, THEN WE CAN SELL IT BACK FOR A PROFIT.
YOU'RE SO SMART...I DON'T HAVE TIME FOR THINGS LIKE THAT AT ALL--
MONDAY I VISIT THE OLD FOLKS' HOME, TUESDAY IS ALL DAY CLASSES, WEDNESDAYS I HAVE TO SHOWER AND CHANGE BETWEEN TENNIS, SOCCER, AND SWIM MEET--
--AND THURSDAYS I TEACH ORPHANS TO...
...READ?
PUSSSSY--
MELODY, THEY WON'T ALLOW ANIMALS AT--
--CAT.
MELODY, OUR RESERVATION IS FOR 9:00, AND I HAD TO HAVE MY GIRL CALL THE MAITRE D' JUST TO GET US IN ON SUCH SHORT NOTICE.
CAT!

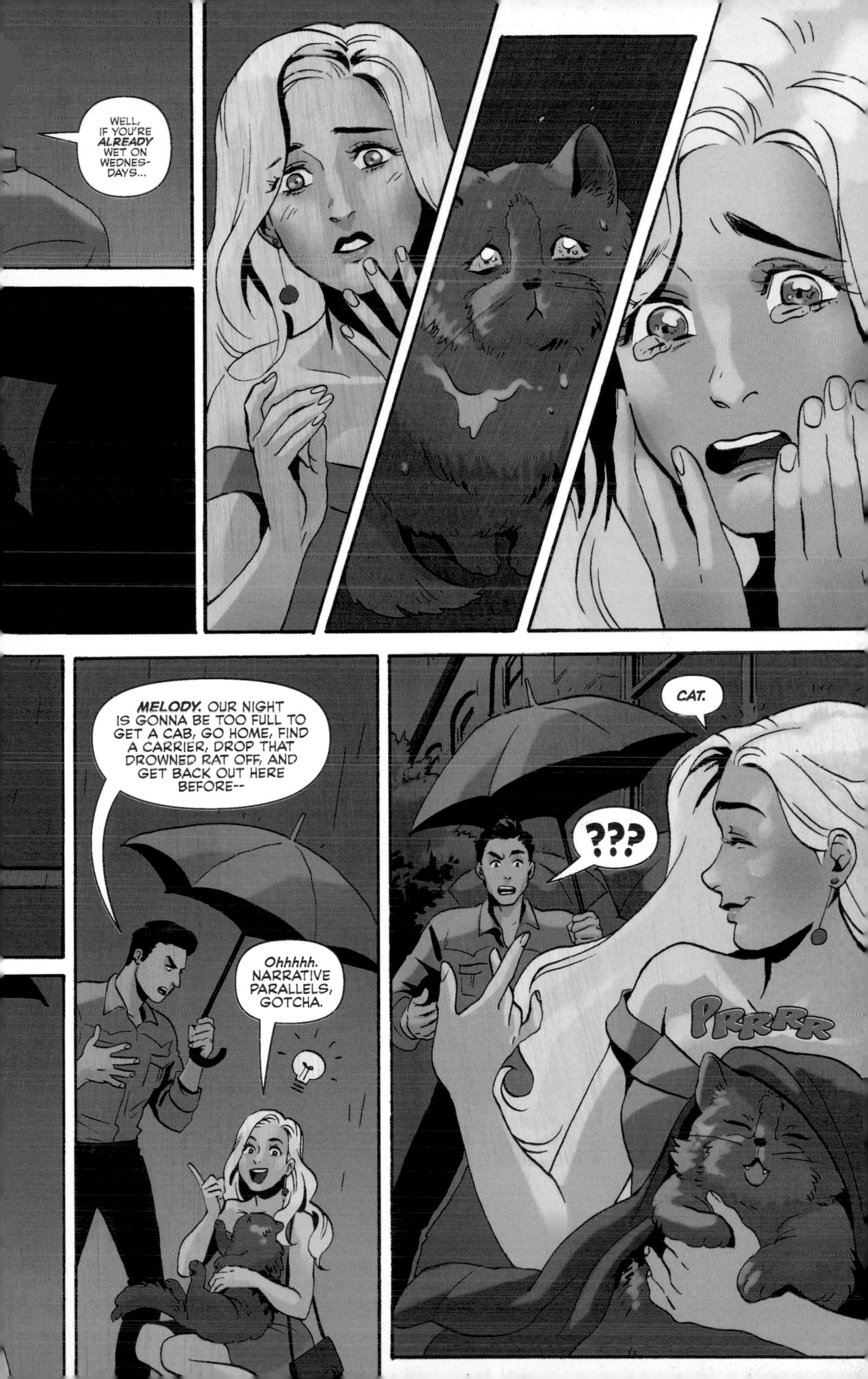
WELL, IF YOU'RE *ALREADY* WET ON WEDNES-DAYS...
MELODY. OUR NIGHT IS GONNA BE TOO FULL TO GET A CAB, GO HOME, FIND A CARRIER, DROP THAT DROWNED RAT OFF, AND GET BACK OUT HERE BEFORE--
Ohhhhh. NARRATIVE PARALLELS, GOTCHA.
CAT.
???
PRRRR

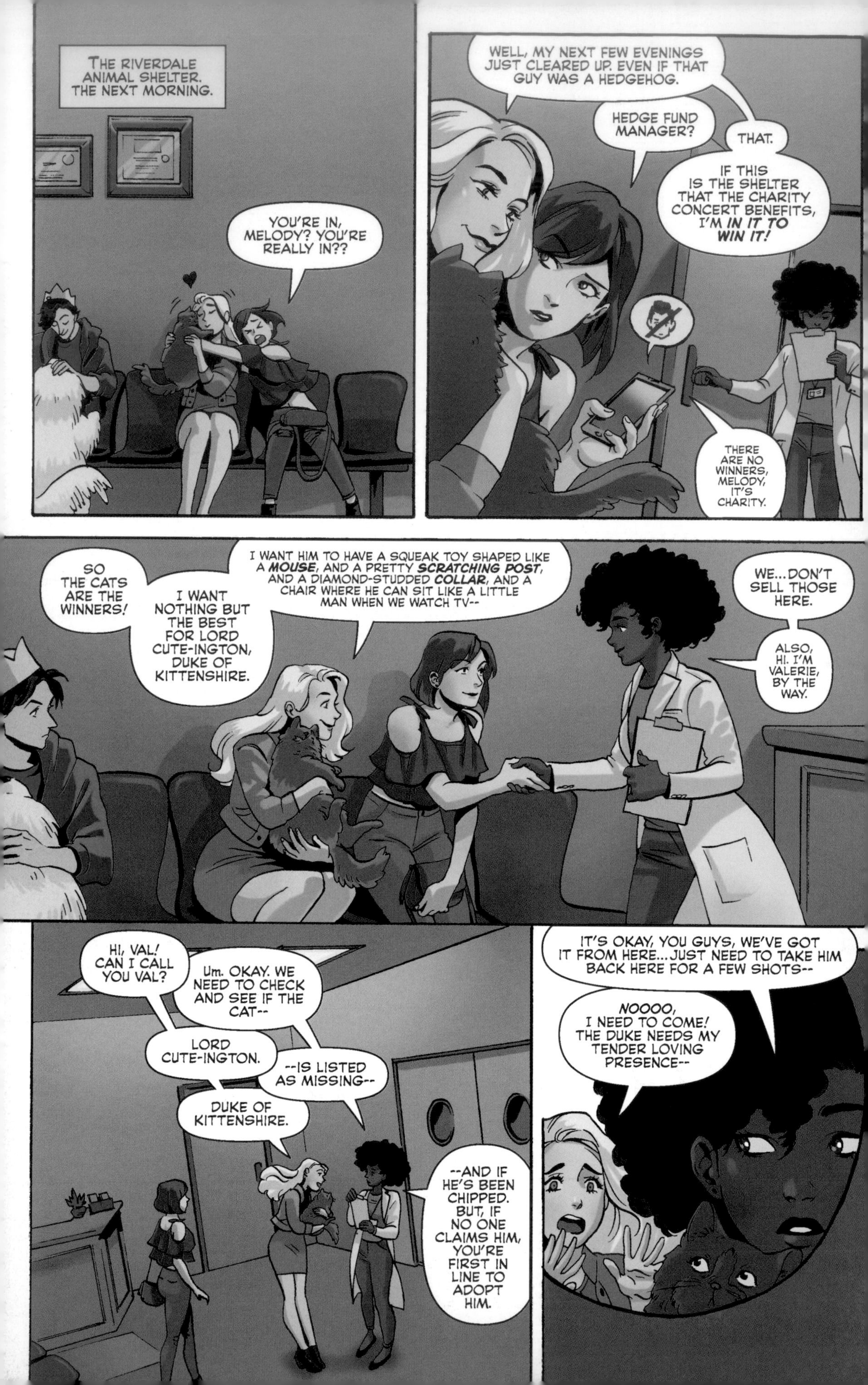
THE RIVERDALE ANIMAL SHELTER. THE NEXT MORNING.
YOU'RE IN, MELODY? YOU'RE REALLY IN??
WELL, MY NEXT FEW EVENINGS JUST CLEARED UP. EVEN IF THAT GUY WAS A HEDGEHOG.
HEDGE FUND MANAGER?
THAT.
IF THIS IS THE SHELTER THAT THE CHARITY CONCERT BENEFITS, I'M *IN IT TO WIN IT!*
THERE ARE NO WINNERS, MELODY, IT'S CHARITY.
SO THE CATS ARE THE WINNERS!
I WANT NOTHING BUT THE BEST FOR LORD CUTE-INGTON, DUKE OF KITTENSHIRE.
I WANT HIM TO HAVE A SQUEAK TOY SHAPED LIKE A ***MOUSE***, AND A PRETTY ***SCRATCHING POST***, AND A DIAMOND-STUDDED ***COLLAR***, AND A CHAIR WHERE HE CAN SIT LIKE A LITTLE MAN WHEN WE WATCH TV--
WE...DON'T SELL THOSE HERE.
ALSO, HI. I'M VALERIE, BY THE WAY.
HI, VAL! CAN I CALL YOU VAL?
Um. OKAY. WE NEED TO CHECK AND SEE IF THE CAT--
LORD CUTE-INGTON.
--IS LISTED AS MISSING--
DUKE OF KITTENSHIRE.
--AND IF HE'S BEEN CHIPPED. BUT, IF NO ONE CLAIMS HIM, YOU'RE FIRST IN LINE TO ADOPT HIM.
IT'S OKAY, YOU GUYS, WE'VE GOT IT FROM HERE...JUST NEED TO TAKE HIM BACK HERE FOR A FEW SHOTS--
NOOOO, I NEED TO COME! THE DUKE NEEDS MY TENDER LOVING PRESENCE--

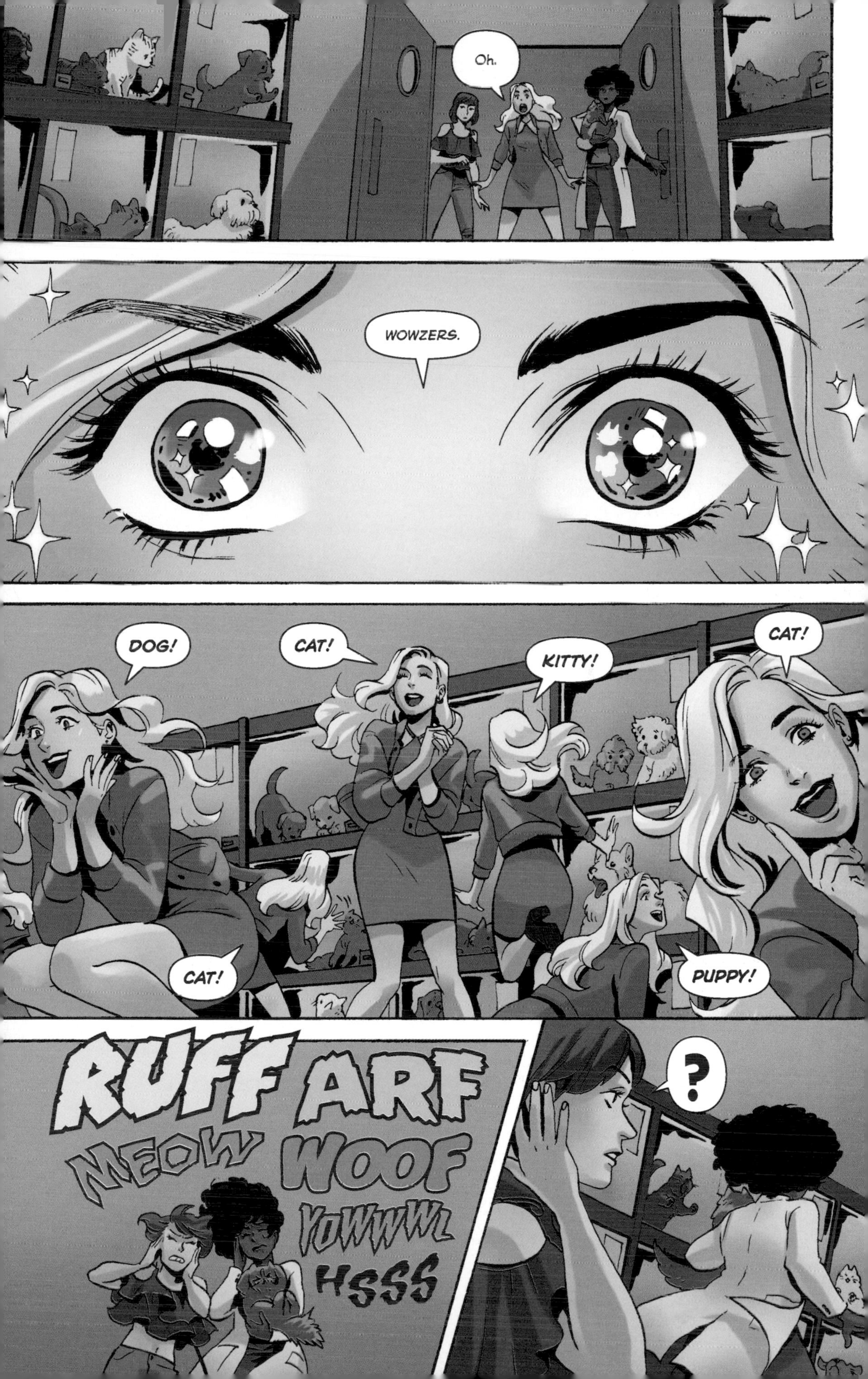

Oh.
WOWZERS.
DOG!
CAT!
KITTY!
CAT!
CAT!
PUPPY!
RUFF ARF
MEOW WOOF
YOWWWL
HSSS
?

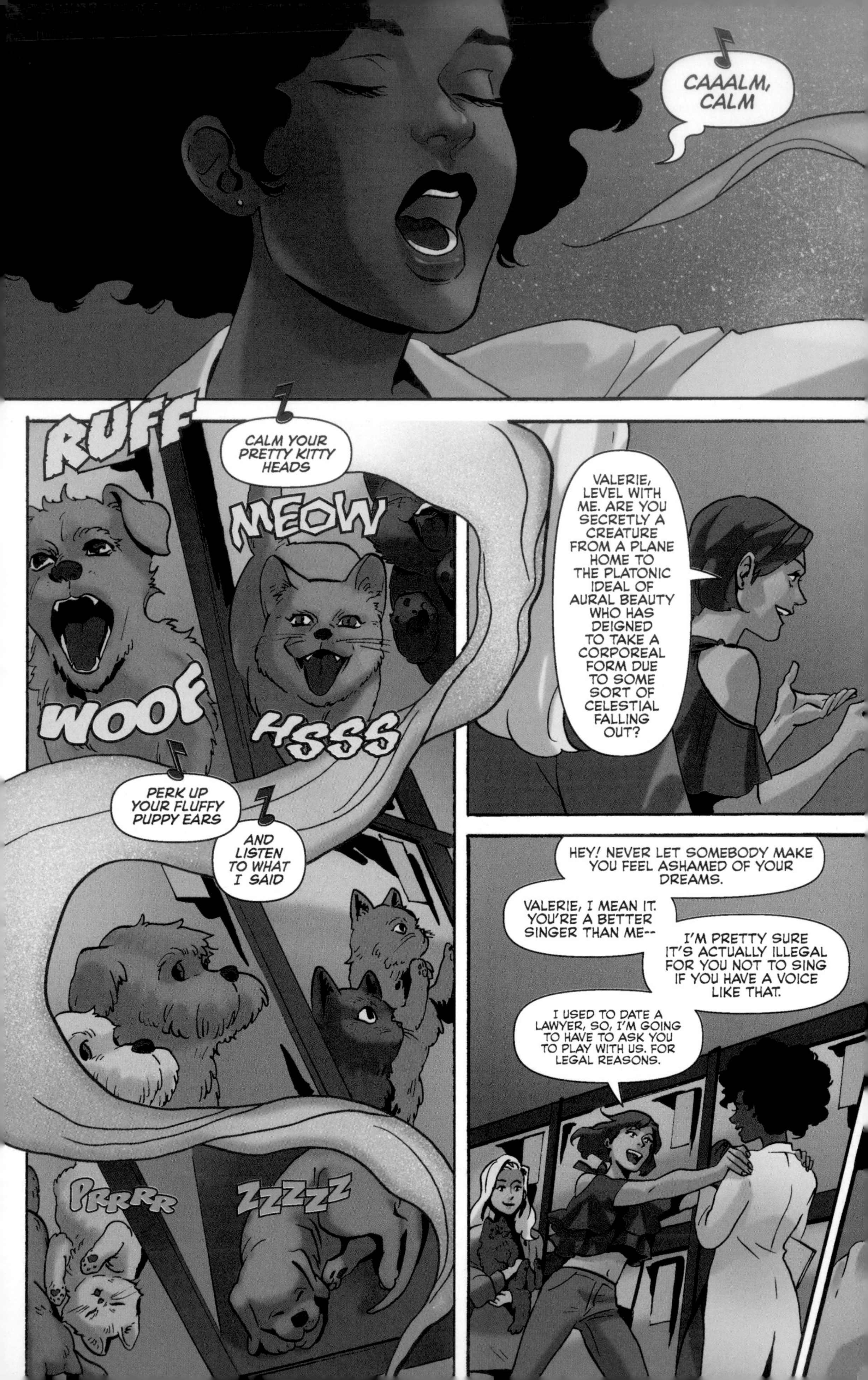
CAAALM, CALM
RUFF
CALM YOUR PRETTY KITTY HEADS
MEOW
WOOF
HSSS
PERK UP YOUR FLUFFY PUPPY EARS
AND LISTEN TO WHAT I SAID
PRRRR
ZZZZZ
VALERIE, LEVEL WITH ME. ARE YOU SECRETLY A CREATURE FROM A PLANE HOME TO THE PLATONIC IDEAL OF AURAL BEAUTY WHO HAS DEIGNED TO TAKE A CORPOREAL FORM DUE TO SOME SORT OF CELESTIAL FALLING OUT?
HEY! NEVER LET SOMEBODY MAKE YOU FEEL ASHAMED OF YOUR DREAMS.
VALERIE, I MEAN IT. YOU'RE A BETTER SINGER THAN ME--
I'M PRETTY SURE IT'S ACTUALLY ILLEGAL FOR YOU NOT TO SING IF YOU HAVE A VOICE LIKE THAT.
I USED TO DATE A LAWYER, SO, I'M GOING TO HAVE TO ASK YOU TO PLAY WITH US. FOR LEGAL REASONS.

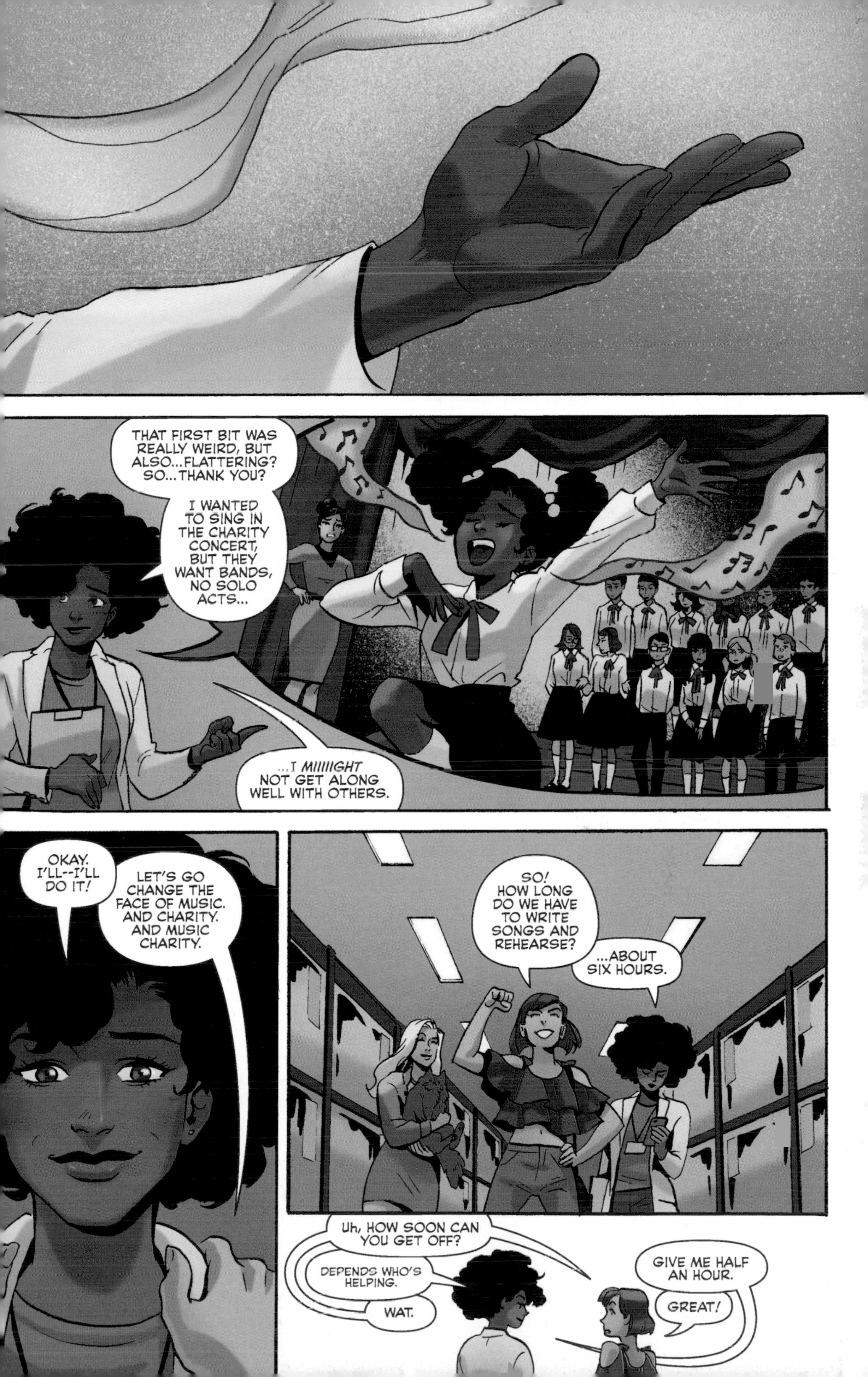
THAT FIRST BIT WAS REALLY WEIRD, BUT ALSO...FLATTERING? SO...THANK YOU?
I WANTED TO SING IN THE CHARITY CONCERT, BUT THEY WANT BANDS, NO SOLO ACTS...
...I *MIIIIIGHT* NOT GET ALONG WELL WITH OTHERS.
OKAY. I'LL--I'LL DO IT!
LET'S GO CHANGE THE FACE OF MUSIC. AND CHARITY. AND MUSIC CHARITY.
SO! HOW LONG DO WE HAVE TO WRITE SONGS AND REHEARSE?
...ABOUT SIX HOURS.
Uh, HOW SOON CAN YOU GET OFF?
DEPENDS WHO'S HELPING.
WAT.
GIVE ME HALF AN HOUR.
GREAT!

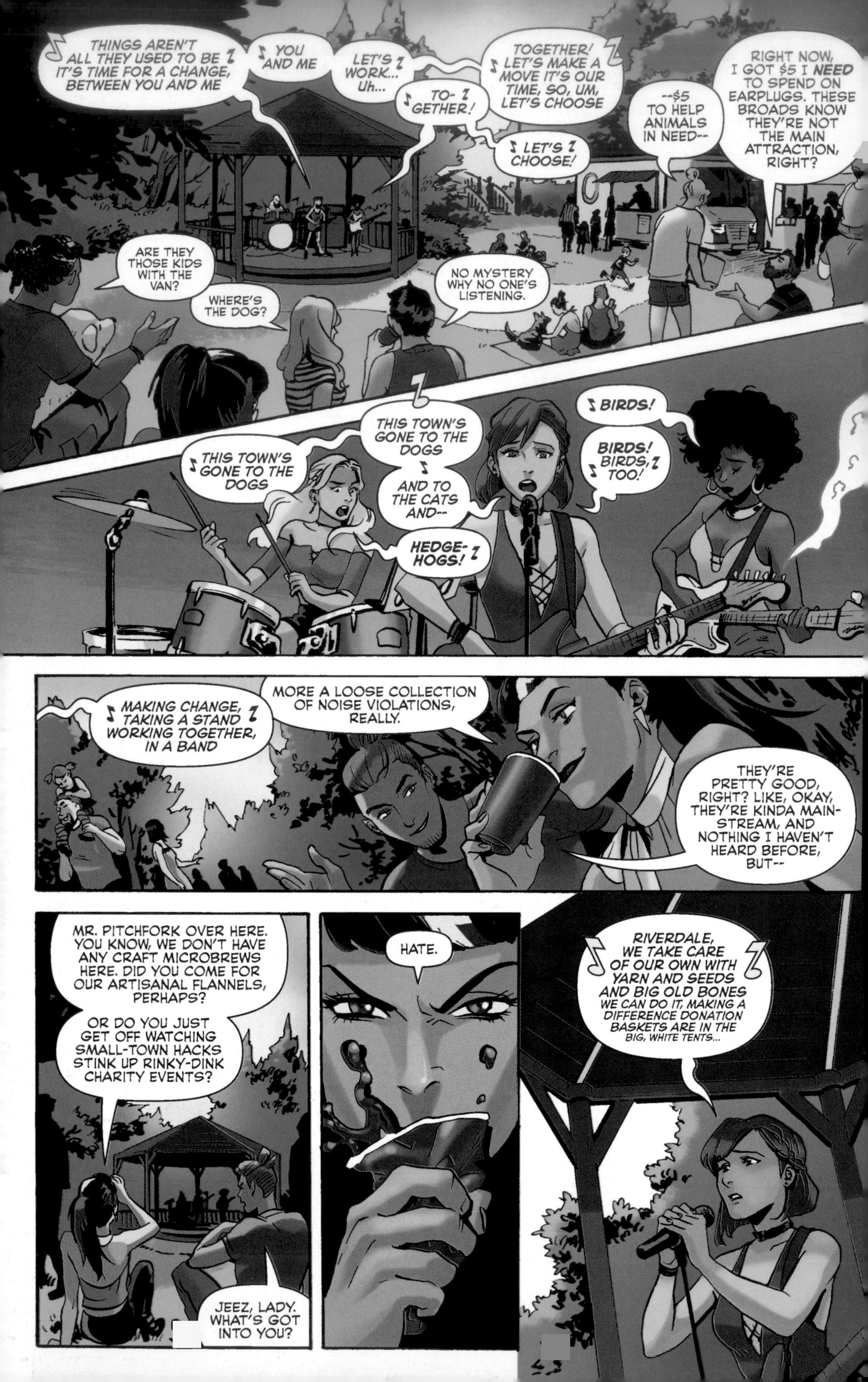
THINGS AREN'T ALL THEY USED TO BE IT'S TIME FOR A CHANGE, BETWEEN YOU AND ME
YOU AND ME
LET'S WORK... Uh...
TO-GETHER!
TOGETHER! LET'S MAKE A MOVE IT'S OUR TIME, SO, UM, LET'S CHOOSE
LET'S CHOOSE!
--$5 TO HELP ANIMALS IN NEED--
RIGHT NOW, I GOT $5 I NEED TO SPEND ON EARPLUGS. THESE BROADS KNOW THEY'RE NOT THE MAIN ATTRACTION, RIGHT?
ARE THEY THOSE KIDS WITH THE VAN?
WHERE'S THE DOG?
NO MYSTERY WHY NO ONE'S LISTENING.
THIS TOWN'S GONE TO THE DOGS
THIS TOWN'S GONE TO THE DOGS
AND TO THE CATS AND--
HEDGE-HOGS!
BIRDS!
BIRDS! BIRDS, TOO!
MAKING CHANGE, TAKING A STAND WORKING TOGETHER, IN A BAND
MORE A LOOSE COLLECTION OF NOISE VIOLATIONS, REALLY.
THEY'RE PRETTY GOOD, RIGHT? LIKE, OKAY, THEY'RE KINDA MAIN-STREAM, AND NOTHING I HAVEN'T HEARD BEFORE, BUT--
MR. PITCHFORK OVER HERE. YOU KNOW, WE DON'T HAVE ANY CRAFT MICROBREWS HERE. DID YOU COME FOR OUR ARTISANAL FLANNELS, PERHAPS?
OR DO YOU JUST GET OFF WATCHING SMALL-TOWN HACKS STINK UP RINKY-DINK CHARITY EVENTS?
JEEZ, LADY. WHAT'S GOT INTO YOU?
HATE.
RIVERDALE, WE TAKE CARE OF OUR OWN WITH YARN AND SEEDS AND BIG OLD BONES WE CAN DO IT, MAKING A DIFFERENCE DONATION BASKETS ARE IN THE BIG, WHITE TENTS...

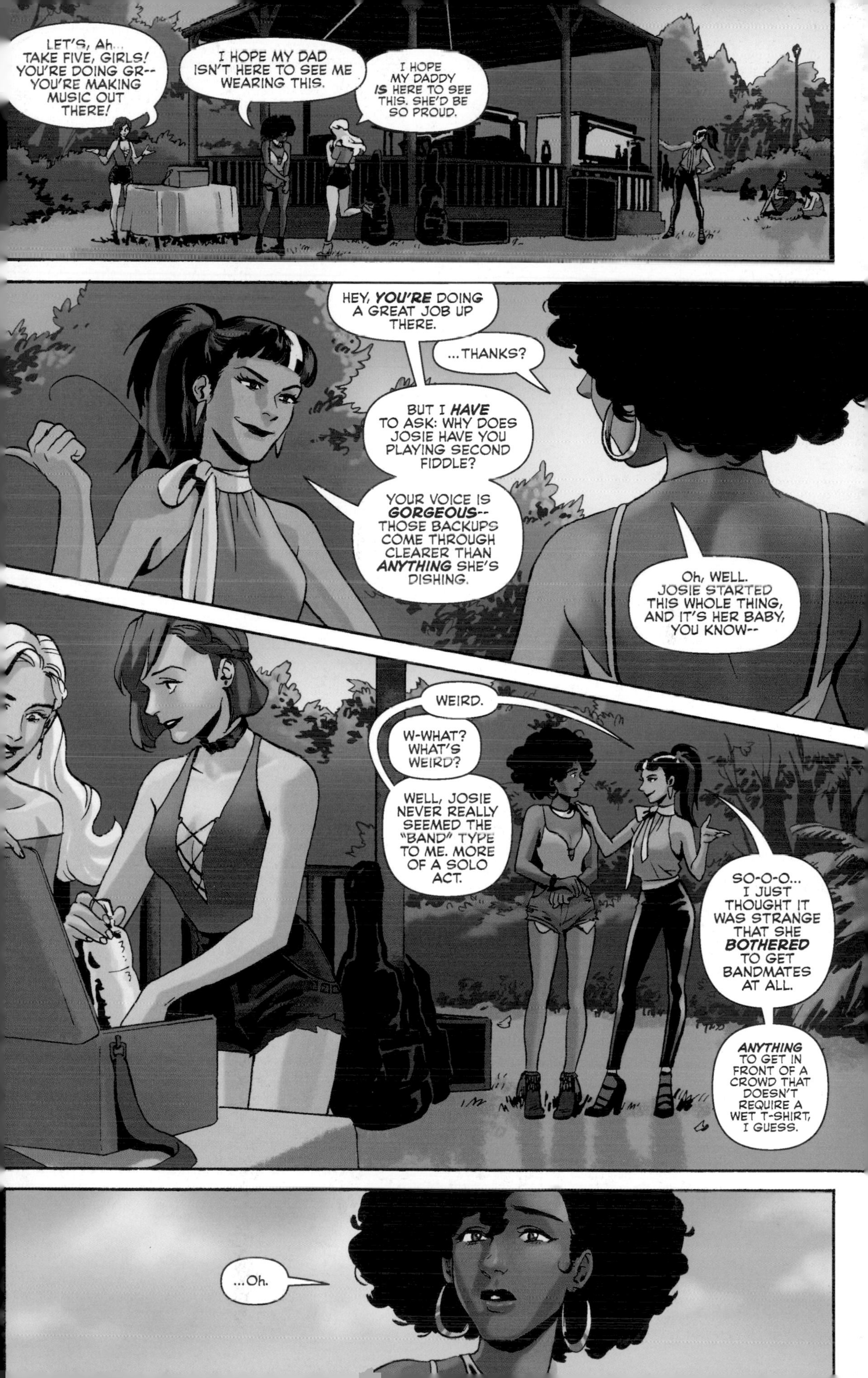
LET'S, Ah... TAKE FIVE, GIRLS! YOU'RE DOING GR-- YOU'RE MAKING MUSIC OUT THERE!
I HOPE MY DAD ISN'T HERE TO SEE ME WEARING THIS.
I HOPE MY DADDY IS HERE TO SEE THIS. SHE'D BE SO PROUD.
HEY, YOU'RE DOING A GREAT JOB UP THERE.
...THANKS?
BUT I HAVE TO ASK: WHY DOES JOSIE HAVE YOU PLAYING SECOND FIDDLE?
YOUR VOICE IS GORGEOUS-- THOSE BACKUPS COME THROUGH CLEARER THAN ANYTHING SHE'S DISHING.
Oh, WELL. JOSIE STARTED THIS WHOLE THING, AND IT'S HER BABY, YOU KNOW--
WEIRD.
W-WHAT? WHAT'S WEIRD?
WELL, JOSIE NEVER REALLY SEEMED THE "BAND" TYPE TO ME. MORE OF A SOLO ACT.
SO-O-O... I JUST THOUGHT IT WAS STRANGE THAT SHE BOTHERED TO GET BANDMATES AT ALL.
ANYTHING TO GET IN FRONT OF A CROWD THAT DOESN'T REQUIRE A WET T-SHIRT, I GUESS.
...Oh.

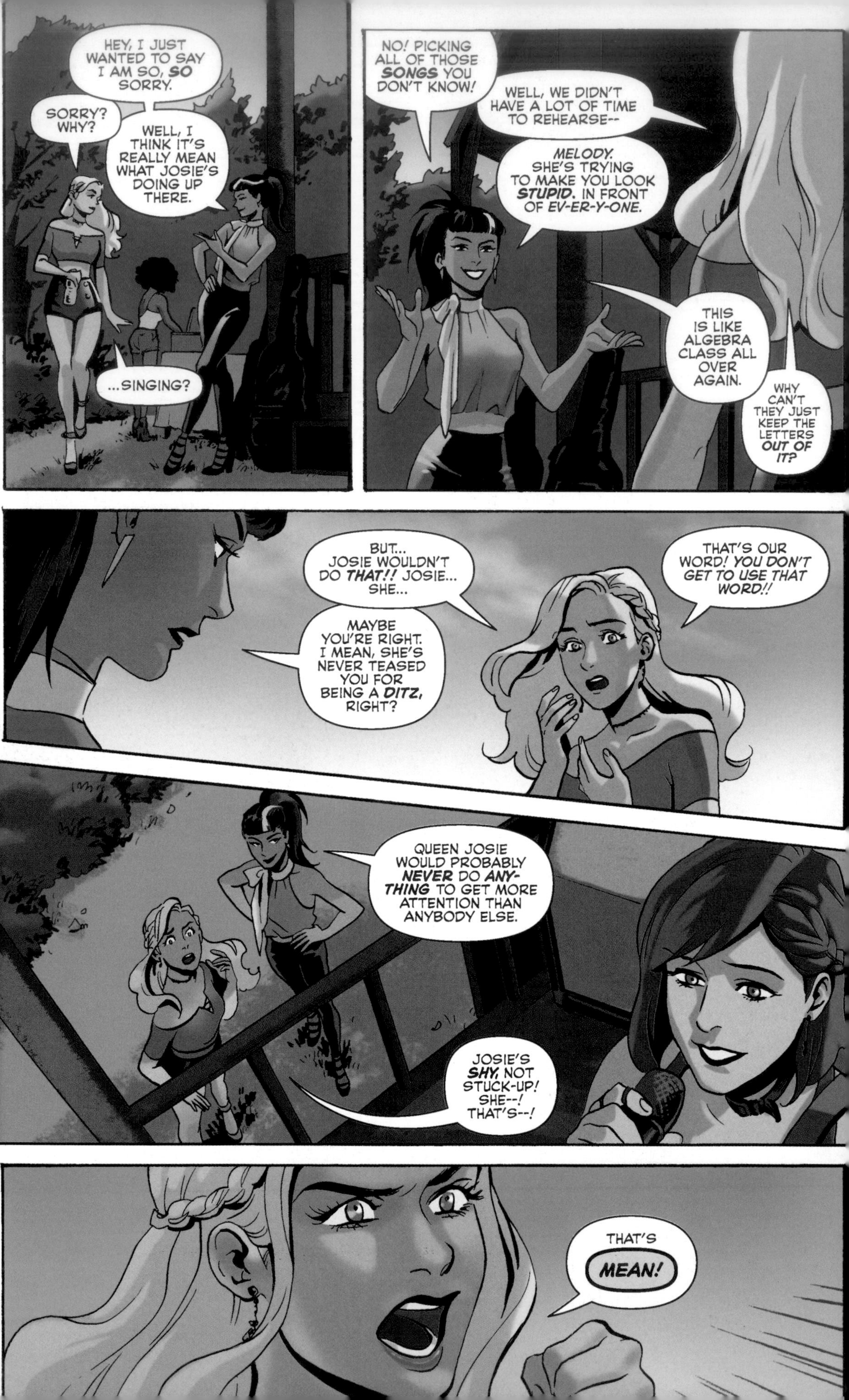
HEY, I JUST WANTED TO SAY I AM SO, SO SORRY.
SORRY? WHY?
WELL, I THINK IT'S REALLY MEAN WHAT JOSIE'S DOING UP THERE.
...SINGING?
NO! PICKING ALL OF THOSE SONGS YOU DON'T KNOW!
WELL, WE DIDN'T HAVE A LOT OF TIME TO REHEARSE--
MELODY. SHE'S TRYING TO MAKE YOU LOOK STUPID. IN FRONT OF EV-ER-Y-ONE.
THIS IS LIKE ALGEBRA CLASS ALL OVER AGAIN.
WHY CAN'T THEY JUST KEEP THE LETTERS OUT OF IT?
BUT... JOSIE WOULDN'T DO THAT!! JOSIE... SHE...
MAYBE YOU'RE RIGHT. I MEAN, SHE'S NEVER TEASED YOU FOR BEING A DITZ, RIGHT?
THAT'S OUR WORD! YOU DON'T GET TO USE THAT WORD!!
QUEEN JOSIE WOULD PROBABLY NEVER DO ANY-THING TO GET MORE ATTENTION THAN ANYBODY ELSE.
JOSIE'S SHY, NOT STUCK-UP! SHE--! THAT'S--!
THAT'S MEAN!

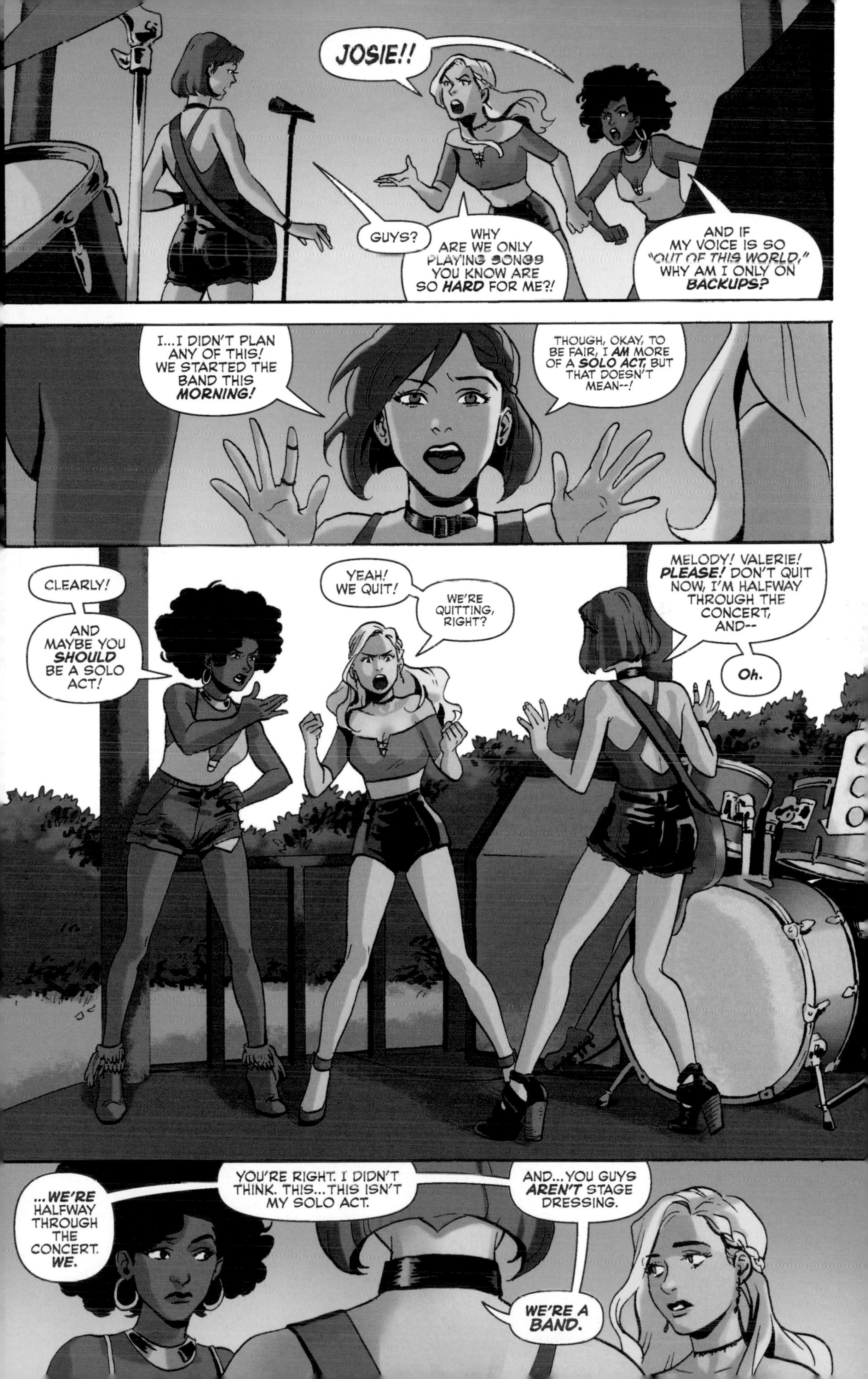
JOSIE!!
GUYS?
WHY ARE WE ONLY PLAYING SONGS YOU KNOW ARE SO HARD FOR ME?!
AND IF MY VOICE IS SO "OUT OF THIS WORLD," WHY AM I ONLY ON BACKUPS?
I...I DIDN'T PLAN ANY OF THIS! WE STARTED THE BAND THIS MORNING!
THOUGH, OKAY, TO BE FAIR, I AM MORE OF A SOLO ACT, BUT THAT DOESN'T MEAN--!
CLEARLY!
AND MAYBE YOU SHOULD BE A SOLO ACT!
YEAH! WE QUIT!
WE'RE QUITTING, RIGHT?
MELODY! VALERIE! PLEASE! DON'T QUIT NOW, I'M HALFWAY THROUGH THE CONCERT, AND--
Oh.
...WE'RE HALFWAY THROUGH THE CONCERT. WE.
YOU'RE RIGHT. I DIDN'T THINK. THIS...THIS ISN'T MY SOLO ACT.
AND...YOU GUYS AREN'T STAGE DRESSING.
WE'RE A BAND.

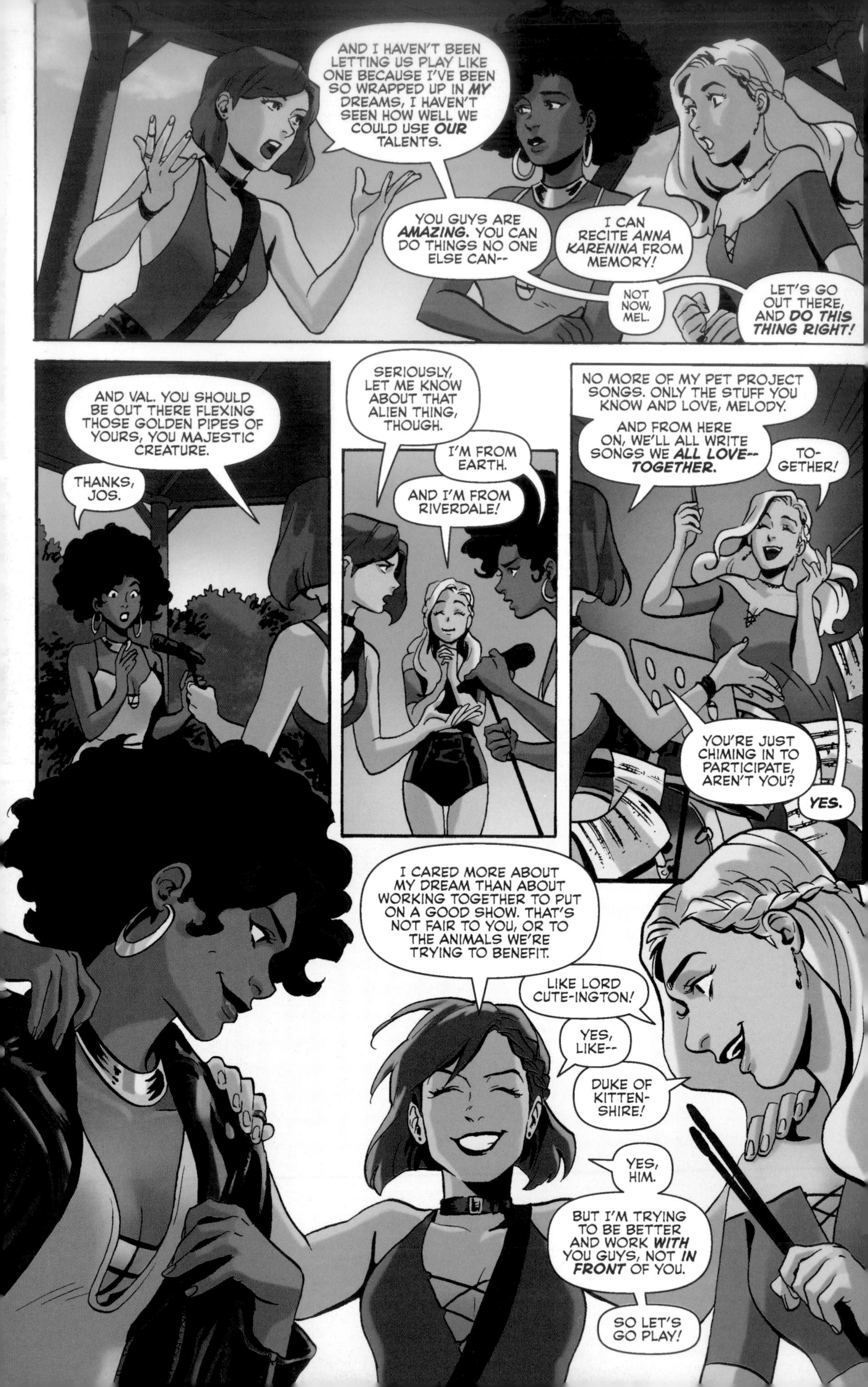

AND I HAVEN'T BEEN LETTING US PLAY LIKE ONE BECAUSE I'VE BEEN SO WRAPPED UP IN *MY* DREAMS, I HAVEN'T SEEN HOW WELL WE COULD USE *OUR* TALENTS.
YOU GUYS ARE *AMAZING.* YOU CAN DO THINGS NO ONE ELSE CAN--
I CAN RECITE *ANNA KARENINA* FROM MEMORY!
NOT NOW, MEL.
LET'S GO OUT THERE, AND *DO THIS THING RIGHT!*
AND VAL. YOU SHOULD BE OUT THERE FLEXING THOSE GOLDEN PIPES OF YOURS, YOU MAJESTIC CREATURE.
THANKS, JOS.
SERIOUSLY, LET ME KNOW ABOUT THAT ALIEN THING, THOUGH.
I'M FROM EARTH.
AND I'M FROM RIVERDALE!
NO MORE OF MY PET PROJECT SONGS. ONLY THE STUFF YOU KNOW AND LOVE, MELODY.
AND FROM HERE ON, WE'LL ALL WRITE SONGS WE *ALL LOVE-- TOGETHER.*
TO-GETHER!
YOU'RE JUST CHIMING IN TO PARTICIPATE, AREN'T YOU?
YES.
I CARED MORE ABOUT MY DREAM THAN ABOUT WORKING TOGETHER TO PUT ON A GOOD SHOW. THAT'S NOT FAIR TO YOU, OR TO THE ANIMALS WE'RE TRYING TO BENEFIT.
LIKE LORD CUTE-INGTON!
YES, LIKE--
DUKE OF KITTEN-SHIRE!
YES, HIM.
BUT I'M TRYING TO BE BETTER AND WORK *WITH* YOU GUYS, NOT *IN FRONT* OF YOU.
SO LET'S GO PLAY!

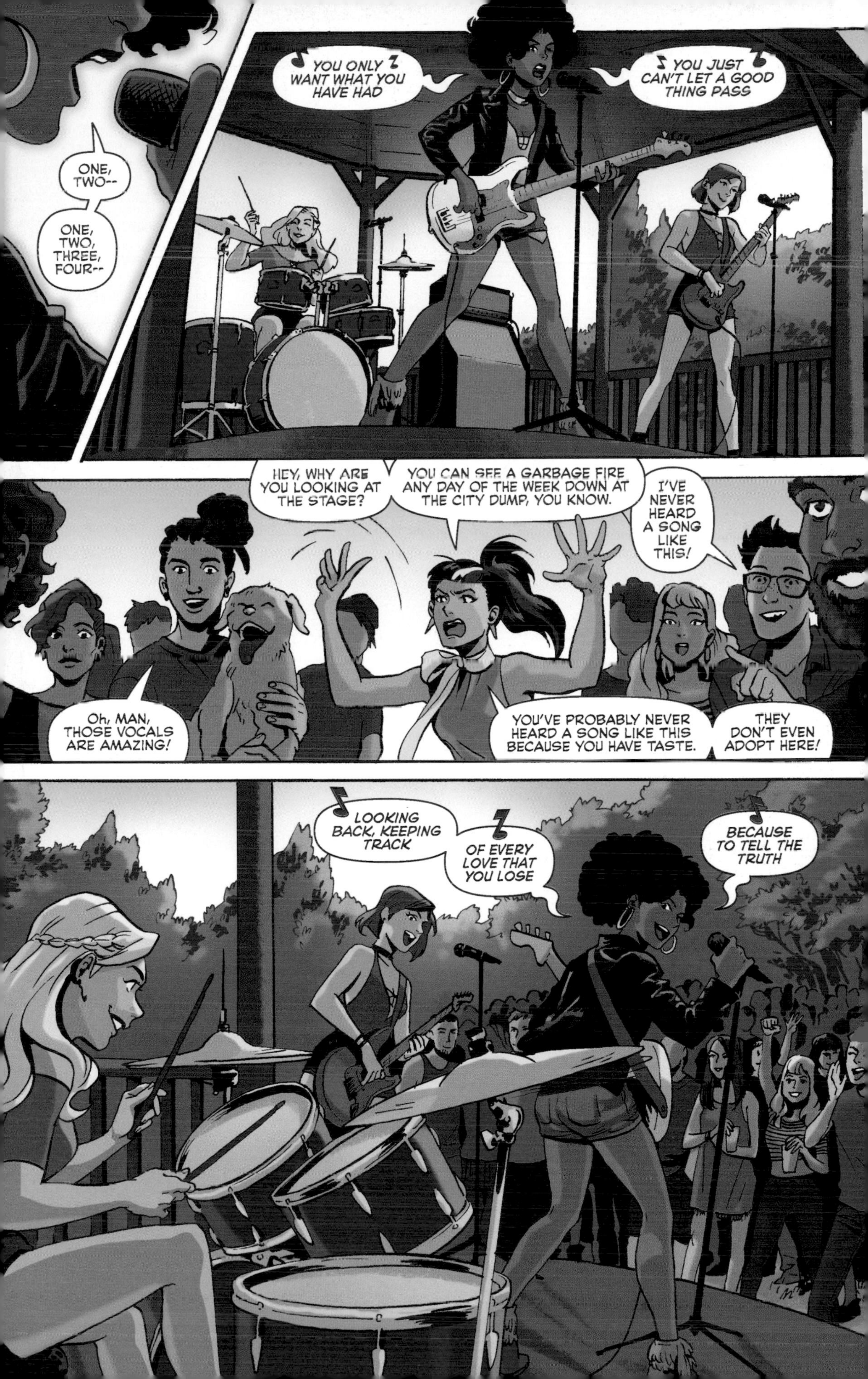
ONE, TWO--
ONE, TWO, THREE, FOUR--
YOU ONLY WANT WHAT YOU HAVE HAD
YOU JUST CAN'T LET A GOOD THING PASS
HEY, WHY ARE YOU LOOKING AT THE STAGE?
YOU CAN SEE A GARBAGE FIRE ANY DAY OF THE WEEK DOWN AT THE CITY DUMP, YOU KNOW.
I'VE NEVER HEARD A SONG LIKE THIS!
Oh, MAN, THOSE VOCALS ARE AMAZING!
YOU'VE PROBABLY NEVER HEARD A SONG LIKE THIS BECAUSE YOU HAVE TASTE.
THEY DON'T EVEN ADOPT HERE!
LOOKING BACK, KEEPING TRACK
OF EVERY LOVE THAT YOU LOSE
BECAUSE TO TELL THE TRUTH

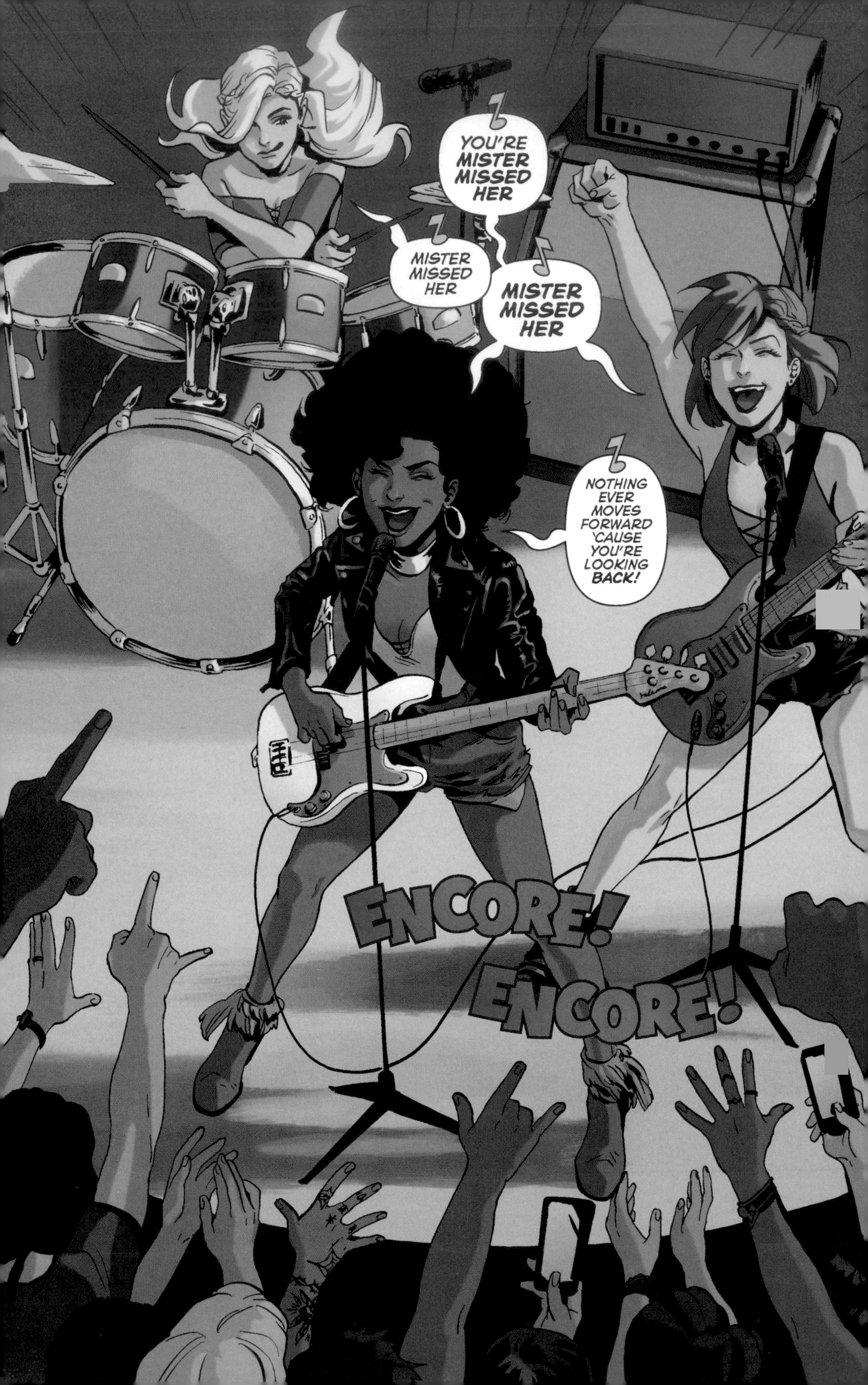
YOU'RE MISTER MISSED HER
MISTER MISSED HER
MISTER MISSED HER
NOTHING EVER MOVES FORWARD 'CAUSE YOU'RE LOOKING BACK!
ENCORE!
ENCORE!

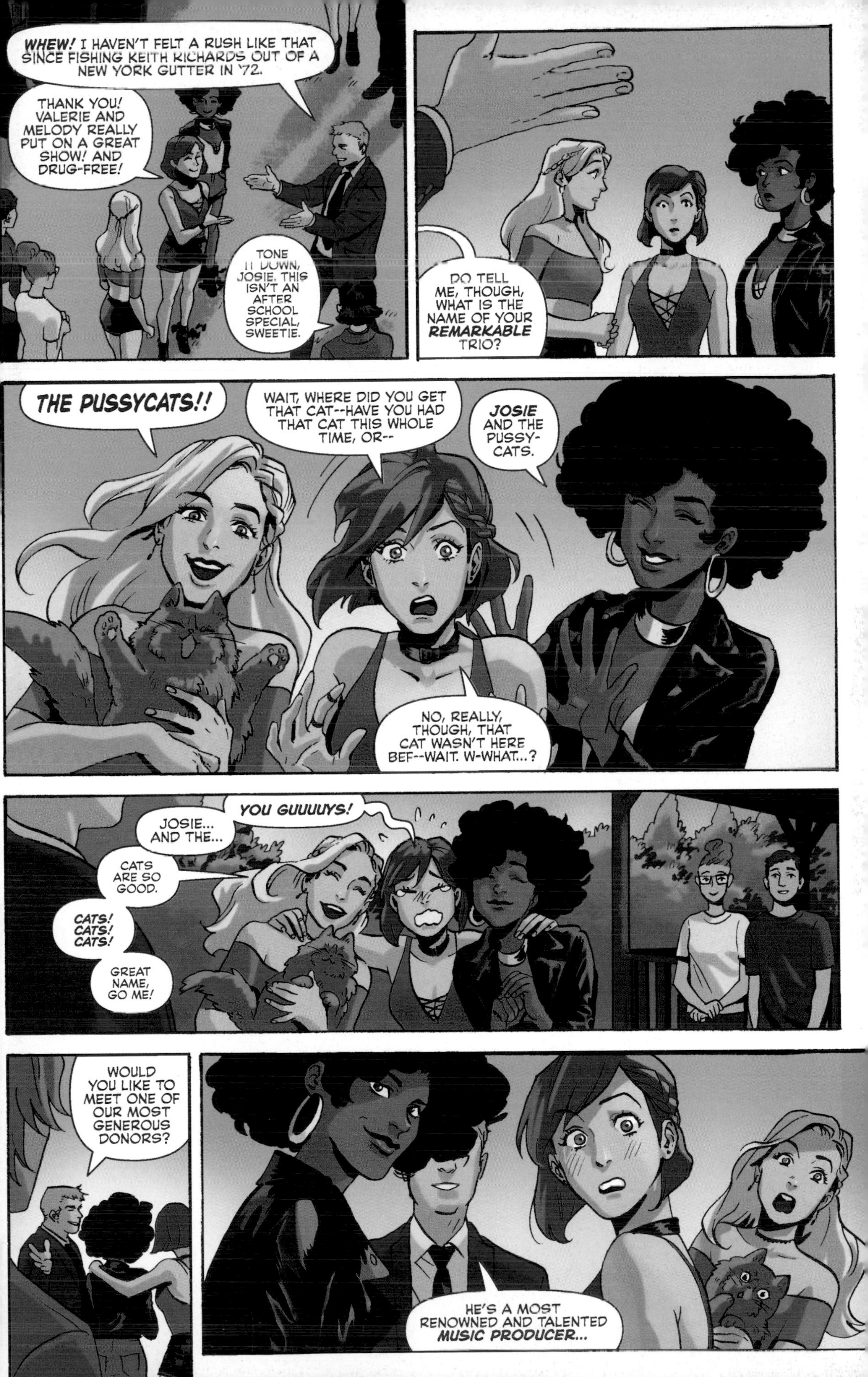
WHEW! I HAVEN'T FELT A RUSH LIKE THAT SINCE FISHING KEITH RICHARDS OUT OF A NEW YORK GUTTER IN '72.
THANK YOU! VALERIE AND MELODY REALLY PUT ON A GREAT SHOW! AND DRUG-FREE!
TONE IT DOWN, JOSIE. THIS ISN'T AN AFTER SCHOOL SPECIAL, SWEETIE.
DO TELL ME, THOUGH, WHAT IS THE NAME OF YOUR REMARKABLE TRIO?
THE PUSSYCATS!!
WAIT, WHERE DID YOU GET THAT CAT--HAVE YOU HAD THAT CAT THIS WHOLE TIME, OR--
JOSIE AND THE PUSSY-CATS.
NO, REALLY, THOUGH, THAT CAT WASN'T HERE BEF--WAIT. W-WHAT...?
JOSIE... AND THE...
YOU GUUUUYS!
CATS ARE SO GOOD.
CATS! CATS! CATS!
GREAT NAME, GO ME!
WOULD YOU LIKE TO MEET ONE OF OUR MOST GENEROUS DONORS?
HE'S A MOST RENOWNED AND TALENTED MUSIC PRODUCER...

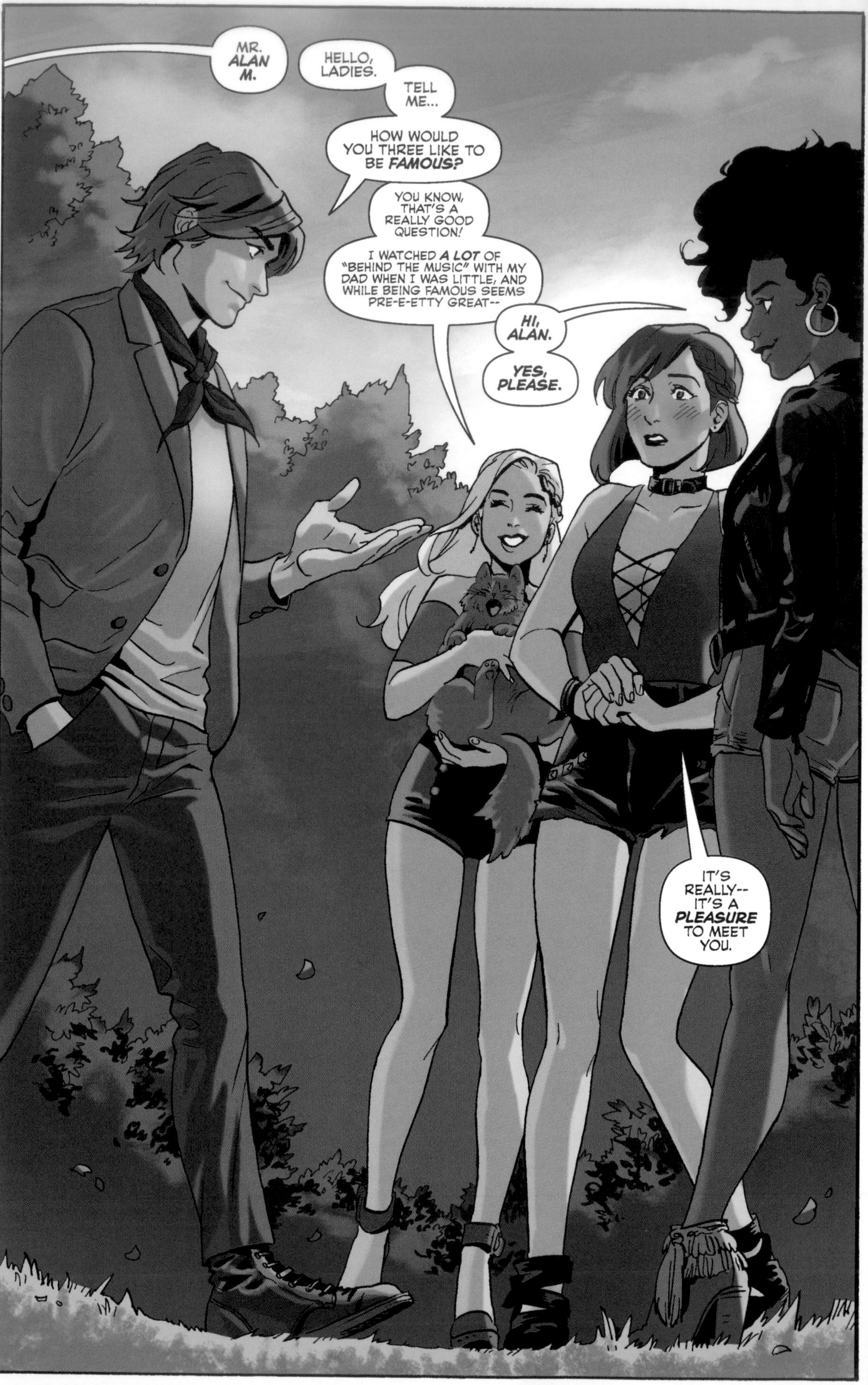
MR. ALAN M.
HELLO, LADIES.
TELL ME...
HOW WOULD YOU THREE LIKE TO BE FAMOUS?
YOU KNOW, THAT'S A REALLY GOOD QUESTION!
I WATCHED A LOT OF "BEHIND THE MUSIC" WITH MY DAD WHEN I WAS LITTLE, AND WHILE BEING FAMOUS SEEMS PRE-E-ETTY GREAT--
HI, ALAN.
YES, PLEASE.
IT'S REALLY-- IT'S A PLEASURE TO MEET YOU.

REGGIE AND ME

Who would have ever guessed that Riverdale's resident mischief-maker would land his own series? Ever the infamous bad boy, Reggie Mantle's life needed to be put under the microscope in a way that a guest-starring role just wouldn't do justice.

Legendary comic writer Tom DeFalco along with the immensely talented Sandy Jarrell have crafted a tale that shows Reggie's human side, all from the perspective of his best friend and trusty companion—his dog, Vader.

It turns out there's a lot more to the king of mean than meets the eye—and as Reggie learns, there's also a lot more to some of the people he knows in Riverdale.

STORY BY
TOM DeFALCO

ART BY
SANDY JARRELL

COLORING BY
KELLY FITZPATRICK

LETTERING BY
JACK MORELLI

ROAD TO RIVERDALE®
REGGIE AND ME

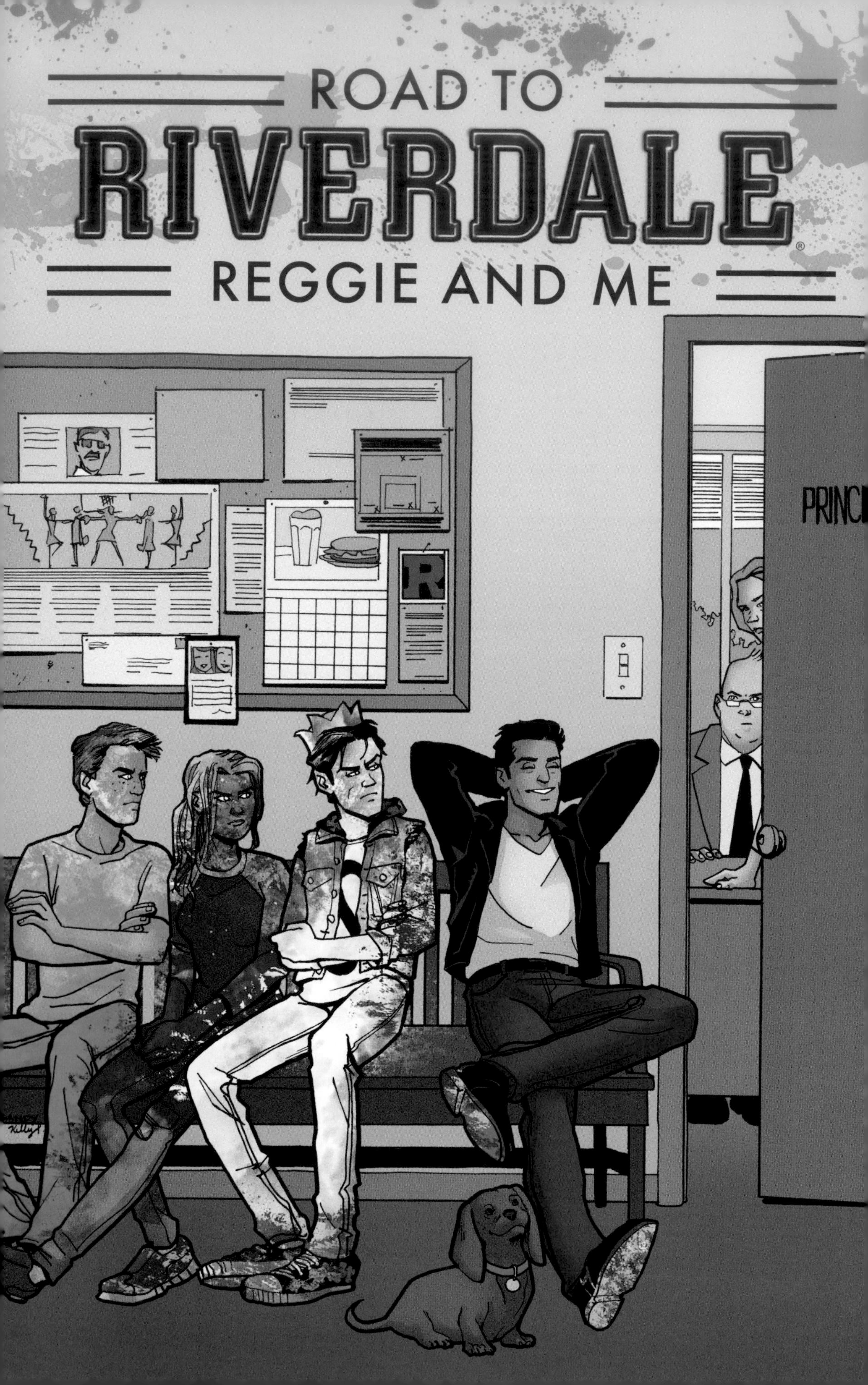
PRINC

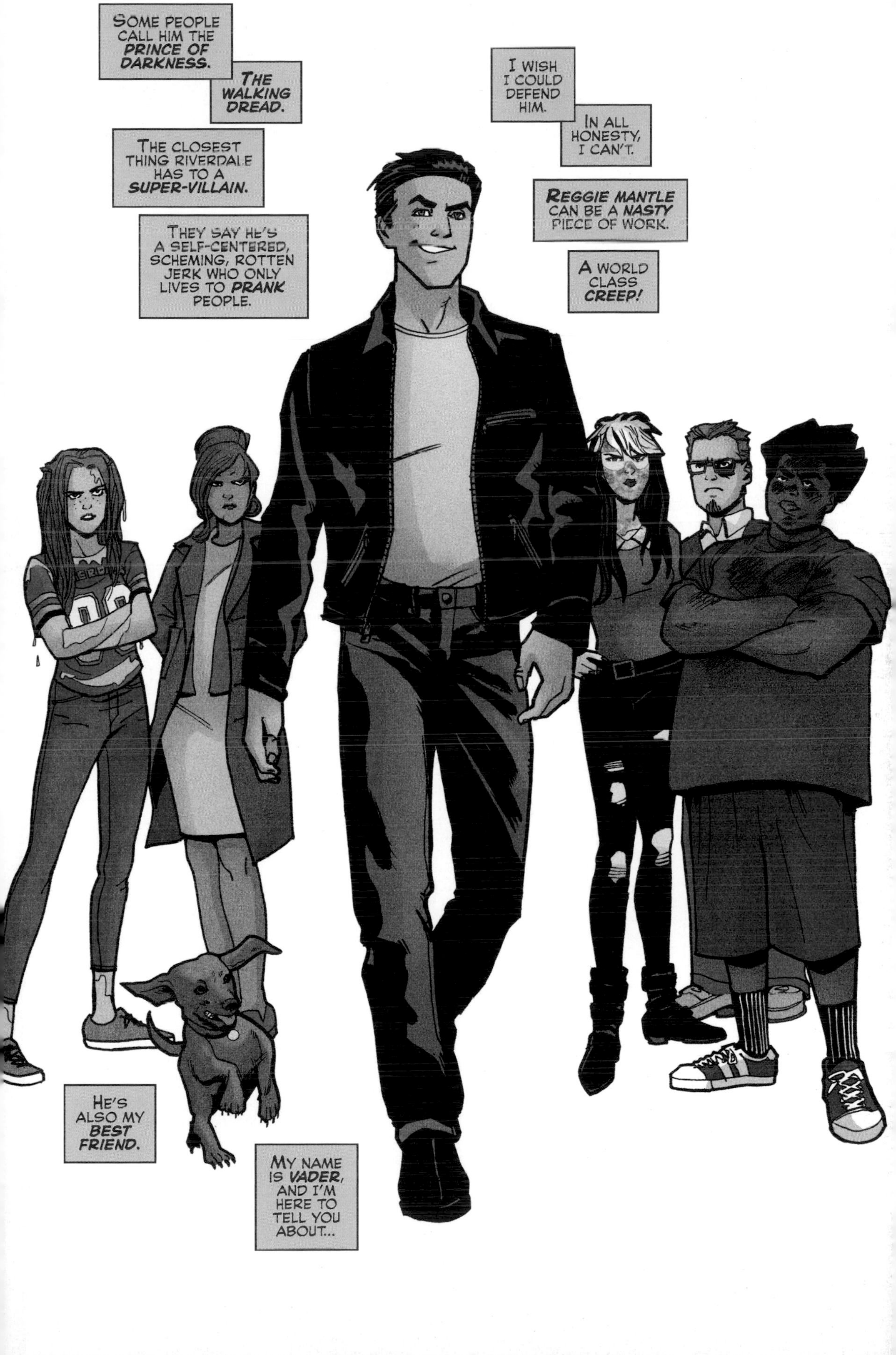
SOME PEOPLE CALL HIM THE PRINCE OF DARKNESS.
THE WALKING DREAD.
THE CLOSEST THING RIVERDALE HAS TO A SUPER-VILLAIN.
THEY SAY HE'S A SELF-CENTERED, SCHEMING, ROTTEN JERK WHO ONLY LIVES TO PRANK PEOPLE.
I WISH I COULD DEFEND HIM.
IN ALL HONESTY, I CAN'T.
REGGIE MANTLE CAN BE A NASTY PIECE OF WORK.
A WORLD CLASS CREEP!
HE'S ALSO MY BEST FRIEND.
MY NAME IS VADER, AND I'M HERE TO TELL YOU ABOUT...

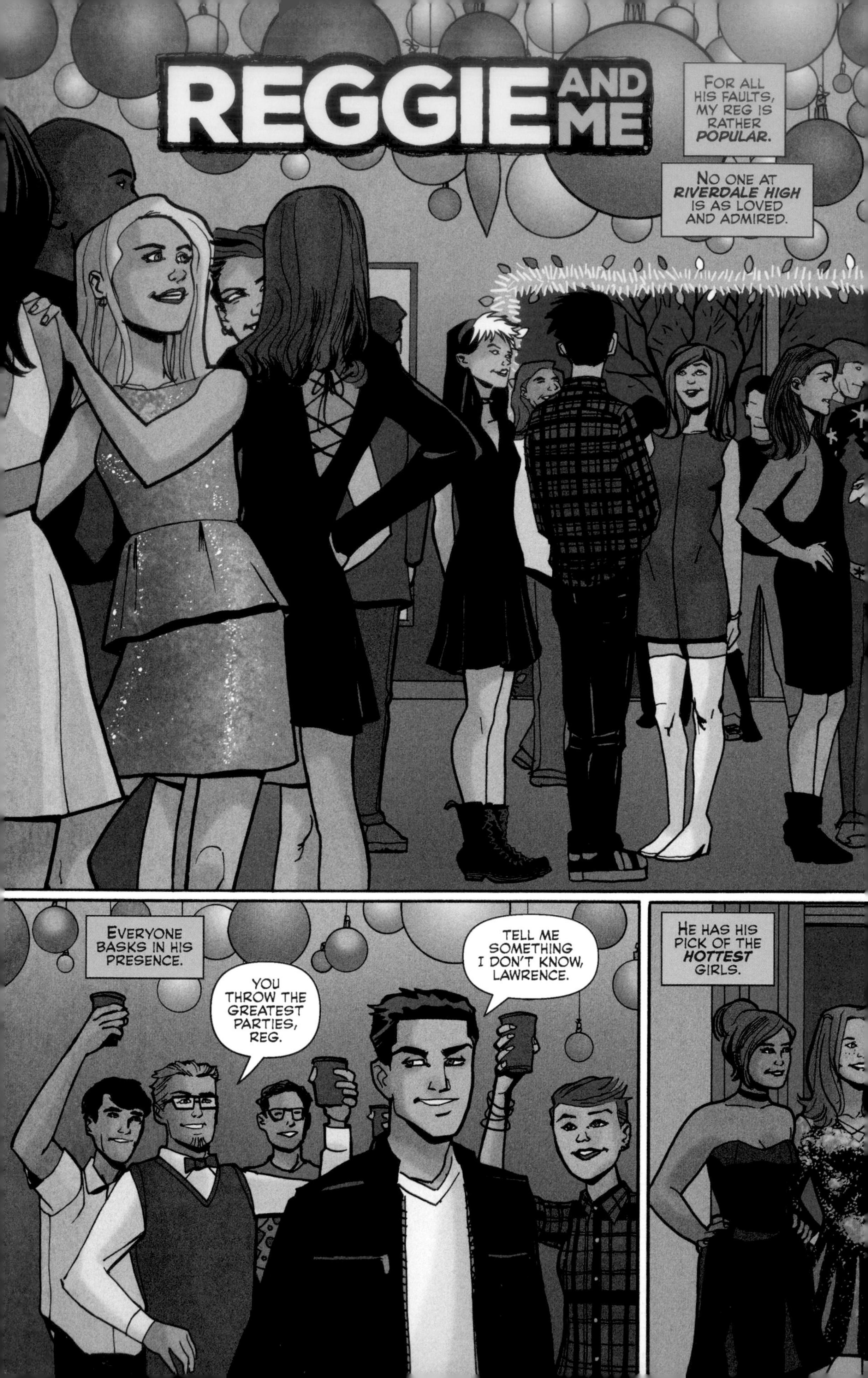
REGGIE AND ME
FOR ALL HIS FAULTS, MY REG IS RATHER POPULAR.
NO ONE AT RIVERDALE HIGH IS AS LOVED AND ADMIRED.
EVERYONE BASKS IN HIS PRESENCE.
YOU THROW THE GREATEST PARTIES, REG.
TELL ME SOMETHING I DON'T KNOW, LAWRENCE.
HE HAS HIS PICK OF THE HOTTEST GIRLS.

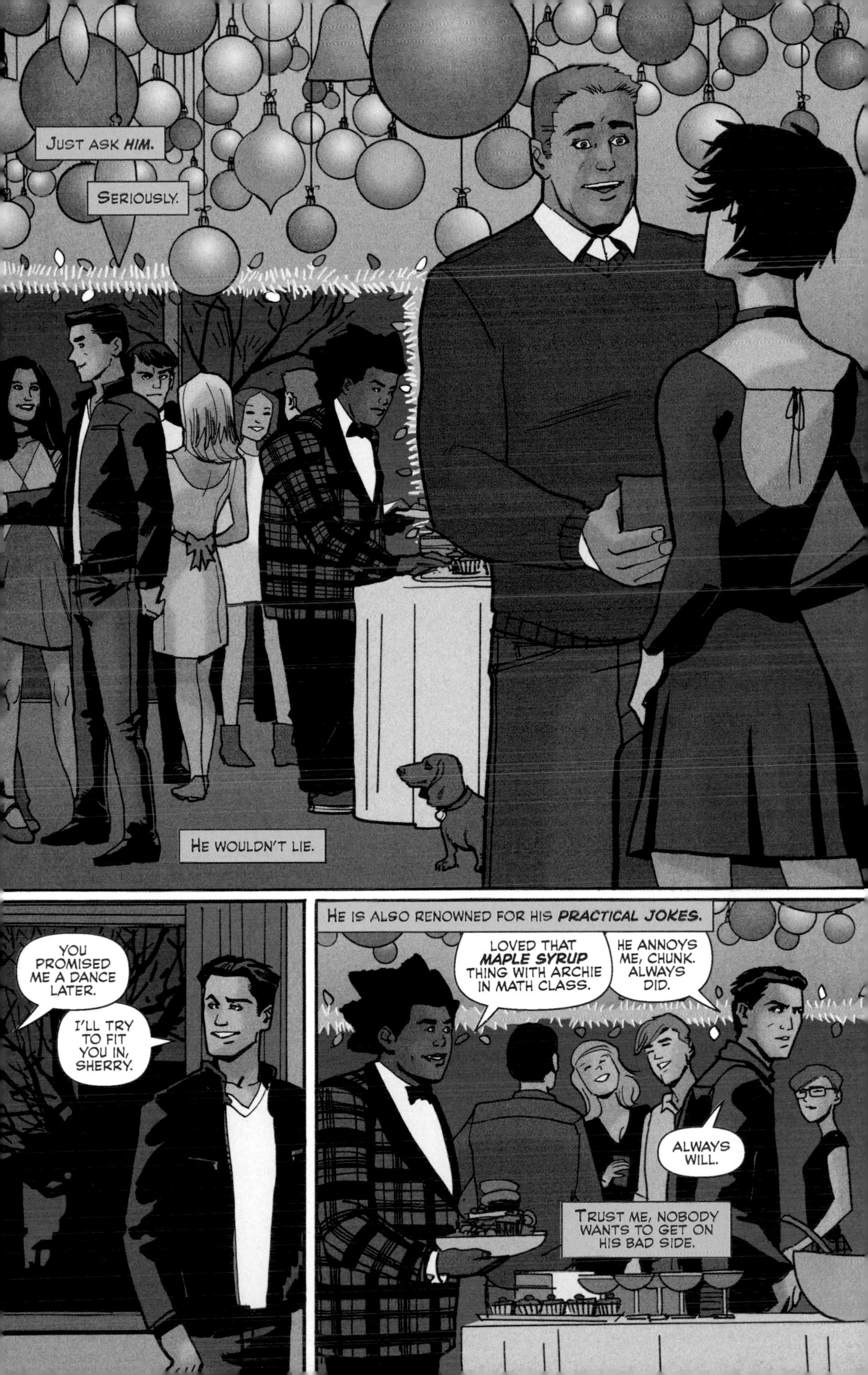
JUST ASK HIM.
SERIOUSLY.
HE WOULDN'T LIE.
YOU PROMISED ME A DANCE LATER.
I'LL TRY TO FIT YOU IN, SHERRY.
HE IS ALSO RENOWNED FOR HIS PRACTICAL JOKES.
LOVED THAT MAPLE SYRUP THING WITH ARCHIE IN MATH CLASS.
HE ANNOYS ME, CHUNK. ALWAYS DID.
ALWAYS WILL.
TRUST ME, NOBODY WANTS TO GET ON HIS BAD SIDE.

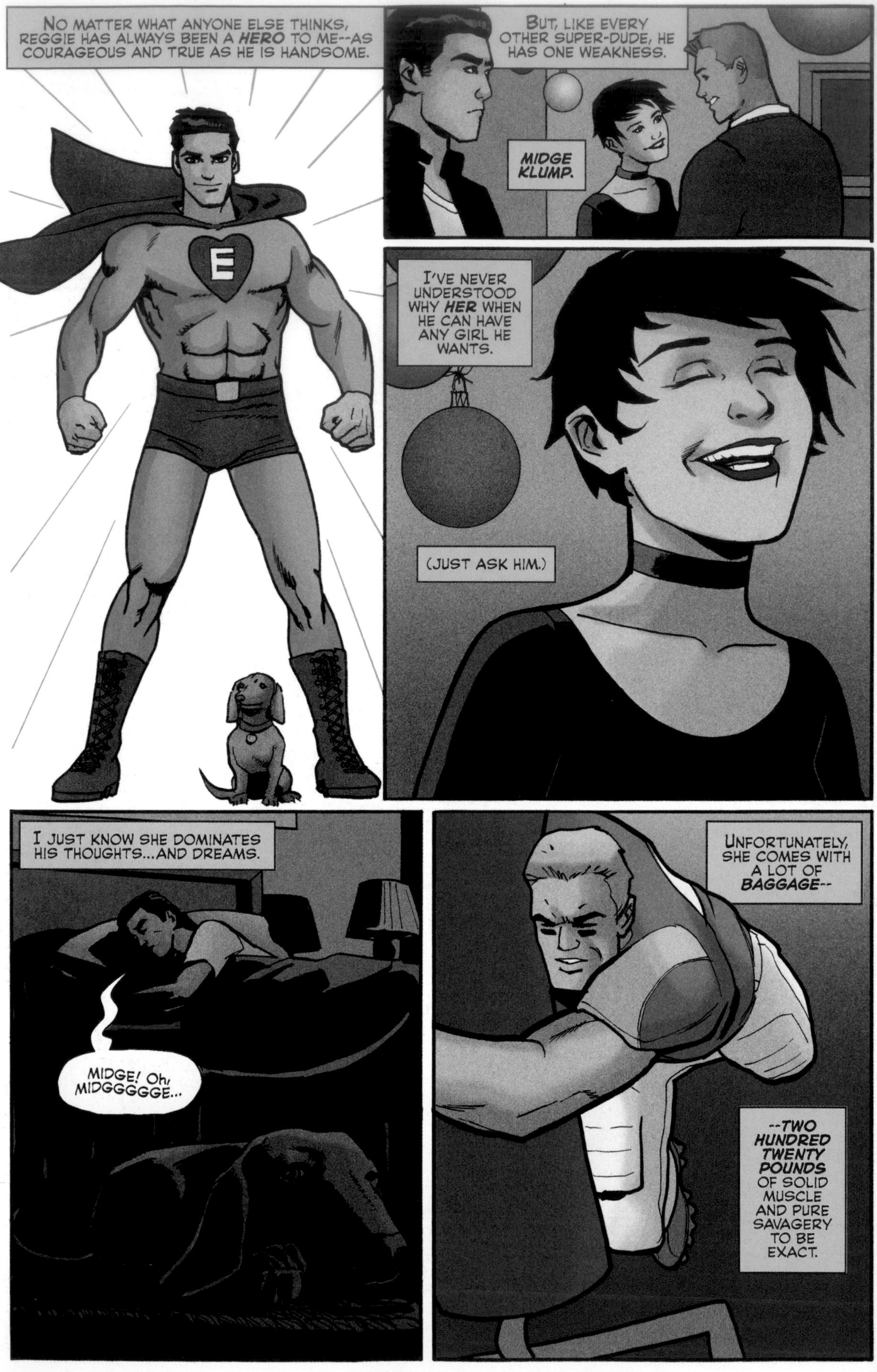

NO MATTER WHAT ANYONE ELSE THINKS, REGGIE HAS ALWAYS BEEN A HERO TO ME--AS COURAGEOUS AND TRUE AS HE IS HANDSOME.
E
BUT, LIKE EVERY OTHER SUPER-DUDE, HE HAS ONE WEAKNESS.
MIDGE KLUMP.
I'VE NEVER UNDERSTOOD WHY HER WHEN HE CAN HAVE ANY GIRL HE WANTS.
(JUST ASK HIM.)
I JUST KNOW SHE DOMINATES HIS THOUGHTS...AND DREAMS.
MIDGE! Oh, MIDGGGGGE...
UNFORTUNATELY, SHE COMES WITH A LOT OF BAGGAGE--
--TWO HUNDRED TWENTY POUNDS OF SOLID MUSCLE AND PURE SAVAGERY TO BE EXACT.

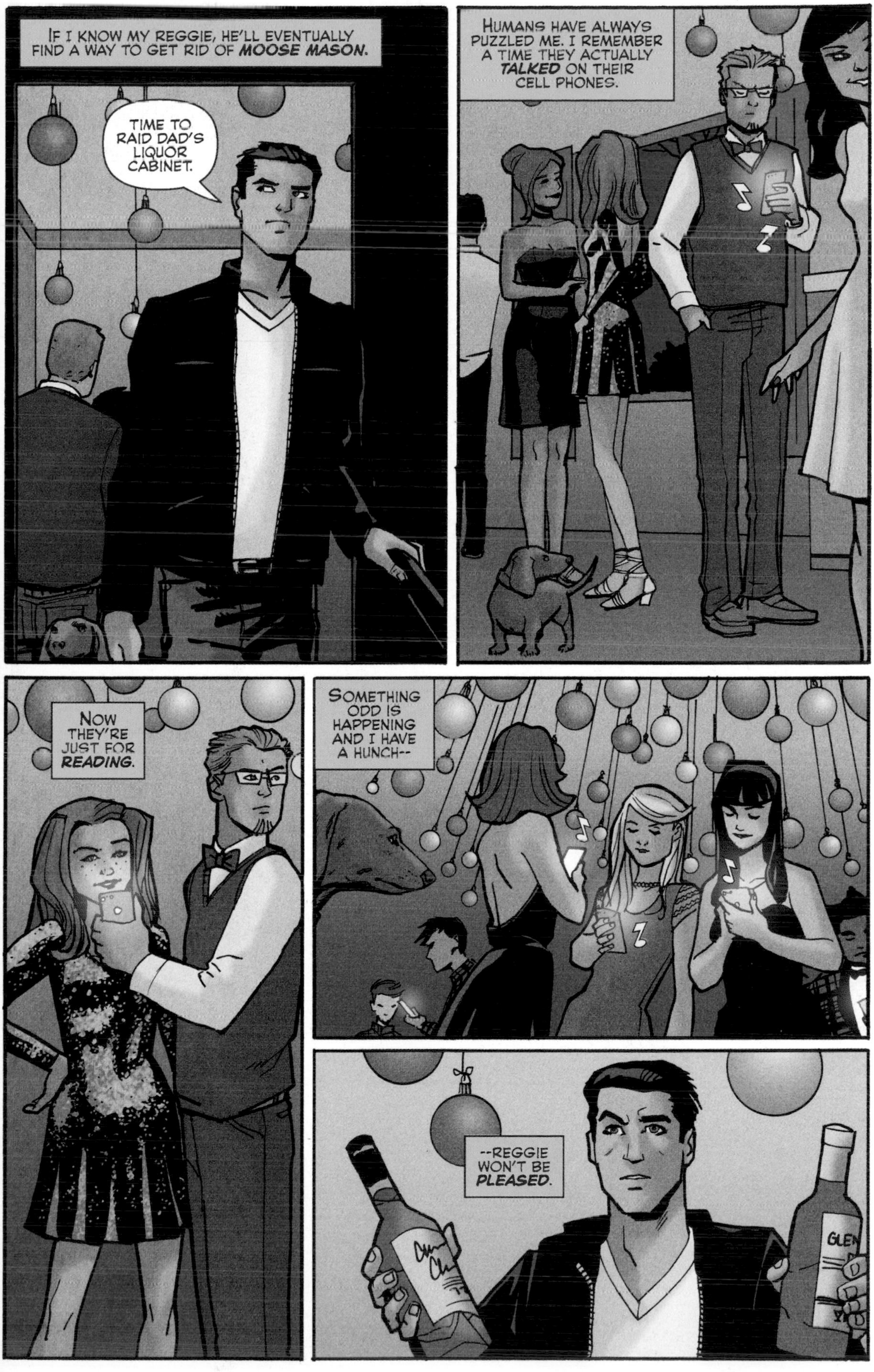
If I know my Reggie, he'll eventually find a way to get rid of MOOSE MASON.
TIME TO RAID DAD'S LIQUOR CABINET.
Humans have always puzzled me. I remember a time they actually TALKED on their cell phones.
Now they're just for READING.
Something odd is happening and I have a hunch--
--Reggie won't be PLEASED.

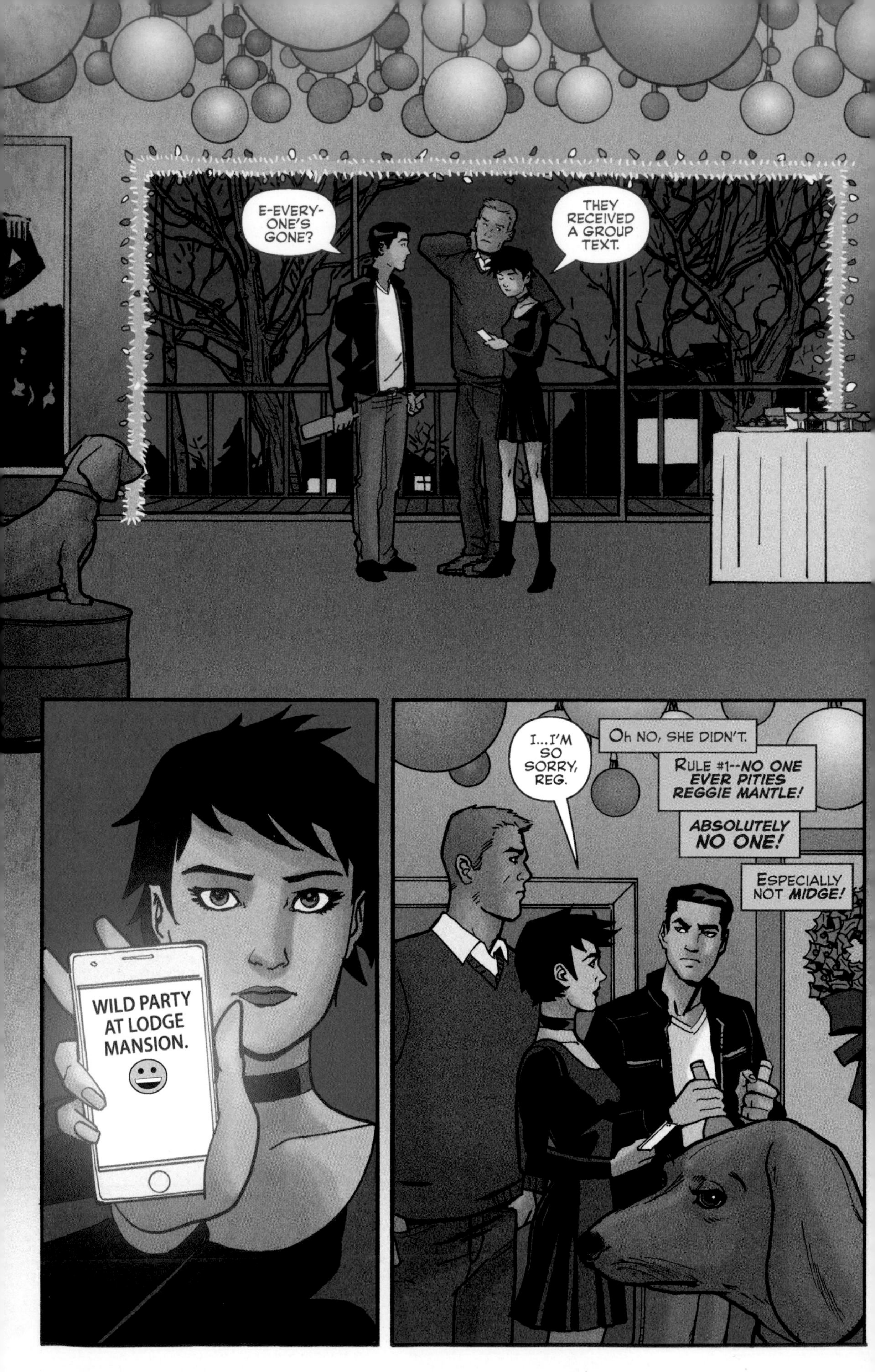
E-EVERY-ONE'S GONE?
THEY RECEIVED A GROUP TEXT.
WILD PARTY AT LODGE MANSION.
I...I'M SO SORRY, REG.
Oh NO, SHE DIDN'T.
RULE #1--NO ONE EVER PITIES REGGIE MANTLE!
ABSOLUTELY NO ONE!
ESPECIALLY NOT MIDGE!

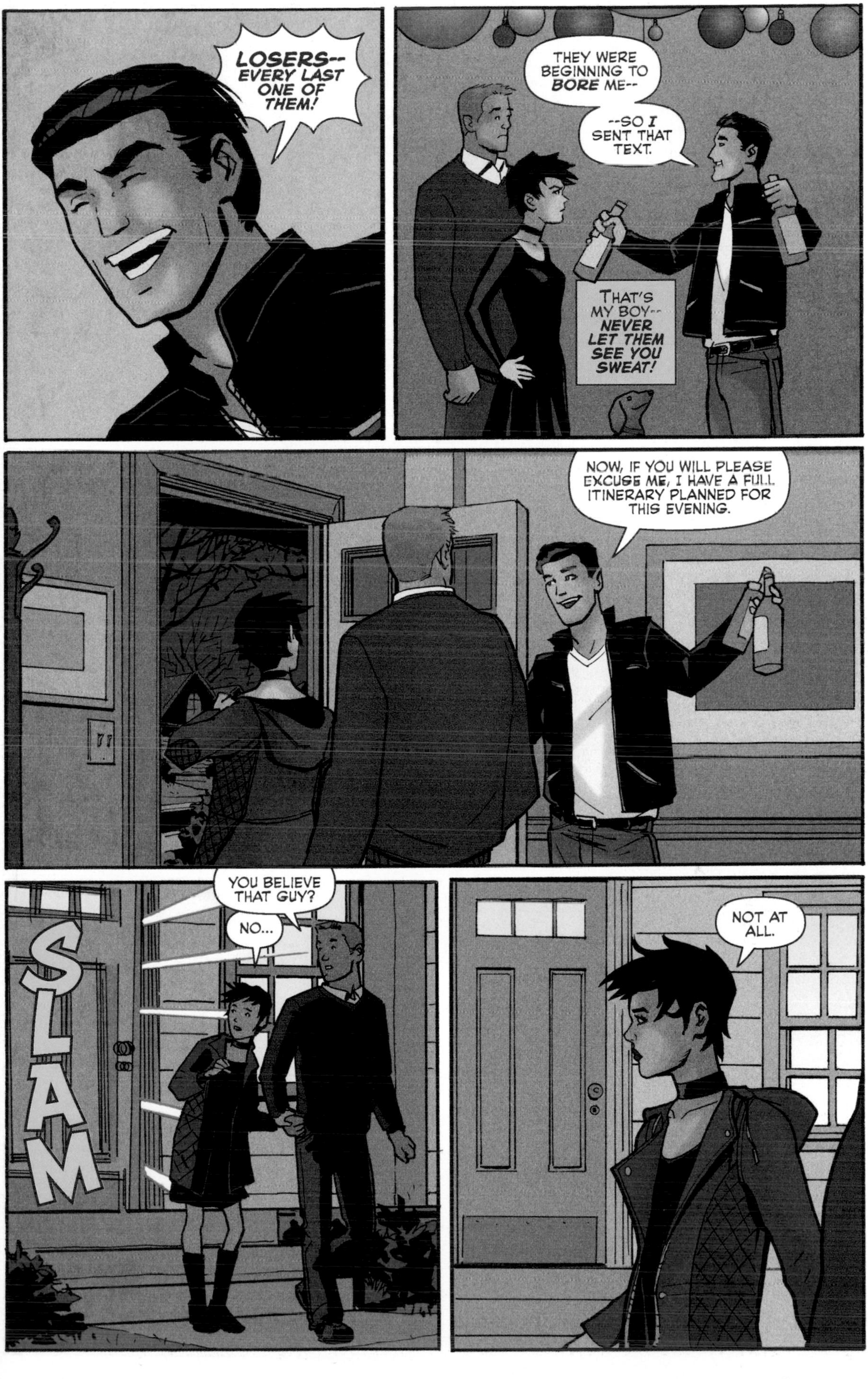
LOSERS-- EVERY LAST ONE OF THEM!
THEY WERE BEGINNING TO BORE ME--
--SO I SENT THAT TEXT.
THAT'S MY BOY-- NEVER LET THEM SEE YOU SWEAT!
NOW, IF YOU WILL PLEASE EXCUSE ME, I HAVE A FULL ITINERARY PLANNED FOR THIS EVENING.
SLAM
YOU BELIEVE THAT GUY?
NO...
NOT AT ALL.

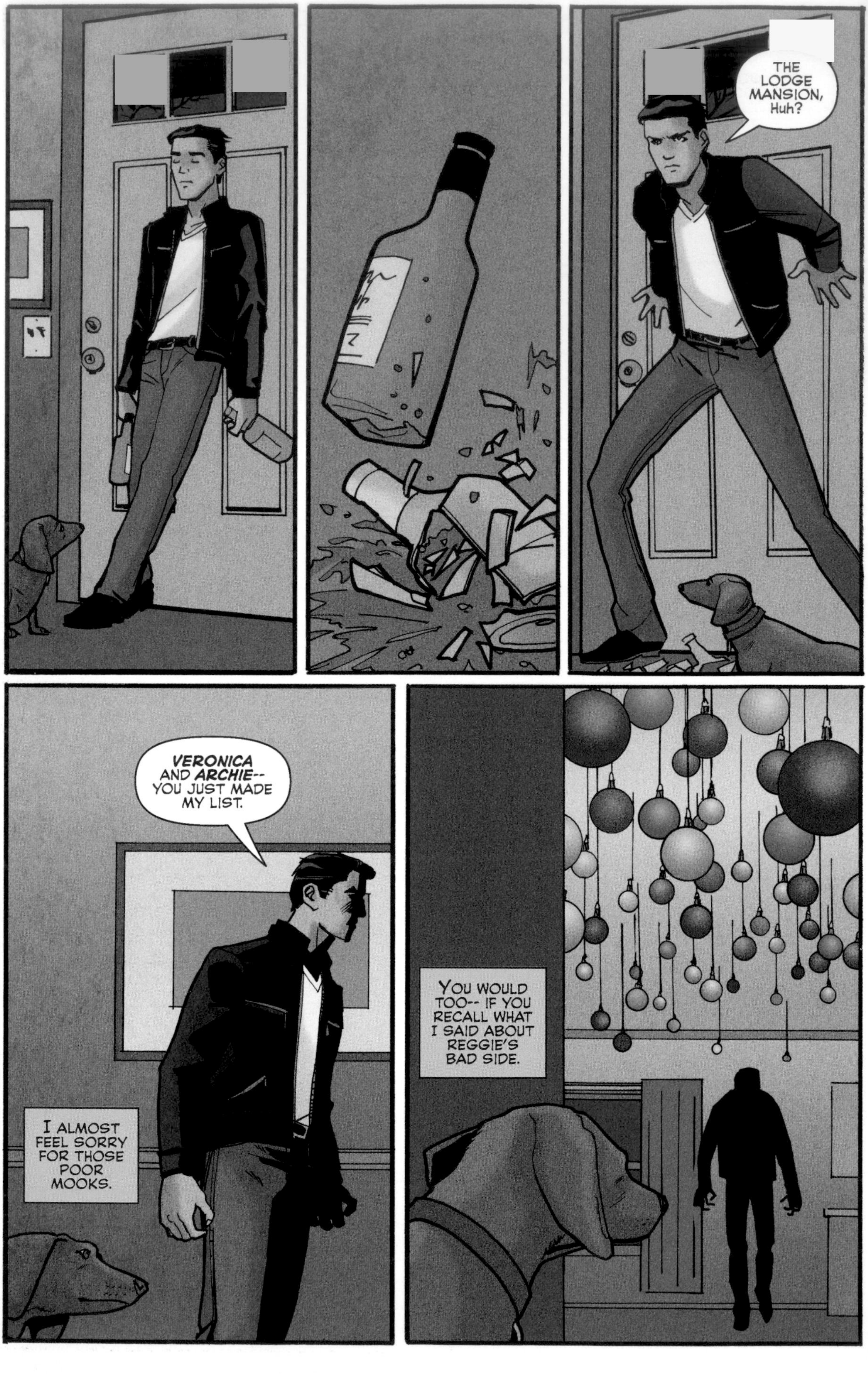
THE LODGE MANSION, Huh?
VERONICA AND ARCHIE-- YOU JUST MADE MY LIST.
I ALMOST FEEL SORRY FOR THOSE POOR MOOKS.
YOU WOULD TOO-- IF YOU RECALL WHAT I SAID ABOUT REGGIE'S BAD SIDE.

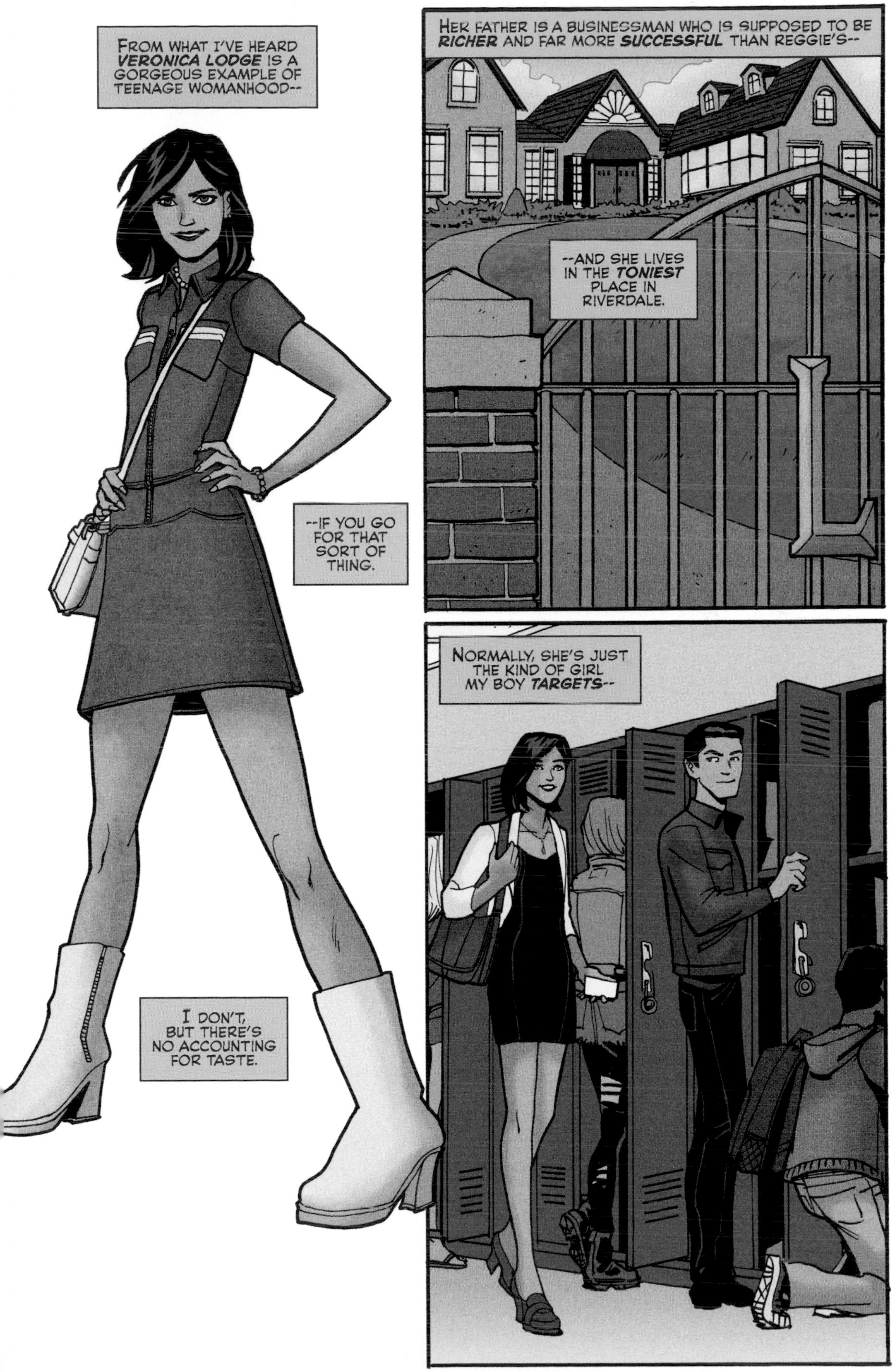
FROM WHAT I'VE HEARD VERONICA LODGE IS A GORGEOUS EXAMPLE OF TEENAGE WOMANHOOD--
--IF YOU GO FOR THAT SORT OF THING.
I DON'T, BUT THERE'S NO ACCOUNTING FOR TASTE.
HER FATHER IS A BUSINESSMAN WHO IS SUPPOSED TO BE RICHER AND FAR MORE SUCCESSFUL THAN REGGIE'S--
--AND SHE LIVES IN THE TONIEST PLACE IN RIVERDALE.
NORMALLY, SHE'S JUST THE KIND OF GIRL MY BOY TARGETS--

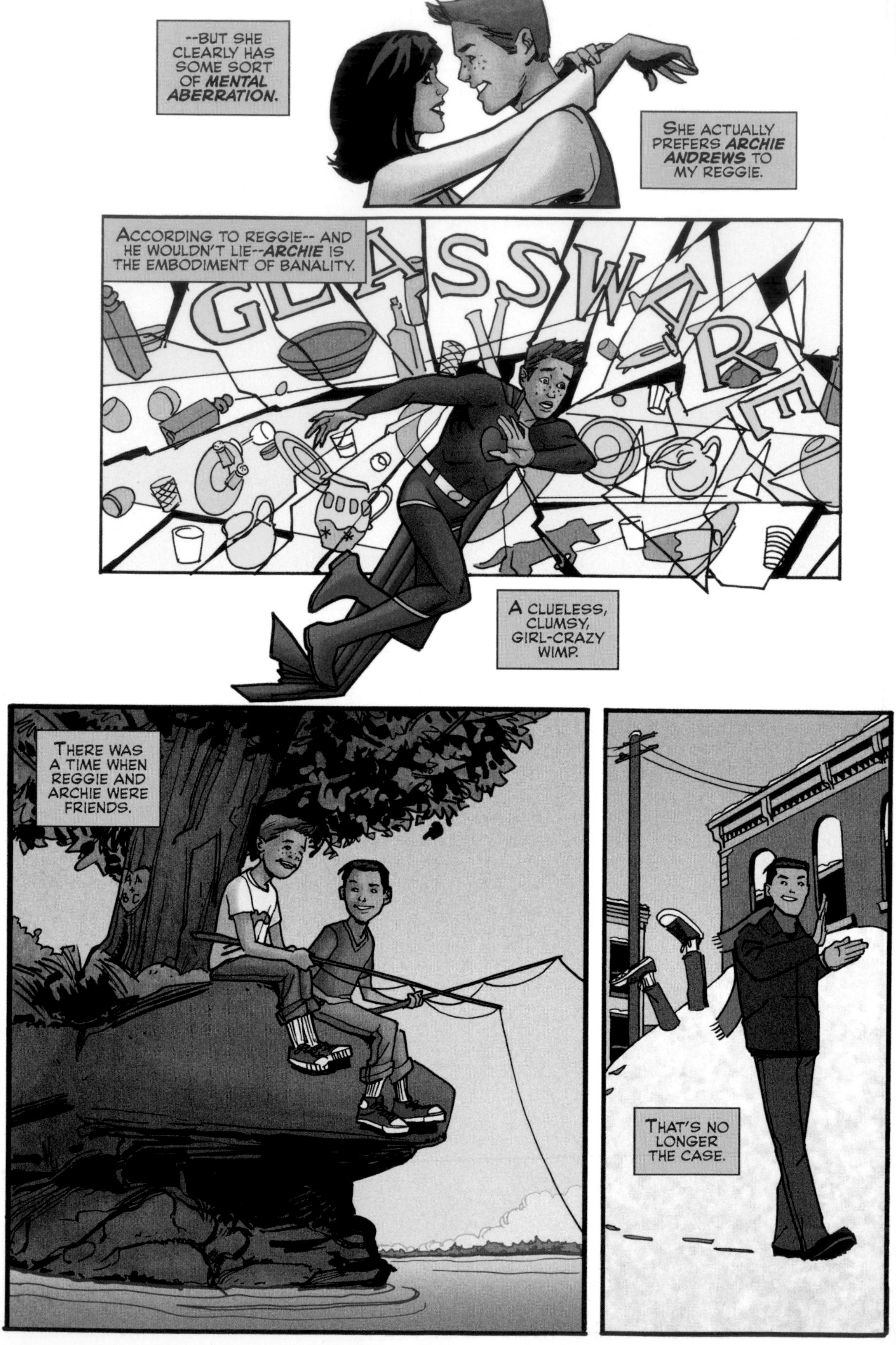
--BUT SHE CLEARLY HAS SOME SORT OF MENTAL ABERRATION.
SHE ACTUALLY PREFERS ARCHIE ANDREWS TO MY REGGIE.
ACCORDING TO REGGIE-- AND HE WOULDN'T LIE--ARCHIE IS THE EMBODIMENT OF BANALITY.
GLASSWARE
A CLUELESS, CLUMSY, GIRL-CRAZY WIMP.
THERE WAS A TIME WHEN REGGIE AND ARCHIE WERE FRIENDS.
THAT'S NO LONGER THE CASE.

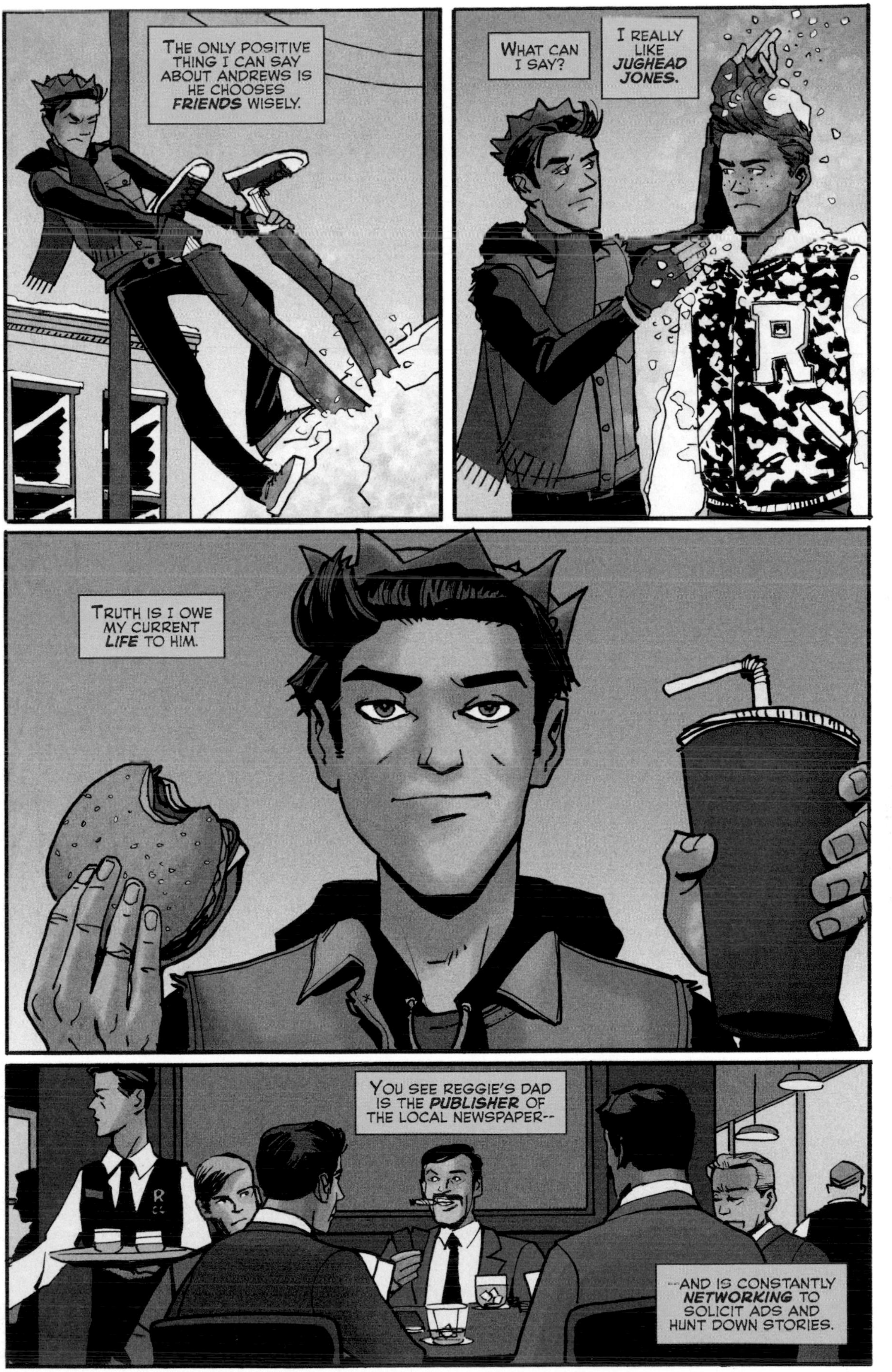
The only positive thing I can say about Andrews is he chooses **friends** wisely.
What can I say?
I really like ***Jughead Jones.***
Truth is I owe my current ***life*** to him.
You see Reggie's dad is the ***publisher*** of the local newspaper--
--and is constantly ***networking*** to solicit ads and hunt down stories.

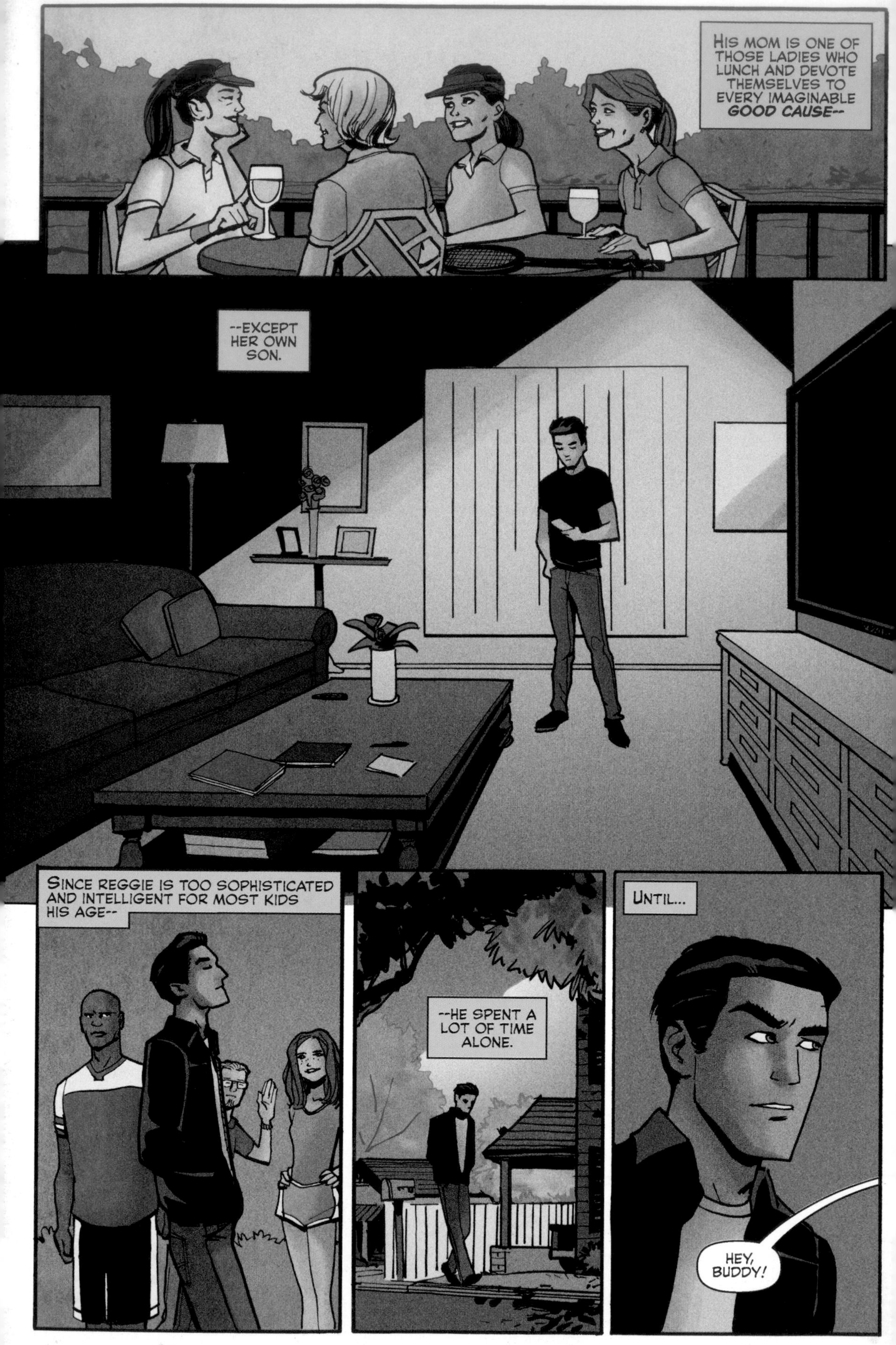
HIS MOM IS ONE OF THOSE LADIES WHO LUNCH AND DEVOTE THEMSELVES TO EVERY IMAGINABLE ***GOOD CAUSE--***
--EXCEPT HER OWN SON.
SINCE REGGIE IS TOO SOPHISTICATED AND INTELLIGENT FOR MOST KIDS HIS AGE--
--HE SPENT A LOT OF TIME ALONE.
UNTIL...
HEY, BUDDY!

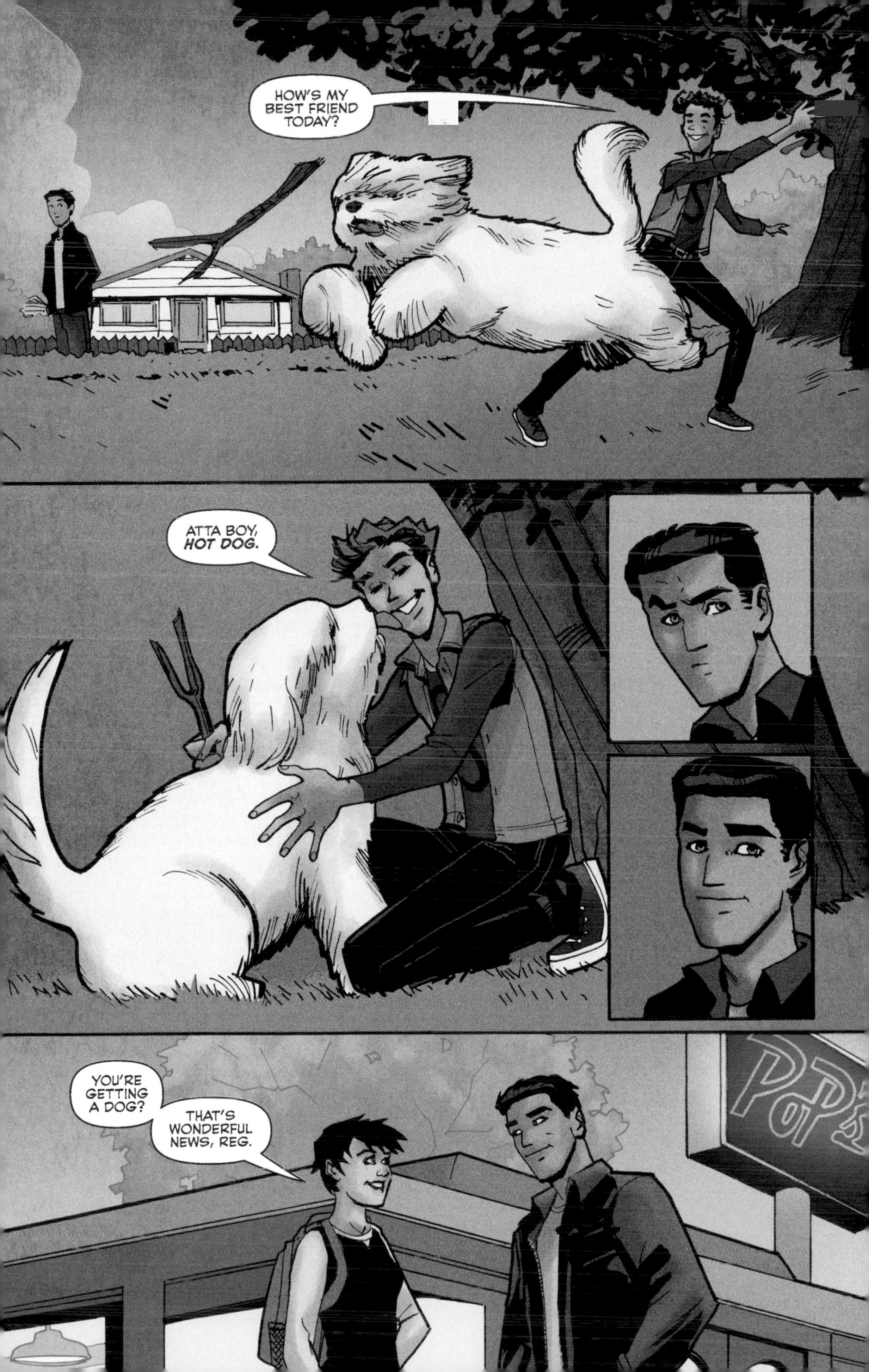
HOW'S MY BEST FRIEND TODAY?
ATTA BOY, HOT DOG.
YOU'RE GETTING A DOG?
THAT'S WONDERFUL NEWS, REG.
POP'S

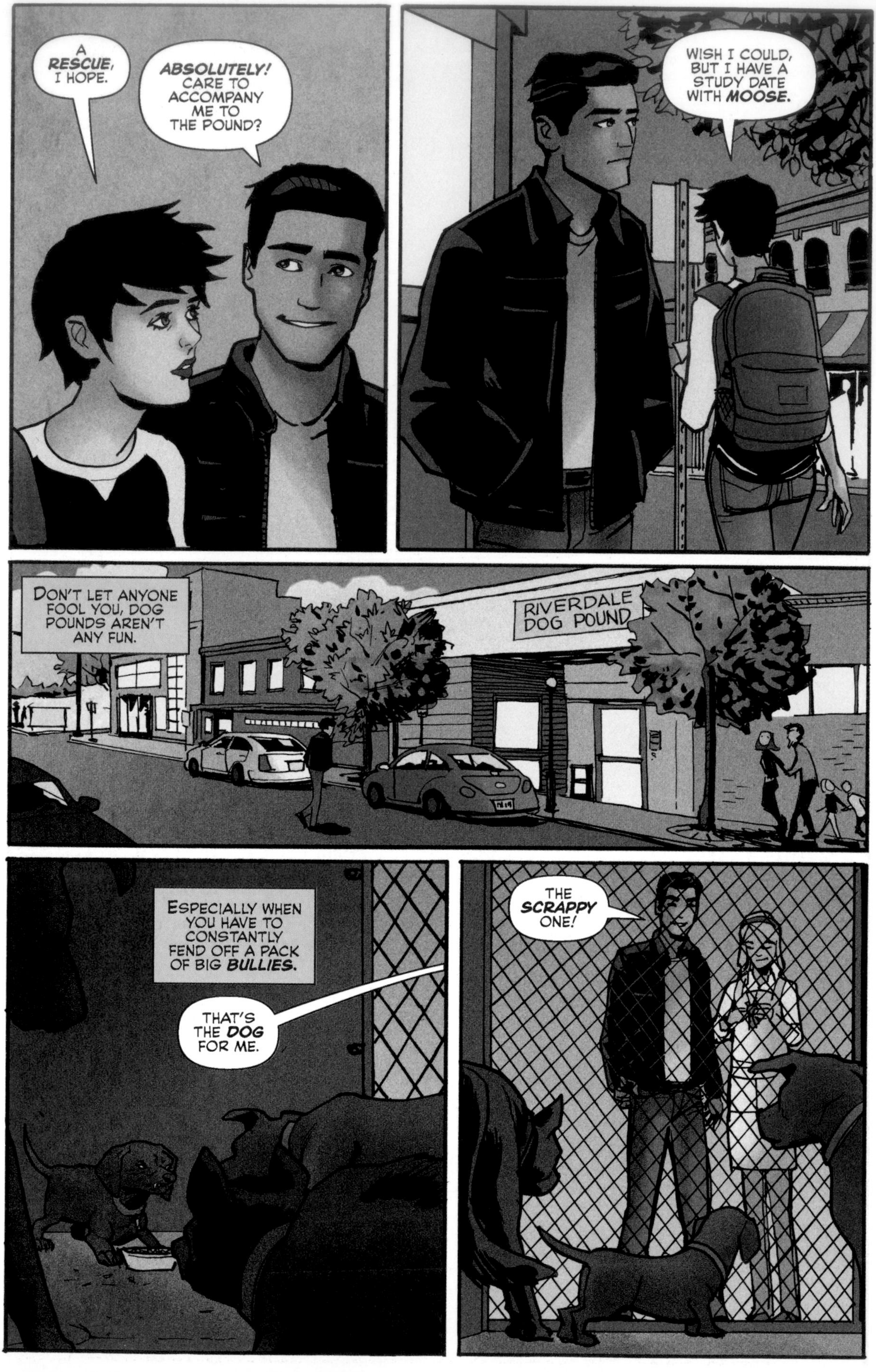
A RESCUE, I HOPE.
ABSOLUTELY! CARE TO ACCOMPANY ME TO THE POUND?
WISH I COULD, BUT I HAVE A STUDY DATE WITH MOOSE.
DON'T LET ANYONE FOOL YOU, DOG POUNDS AREN'T ANY FUN.
RIVERDALE DOG POUND
ESPECIALLY WHEN YOU HAVE TO CONSTANTLY FEND OFF A PACK OF BIG BULLIES.
THAT'S THE DOG FOR ME.
THE SCRAPPY ONE!

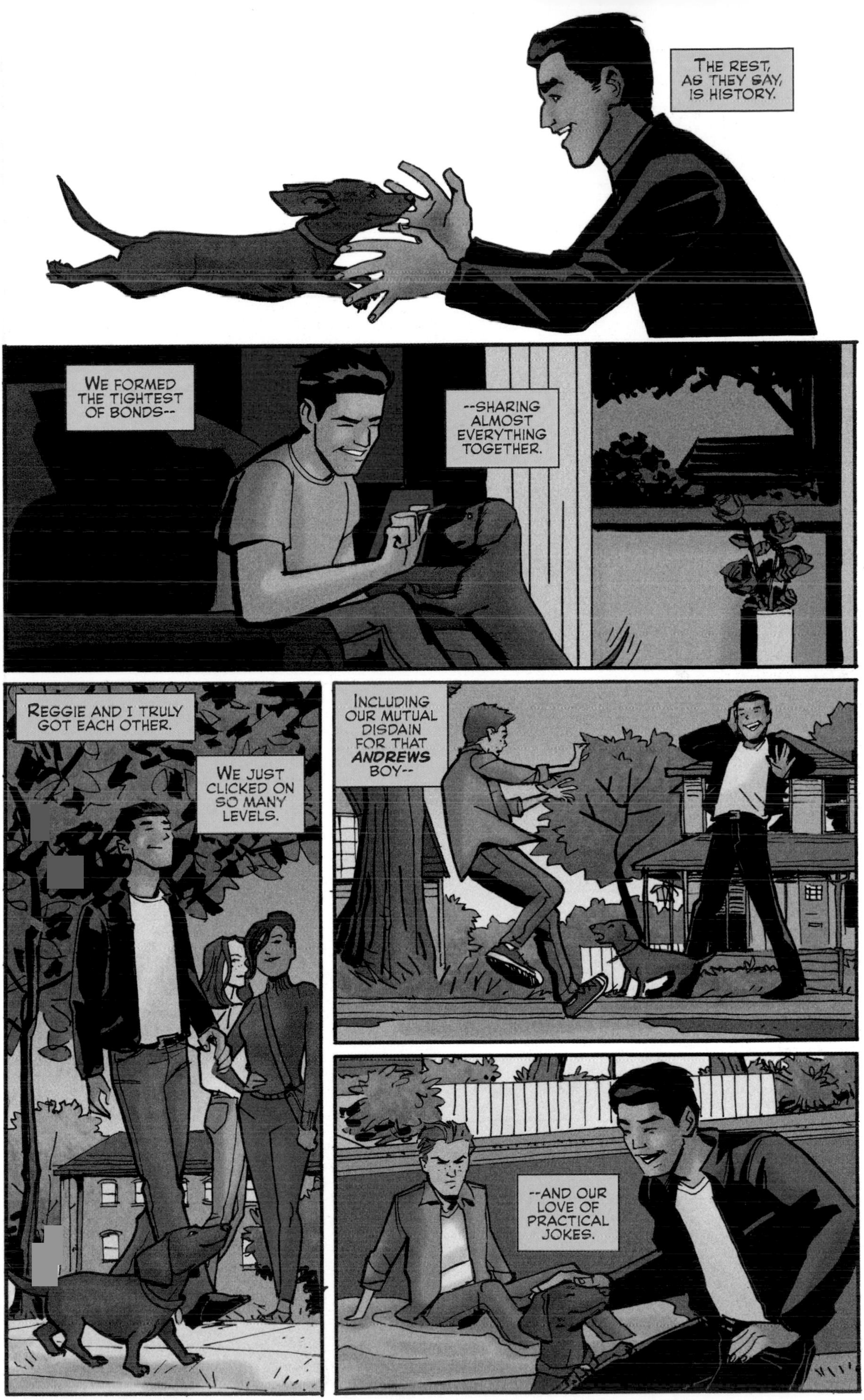
THE REST, AS THEY SAY, IS HISTORY.
WE FORMED THE TIGHTEST OF BONDS--
--SHARING ALMOST EVERYTHING TOGETHER.
REGGIE AND I TRULY GOT EACH OTHER.
WE JUST CLICKED ON SO MANY LEVELS.
INCLUDING OUR MUTUAL DISDAIN FOR THAT ANDREWS BOY--
--AND OUR LOVE OF PRACTICAL JOKES.

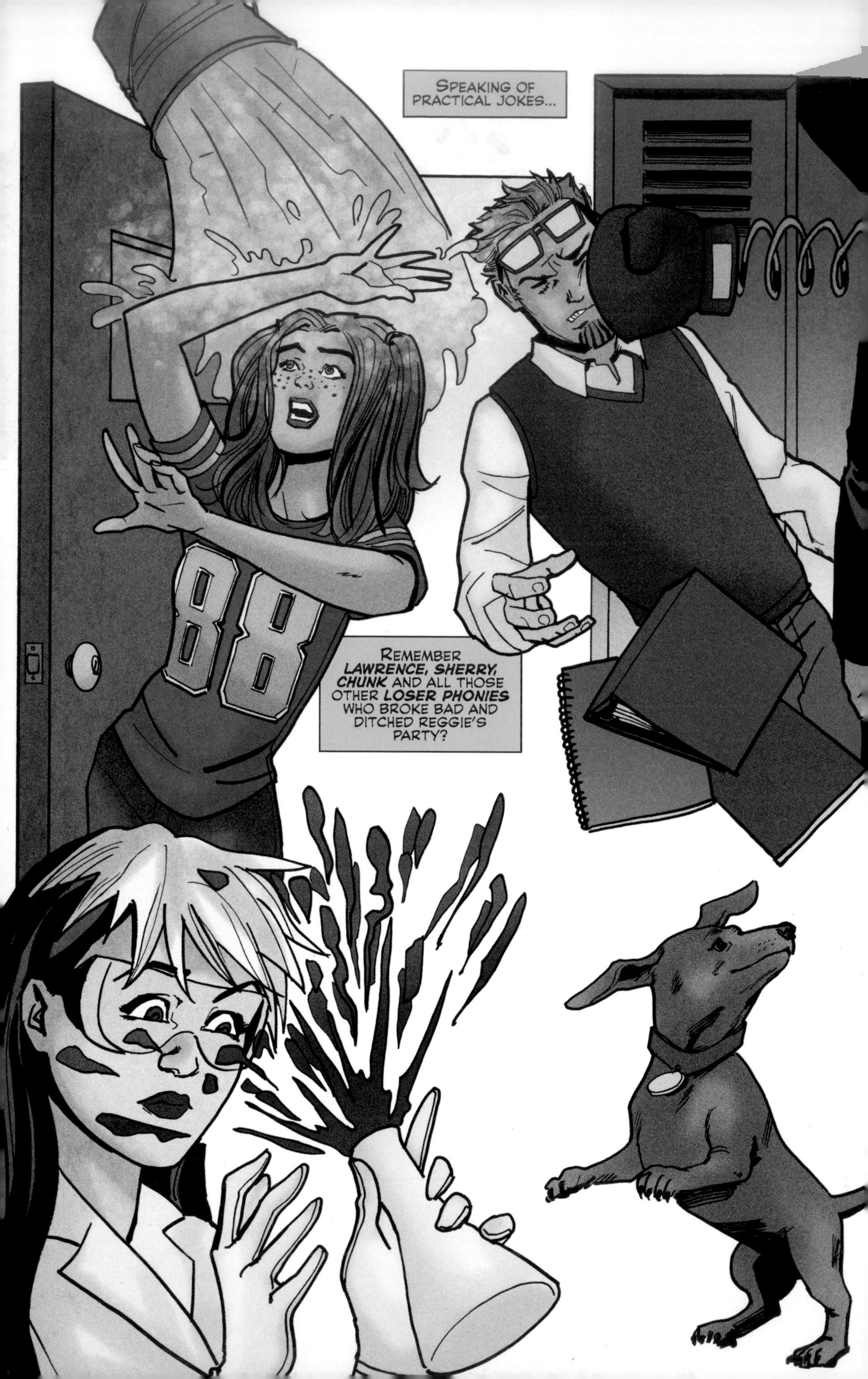
SPEAKING OF PRACTICAL JOKES...
REMEMBER LAWRENCE, SHERRY, CHUNK AND ALL THOSE OTHER LOSER PHONIES WHO BROKE BAD AND DITCHED REGGIE'S PARTY?

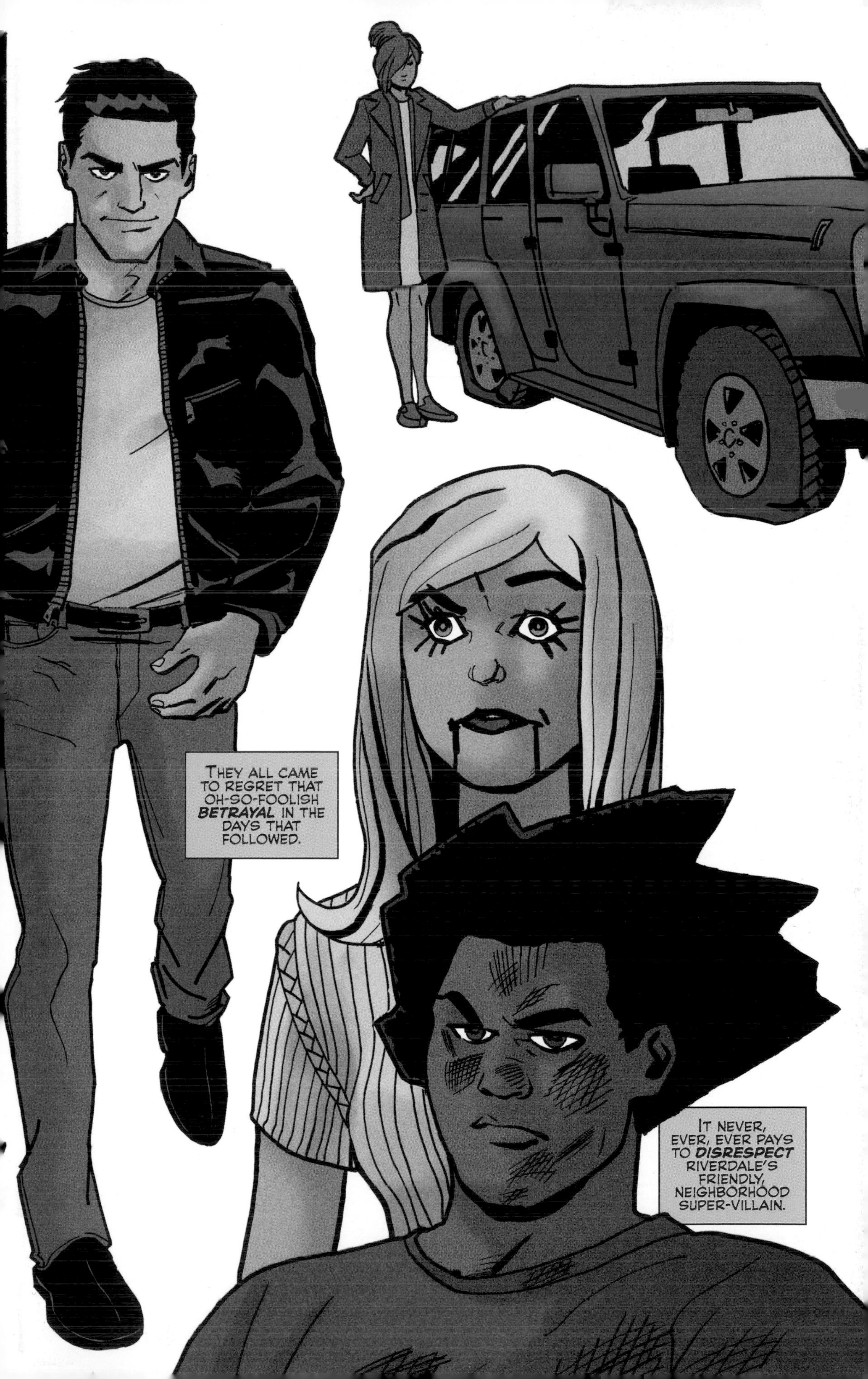
THEY ALL CAME TO REGRET THAT OH-SO-FOOLISH BETRAYAL IN THE DAYS THAT FOLLOWED.
IT NEVER, EVER, EVER PAYS TO DISRESPECT RIVERDALE'S FRIENDLY, NEIGHBORHOOD SUPER-VILLAIN.

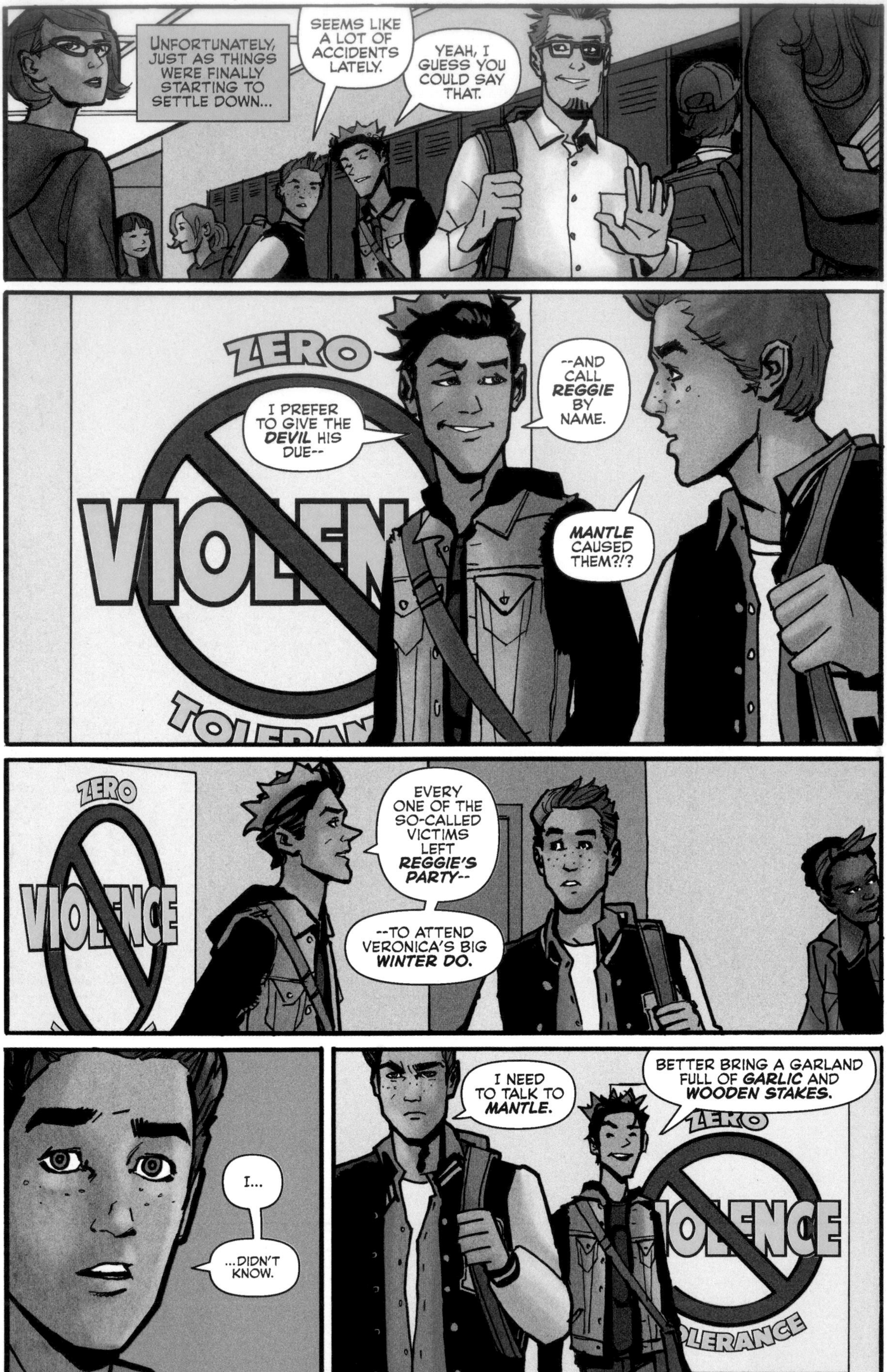
UNFORTUNATELY, JUST AS THINGS WERE FINALLY STARTING TO SETTLE DOWN...
SEEMS LIKE A LOT OF ACCIDENTS LATELY.
YEAH, I GUESS YOU COULD SAY THAT.
ZERO VIOLEN TOLERAN
I PREFER TO GIVE THE DEVIL HIS DUE--
--AND CALL REGGIE BY NAME.
MANTLE CAUSED THEM?!?
ZERO VIOLENCE
EVERY ONE OF THE SO-CALLED VICTIMS LEFT REGGIE'S PARTY--
--TO ATTEND VERONICA'S BIG WINTER DO.
I...
...DIDN'T KNOW.
I NEED TO TALK TO MANTLE.
BETTER BRING A GARLAND FULL OF GARLIC AND WOODEN STAKES.
ZERO VIOLENCE TOLERANCE

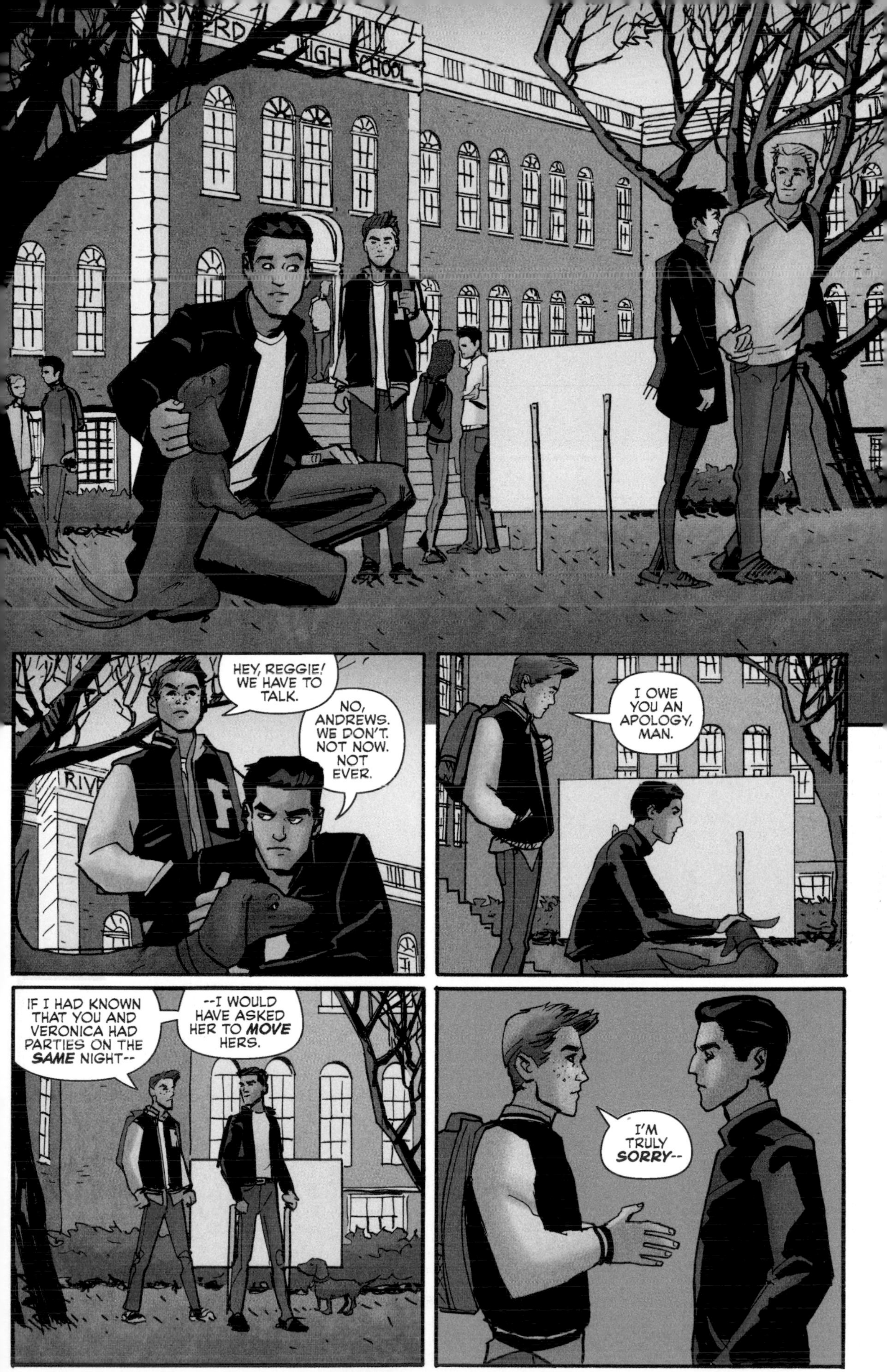

RIVERDALE HIGH SCHOOL
HEY, REGGIE! WE HAVE TO TALK.
NO, ANDREWS. WE DON'T. NOT NOW. NOT EVER.
I OWE YOU AN APOLOGY, MAN.
IF I HAD KNOWN THAT YOU AND VERONICA HAD PARTIES ON THE SAME NIGHT--
--I WOULD HAVE ASKED HER TO MOVE HERS.
I'M TRULY SORRY--

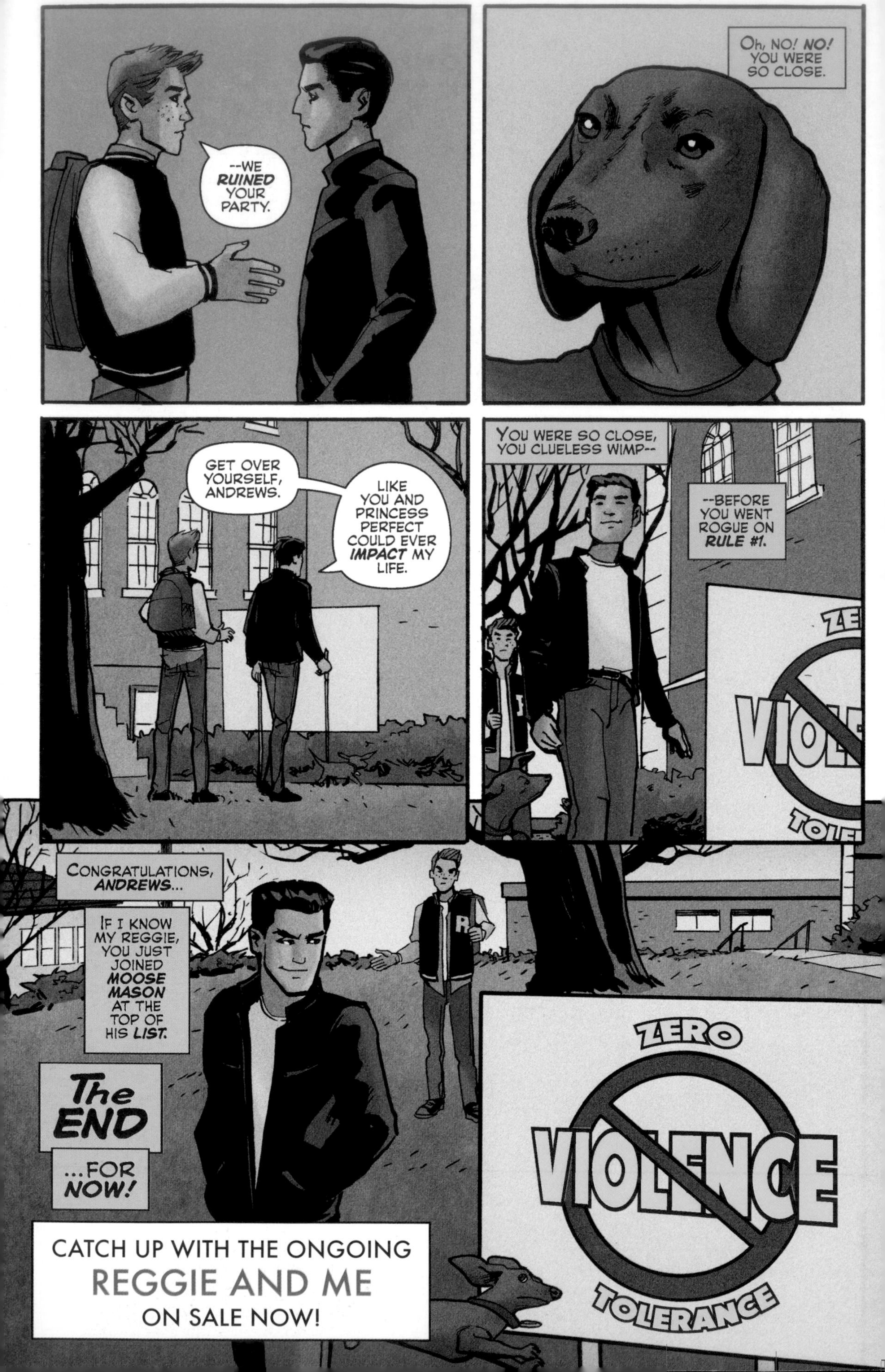
--WE RUINED YOUR PARTY.
Oh, NO! NO! YOU WERE SO CLOSE.
GET OVER YOURSELF, ANDREWS.
LIKE YOU AND PRINCESS PERFECT COULD EVER IMPACT MY LIFE.
YOU WERE SO CLOSE, YOU CLUELESS WIMP--
--BEFORE YOU WENT ROGUE ON RULE #1.
CONGRATULATIONS, ANDREWS...
IF I KNOW MY REGGIE, YOU JUST JOINED MOOSE MASON AT THE TOP OF HIS LIST.
ZERO VIOLENCE TOLERANCE
The END
...FOR NOW!
CATCH UP WITH THE ONGOING
REGGIE AND ME
ON SALE NOW!

ROAD TO

RIVERDALE®

SPECIAL FEATURES

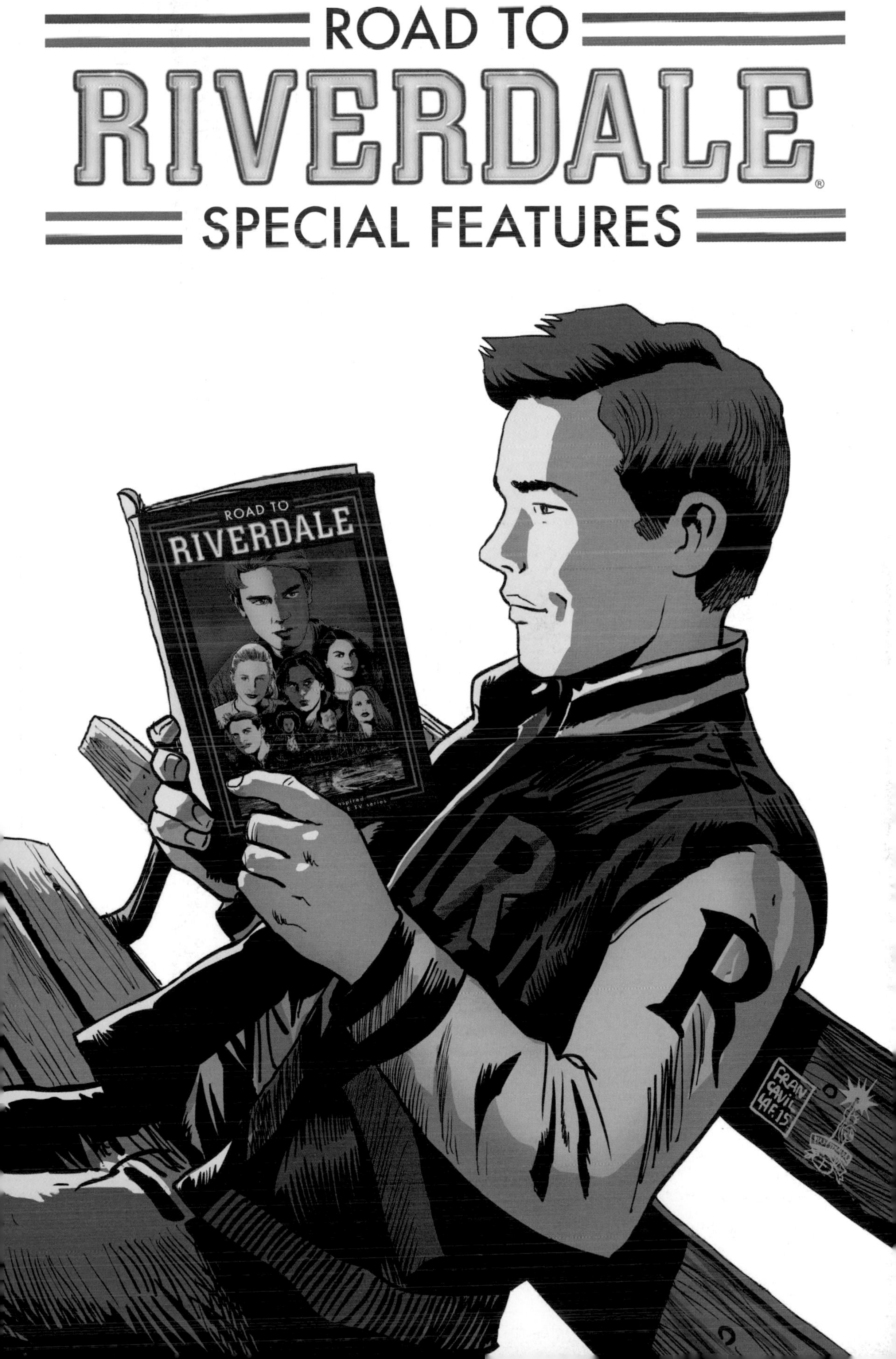
ROAD TO
RIVERDALE

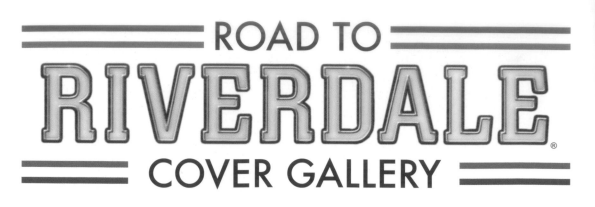

ROAD TO RIVERDALE® COVER GALLERY

After the announcement of the CW's *Riverdale* TV series, it only made sense that we would want to follow it up with a comic series set in the same world as the show.

Coming this winter, you can read a special *Riverdale* one-shot that takes place before the events of the pilot, featuring stories from the writers of the CW series along with art from Alitha Martinez, Elliott Fernandez, Jim Towe, Thomas Pitilli, Thomas Chu, Andre Szymanowicz, Janice Chiang and John Workman. Then, get ready for an all-new, ongoing *Riverdale* comic series!

Check out a few of the amazing covers from both the upcoming *Riverdale* one-shot and the *Riverdale* ongoing series.

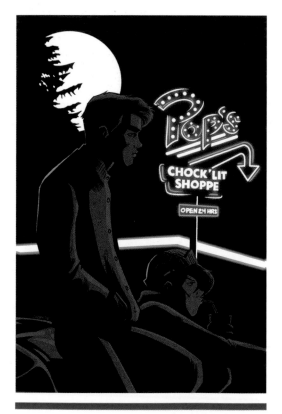

Pop's
CHOCK'LIT SHOPPE
OPEN 24 HRS

Riverdale One-Shot variant by
DEREK CHARM

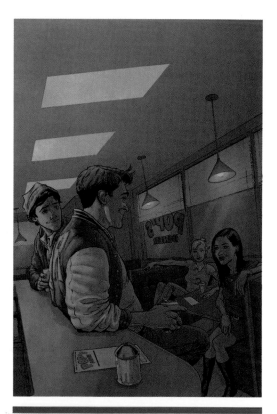

Riverdale One-Shot variant by
ADAM GORHAM

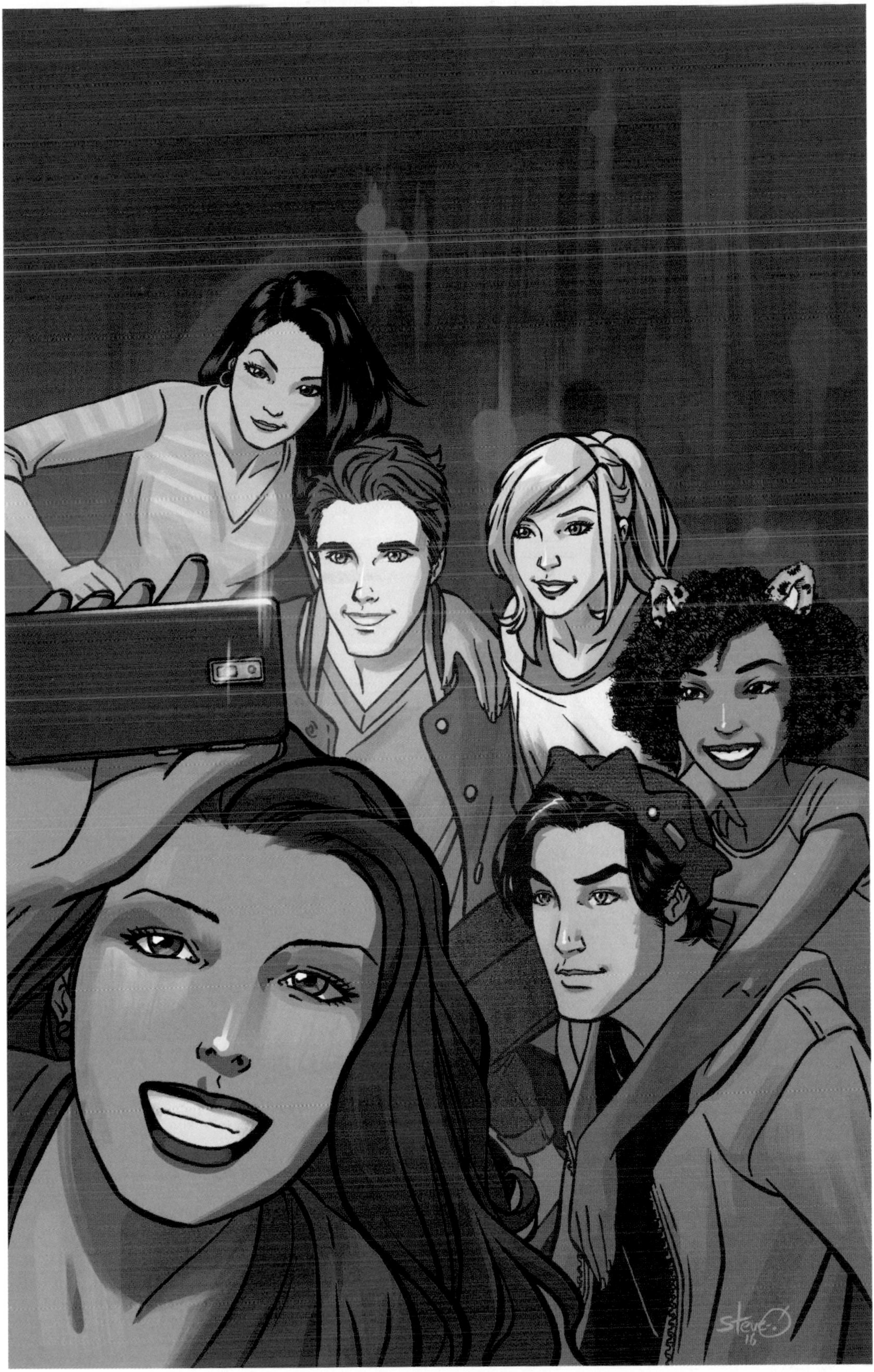

Riverdale One-Shot main cover by
ALITHA MARTINEZ with STEVE DOWNER

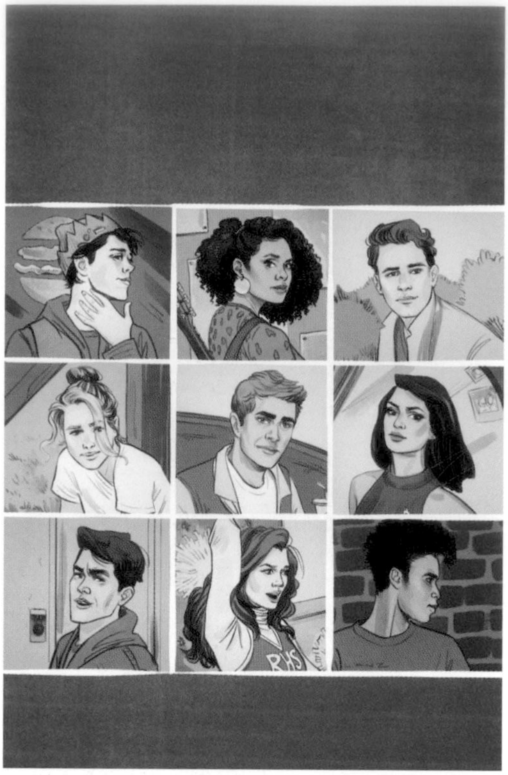

Riverdale One-Shot variant by
SANDRA LANZ

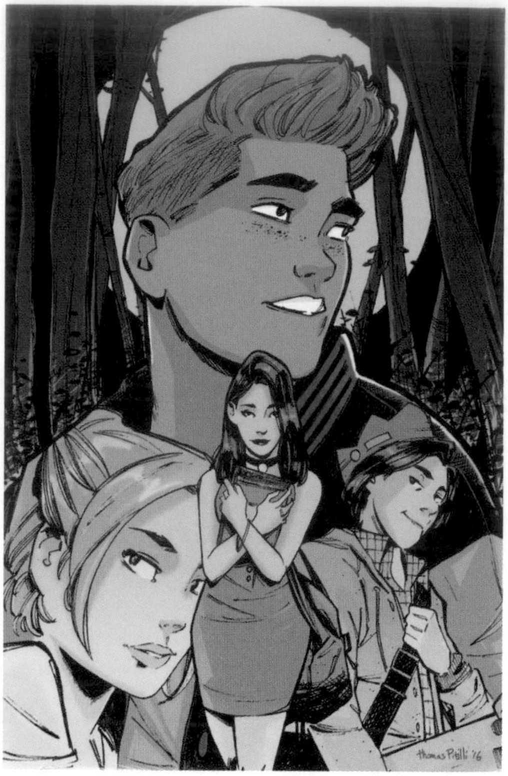

Riverdale One-Shot variant by
THOMAS PITILLI

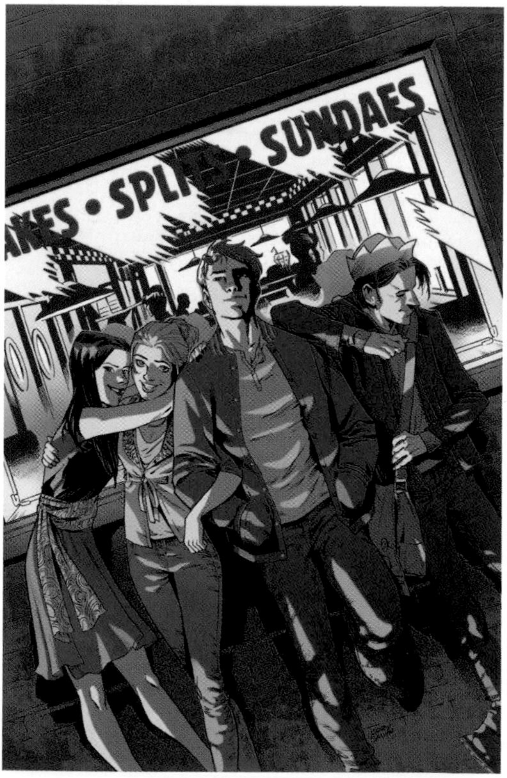
SUNDAES

Riverdale One-Shot variant by
CORY SMITH

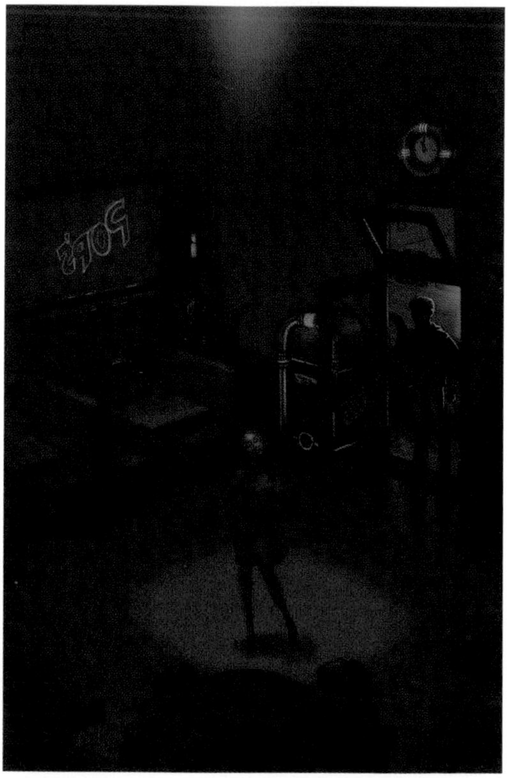

Riverdale One-Shot variant by
MORITAT

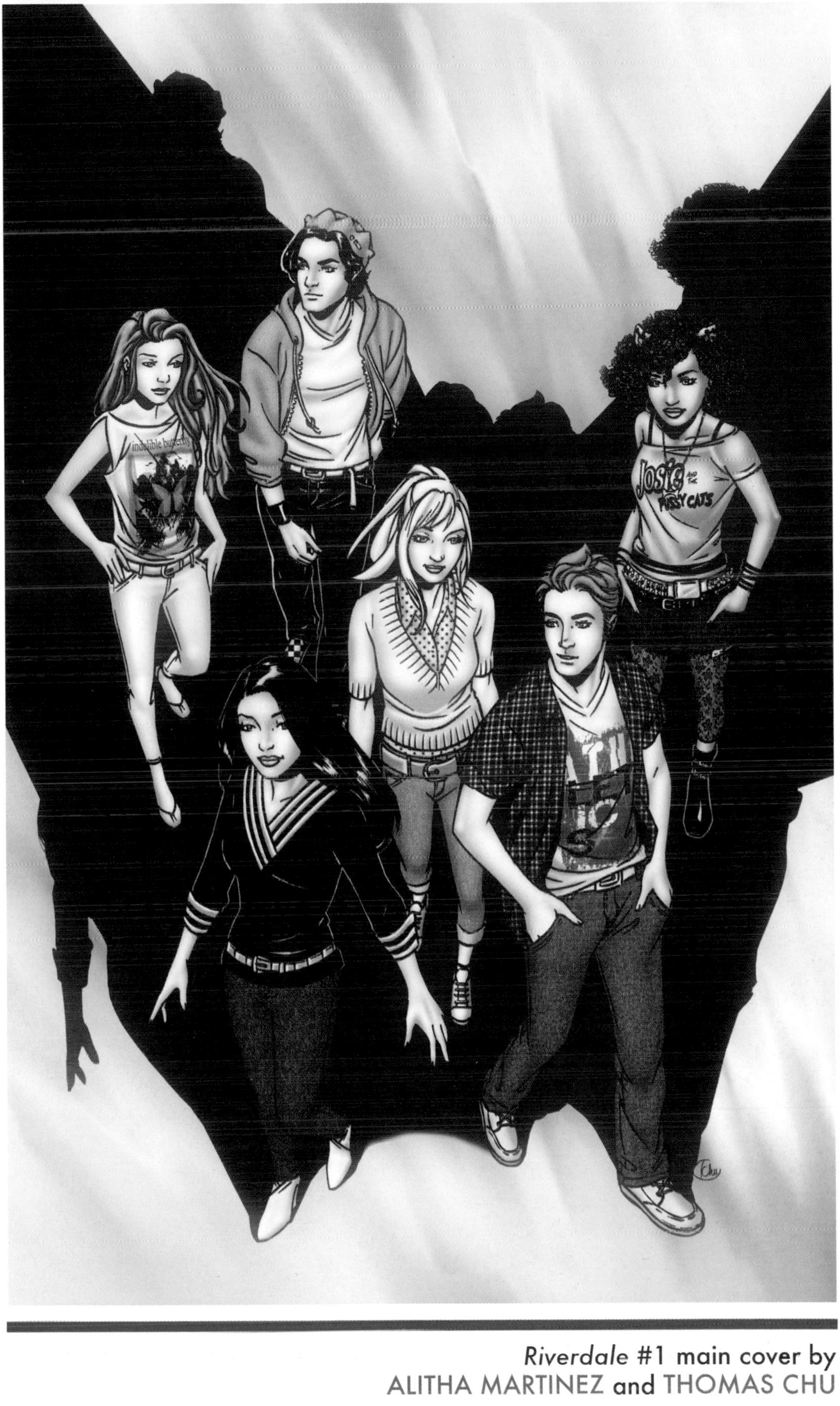
indelible butterfly
Josie AND THE PUSSY CATS

Riverdale #1 main cover by
ALITHA MARTINEZ and THOMAS CHU

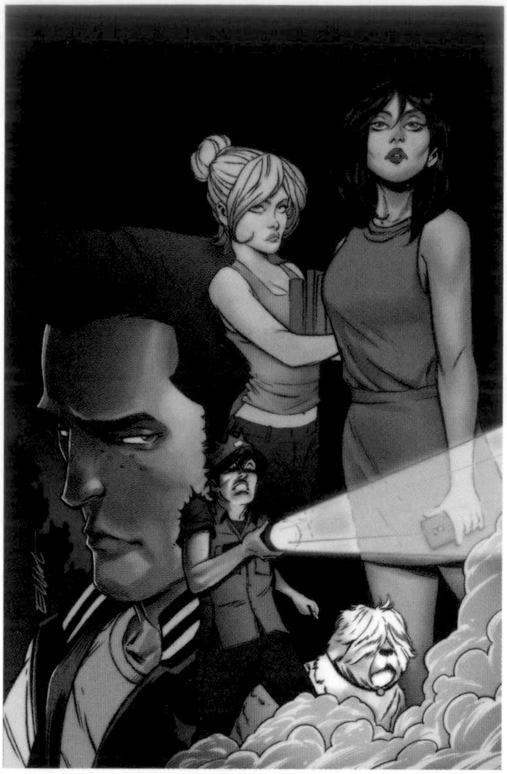

Riverdale #1 variant by
ELLIOTT FERNANDEZ

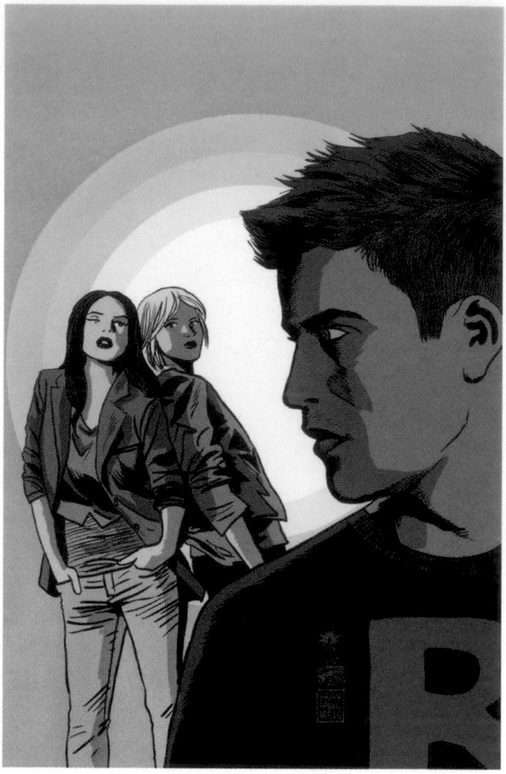

Riverdale #1 variant by
FRANCESCO FRANCAVILLA

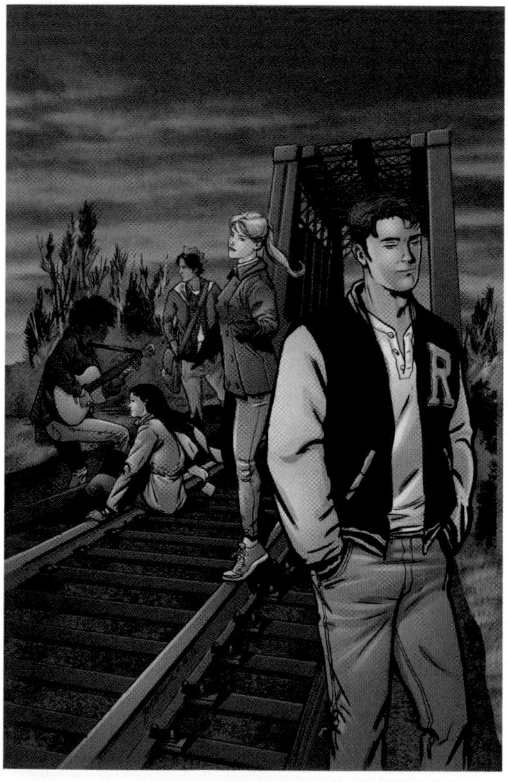

Riverdale #1 variant by
PETER KRAUSE

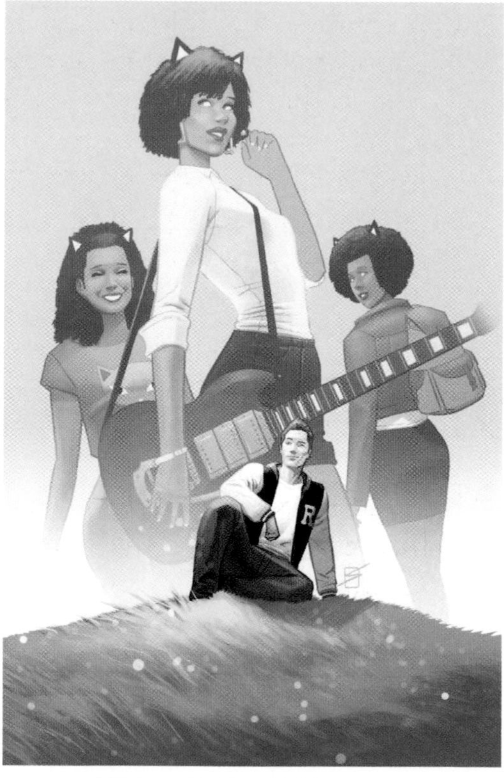

Riverdale #1 variant by
RON SALAS

ROAD TO
RIVERDALE
PHOTO GALLERY

Now that you're all caught up on the world of the NEW RIVERDALE, it's time to introduce you to the CW *Riverdale* universe. All of the stories you just read are a part of the new vision of Riverdale—the characters' personalities and aspects are the same as they've been for the past 75 years, but the situations and settings are modern, something both kids and adults can connect with in today's society.

This new version of *Riverdale* was not only groundbreaking for the comics, but also led to the media opportunity of a lifetime: the whole Archie universe starring in their own primetime drama on the CW network. The aptly-named Riverdale is spearheaded by Archie Comics Chief Creative Officer, Roberto Aguirre-Sacasa, the genius writer behind the smash-hit *Afterlife with Archie* and *Chilling Adventures of Sabrina* comic series.

This one-hour, live-action drama premieres January 2017. While the tone and storylines are very unique from the comics, you'll notice that everything you love about the characters remain the same.

Here is a special peek at some behind-the-scenes shots from the series, as well as some stand-out covers and panels from the New Riverdale universe.

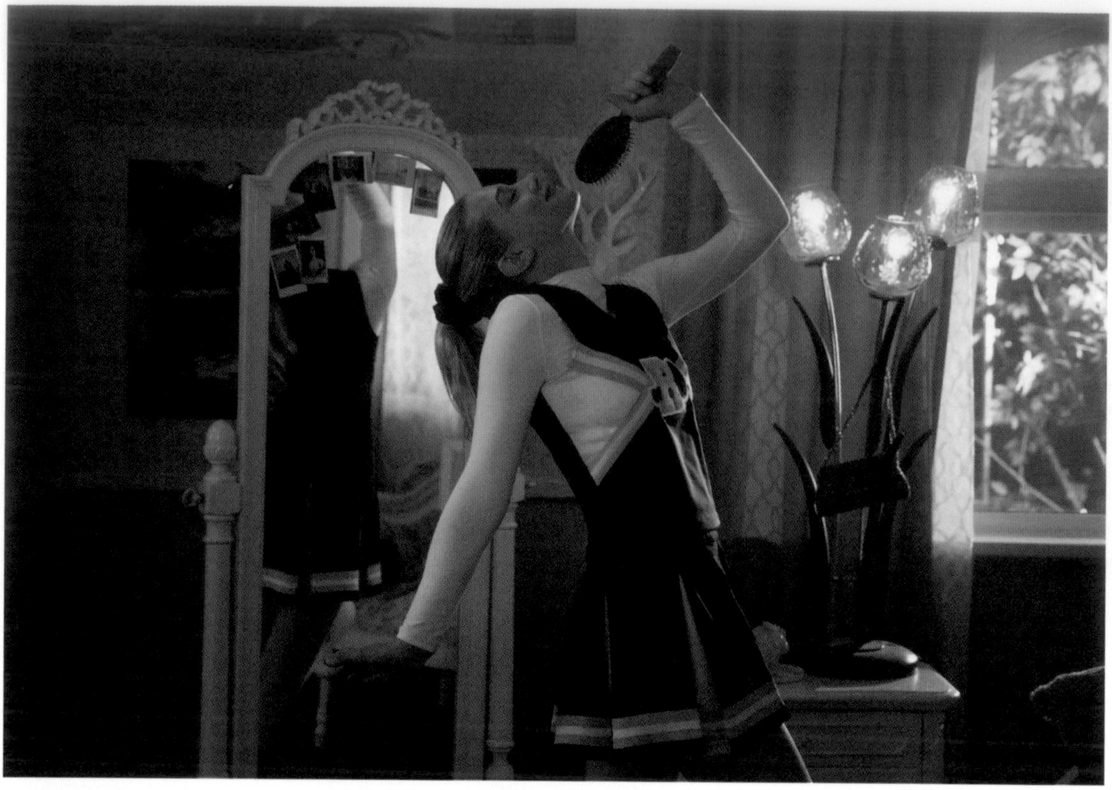

LILI REINHART as an exuberant Betty Cooper in her Riverdale High cheerleading uniform.

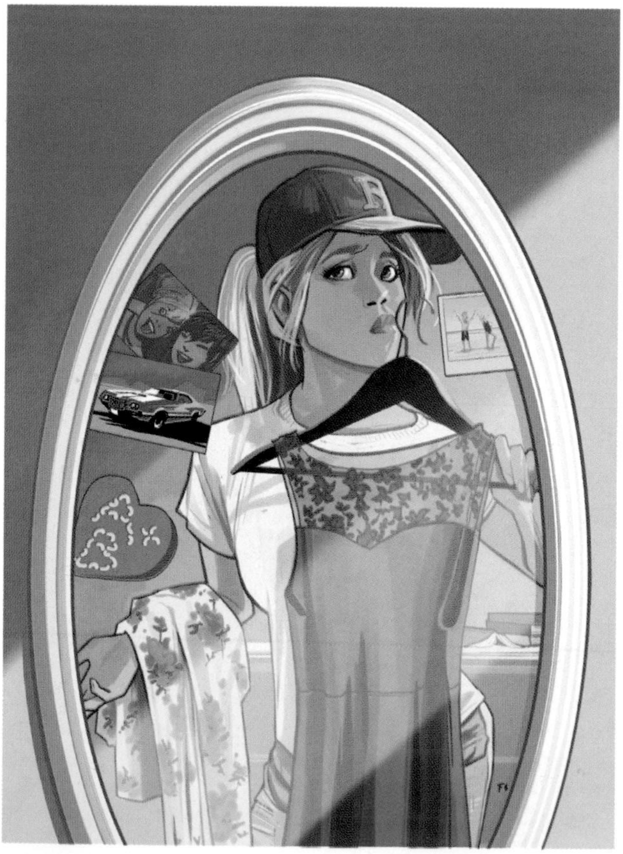

The cover of *Archie* #2 by FIONA STAPLES.

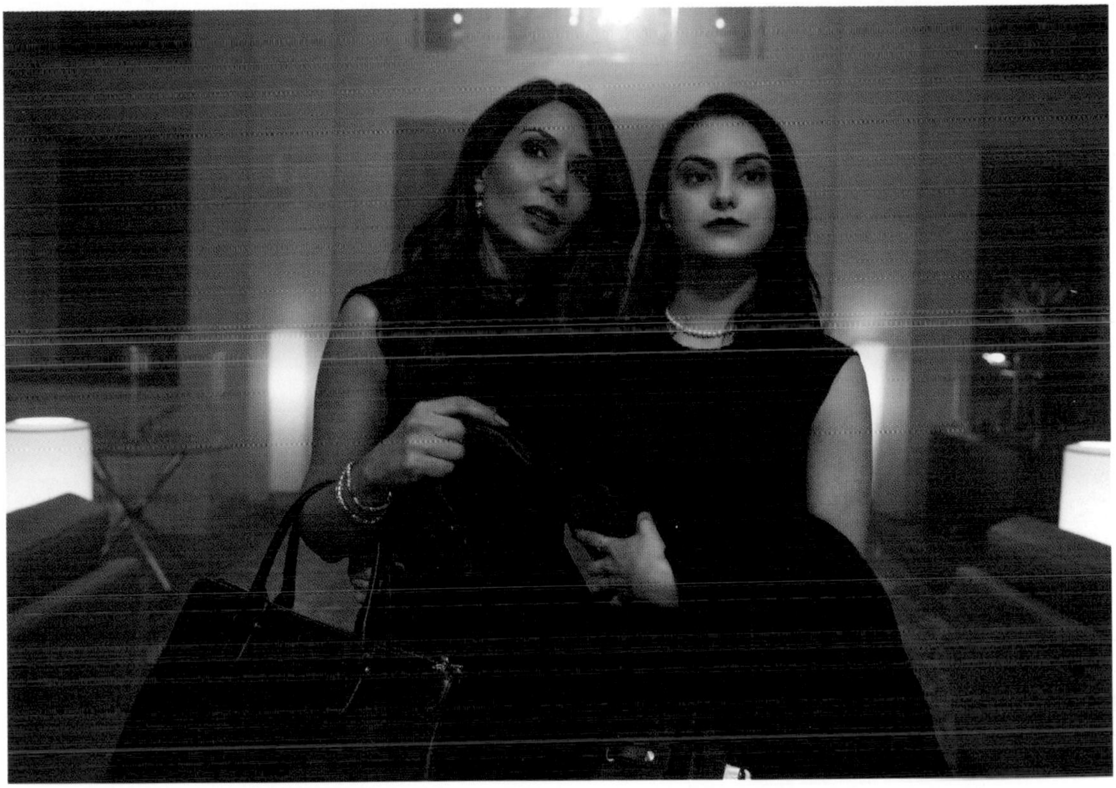

CAMILA MENDES as Veronica Lodge and MARISOL NICHOLS as her mother, Hermione. The two have just moved to Riverdale.

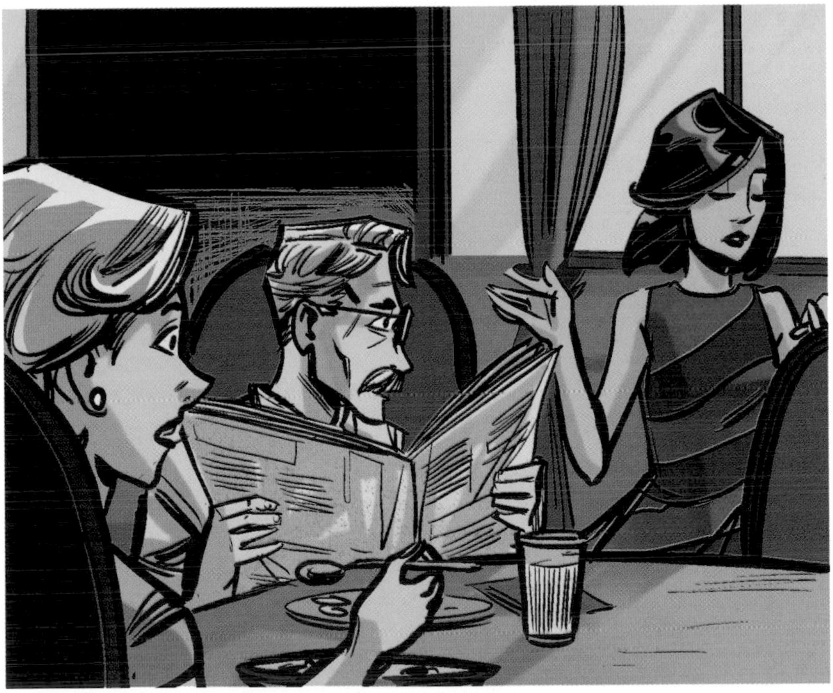

Veronica, Mr. Lodge and Mrs. Lodge from *Archie* #12, drawn by RYAN JAMPOLE and THOMAS PITILLI.

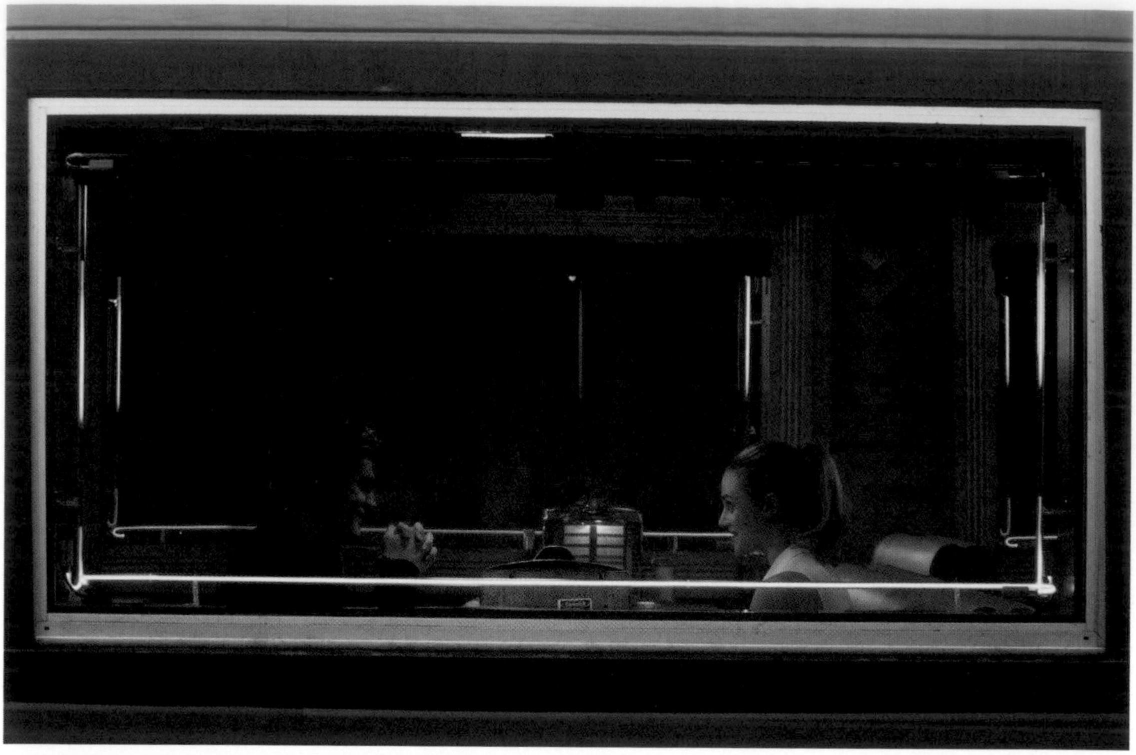

KJ APA as Archie Andrews and Betty, sharing a milkshake at Pop's.

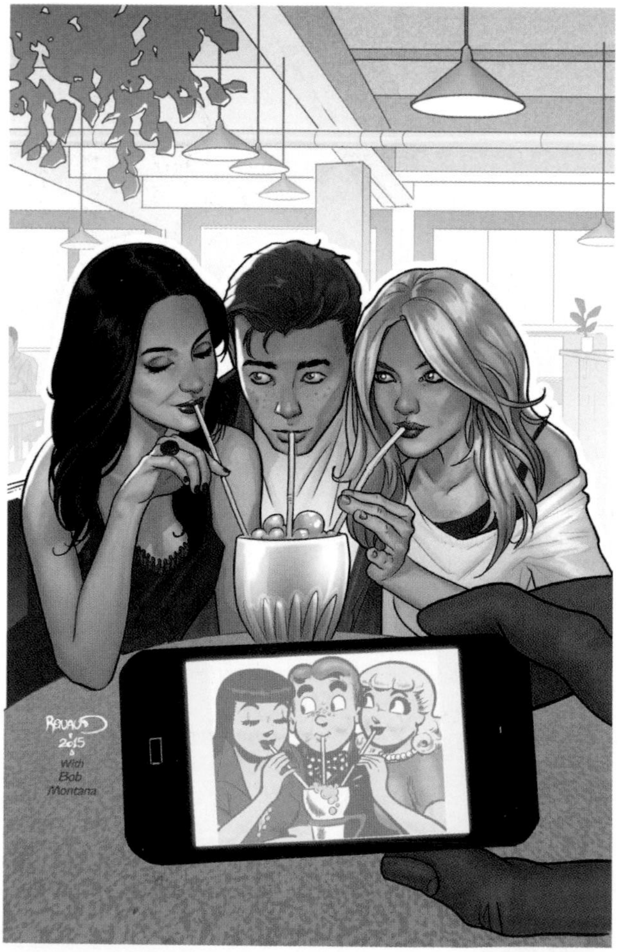
Renaud
2015
With
Bob
Montana

Three-on-a-milkshake variant cover for *Archie* #4 by PAUL RENAUD.

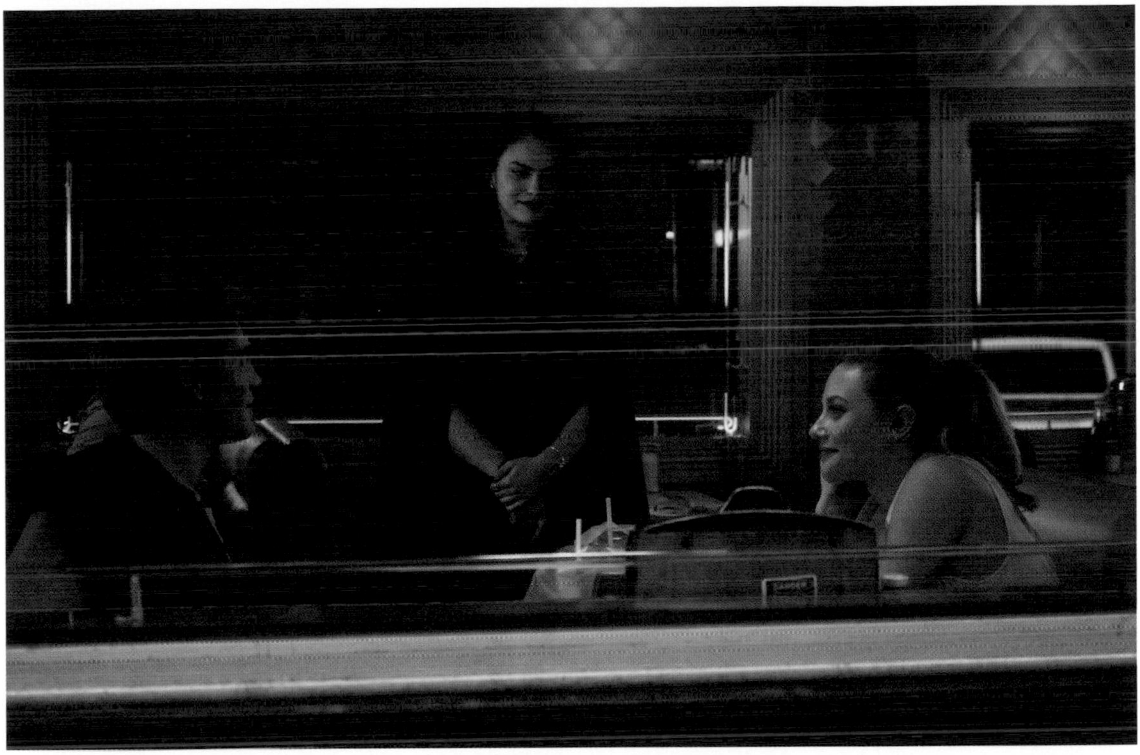

Veronica, introducing herself to Archie and Betty.

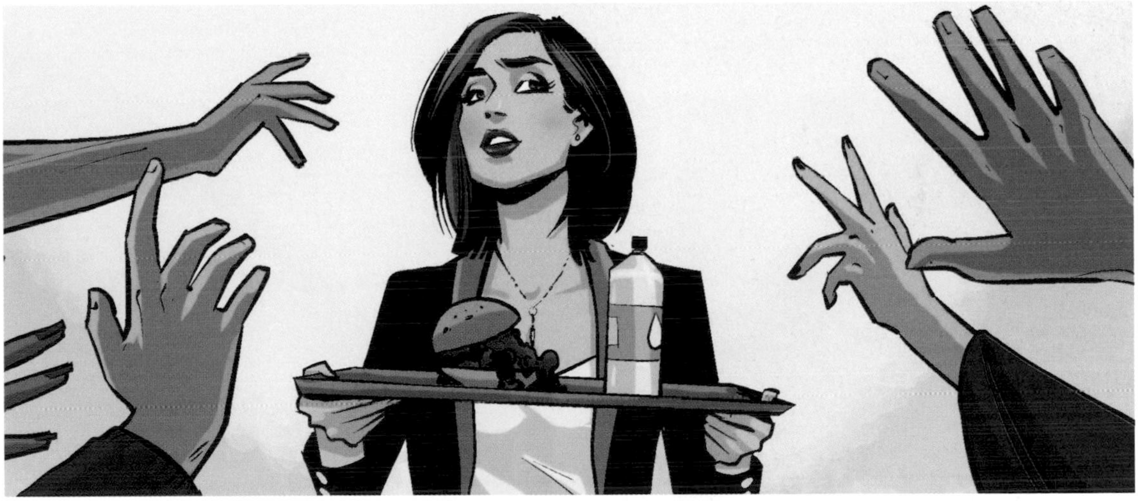

Veronica in the Riverdale High cafeteria on her first day, from *Archie* #3. Art by FIONA STAPLES.

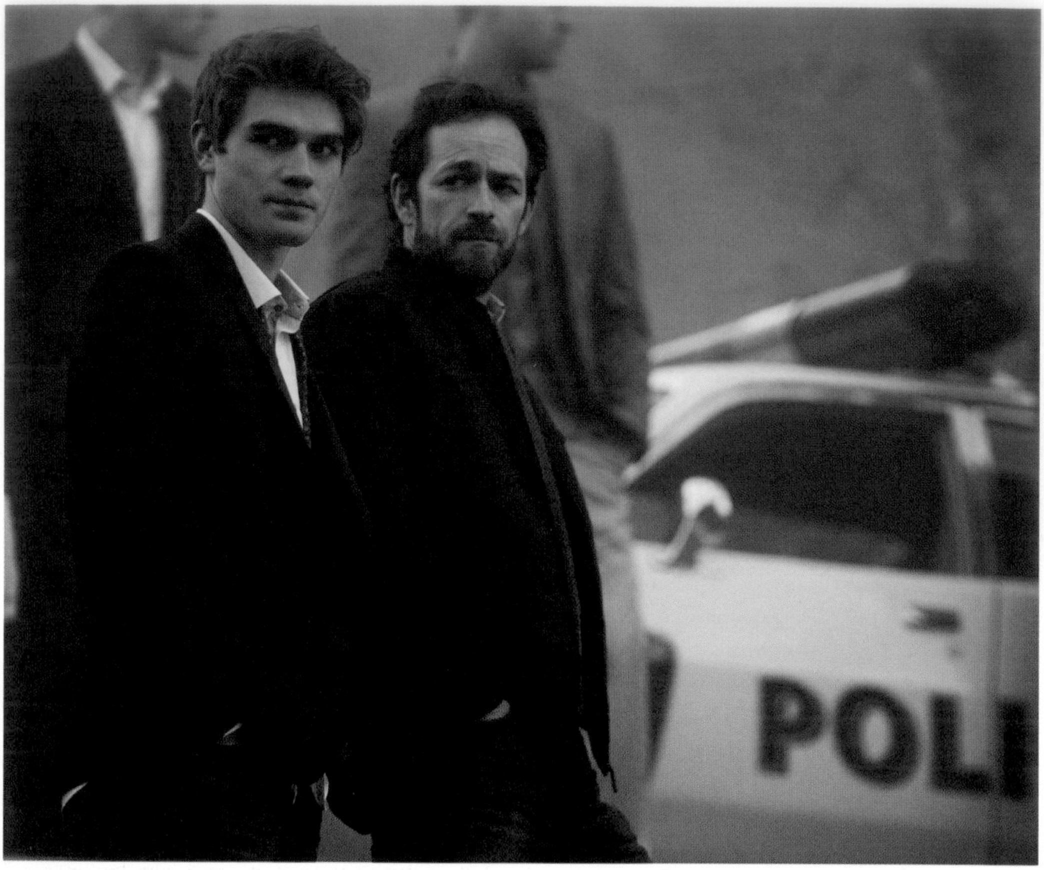
POLI

Even Fred Andrews got an updated look! Archie and LUKE PERRY as Archie's dad, Fred.

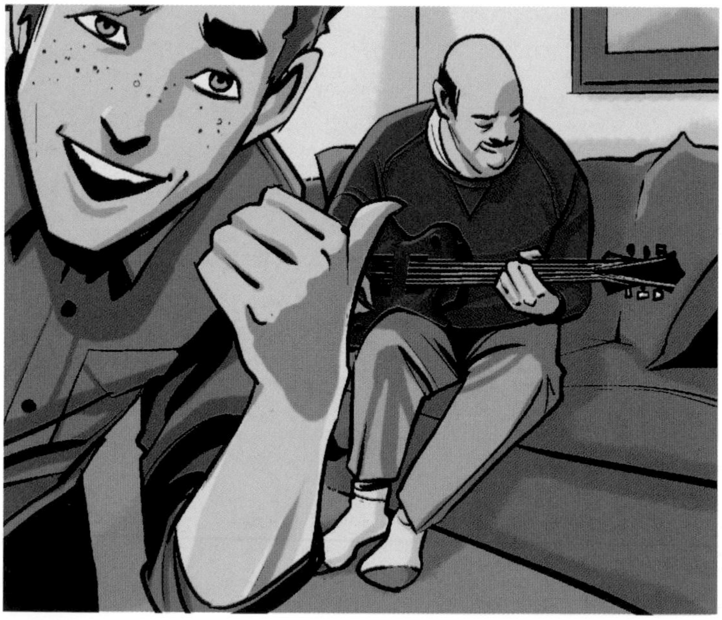

Archie jamming with his dad from *Archie* #1. Art by FIONA STAPLES.

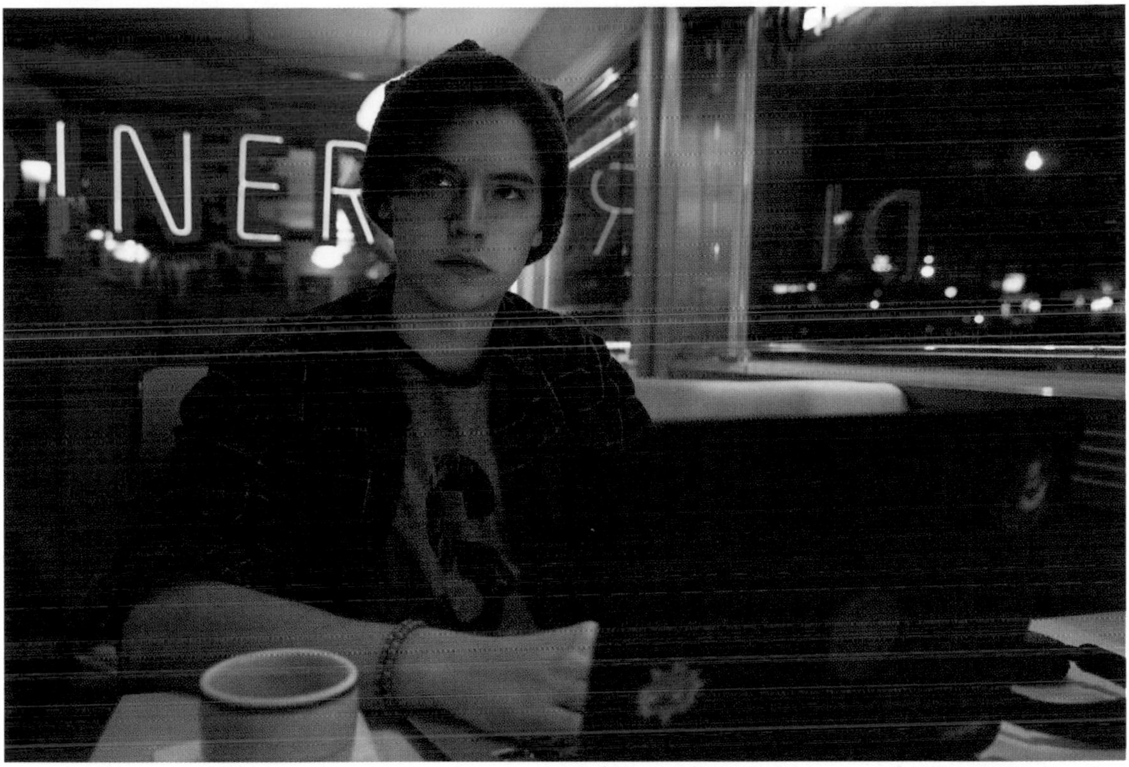
INER

COLE SPROUSE as Jughead Jones can be found writing away on his trusty laptop when he's not chomping away on burgers.

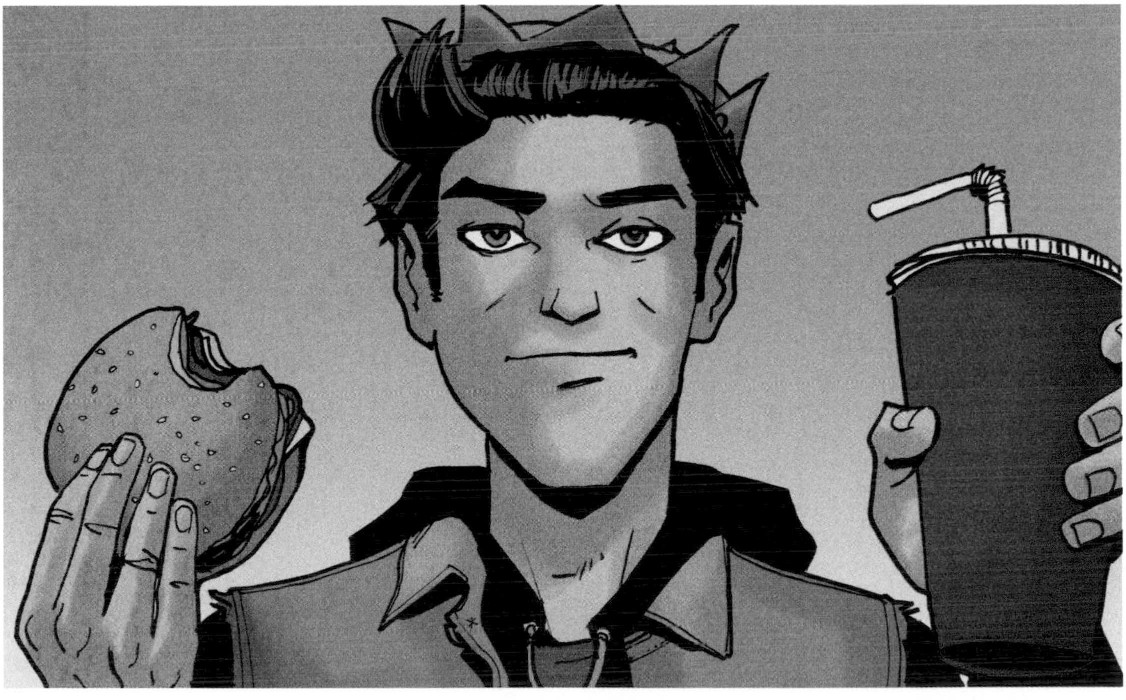

Jughead, armed with his weapons of choice, from *Reggie and Me* #1. Art by SANDY JARRELL.

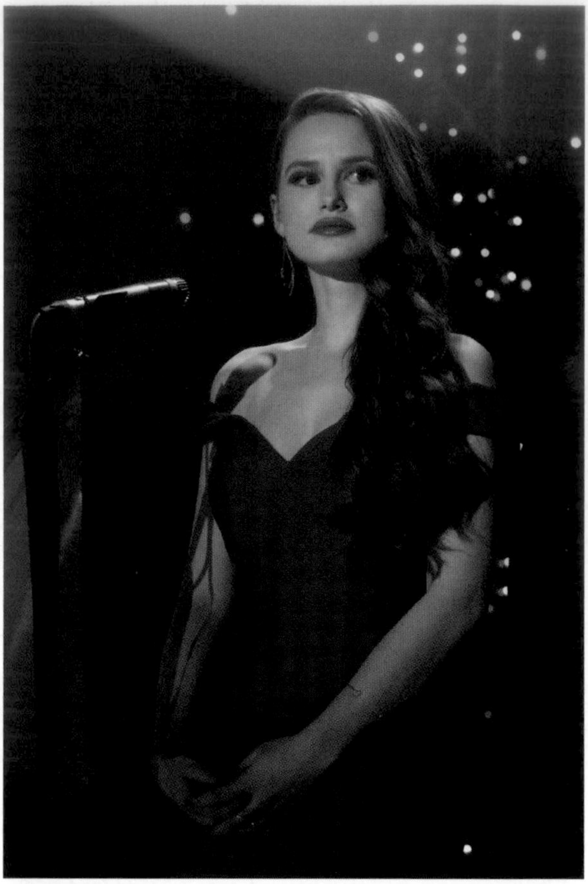

MADELAINE PETSCH looking stunning as Cheryl Blossom.

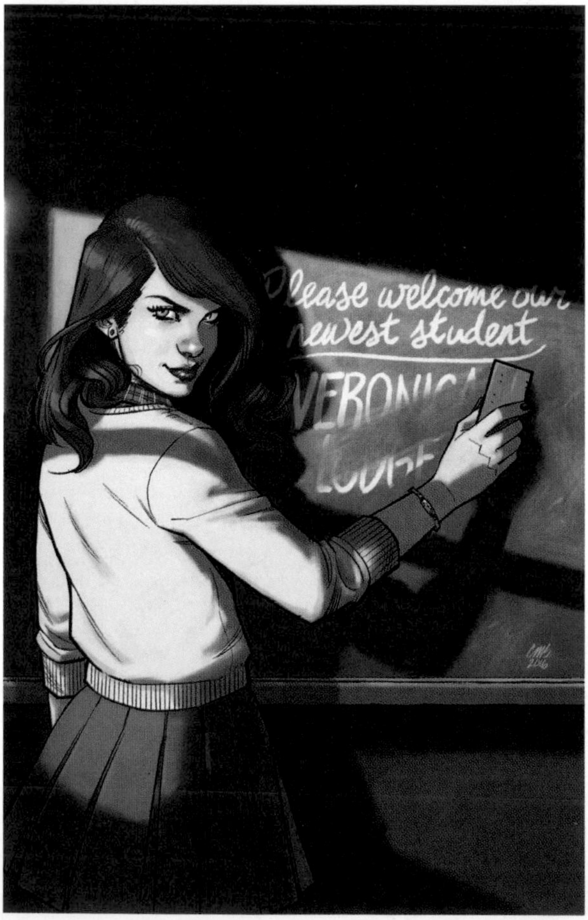

Please welcome our
newest student

Cheryl Blossom makes her debut in the New Riverdale. *Archie* #14 variant cover by CAMERON STEWART.

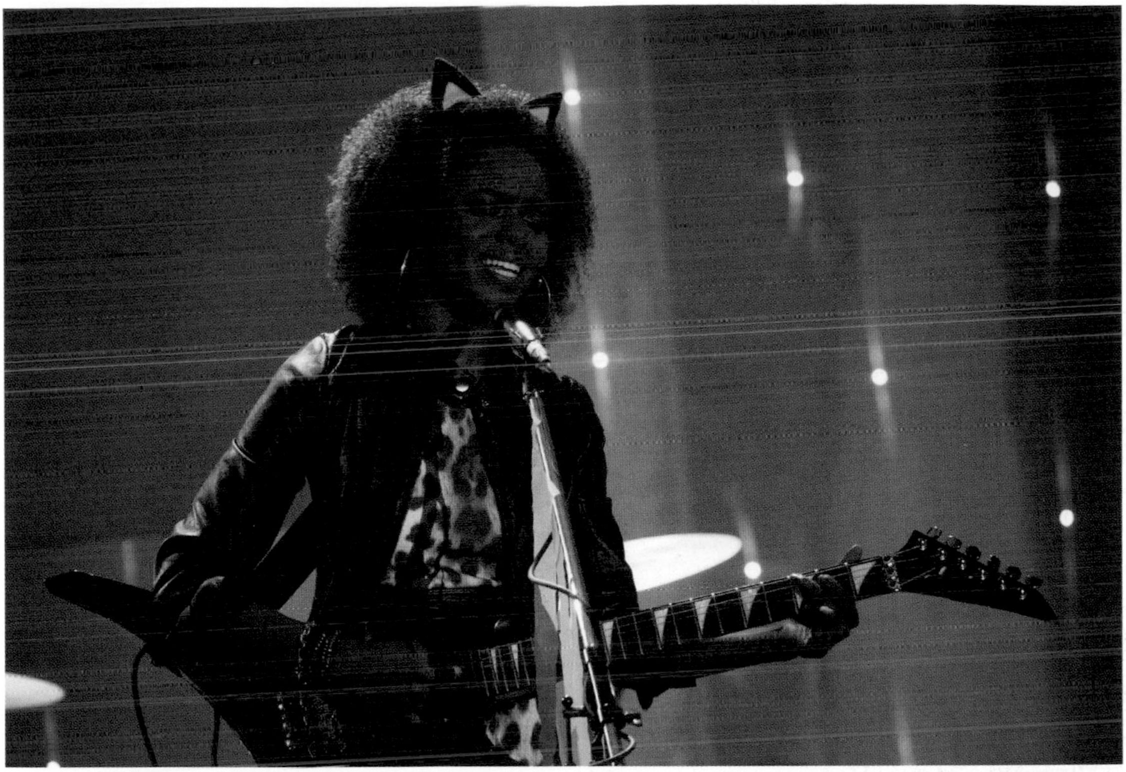

Say hello to Josie McCoy! ASHLEIGH MURRAY is donning the cat ears as the lead singer of the Pussycats.

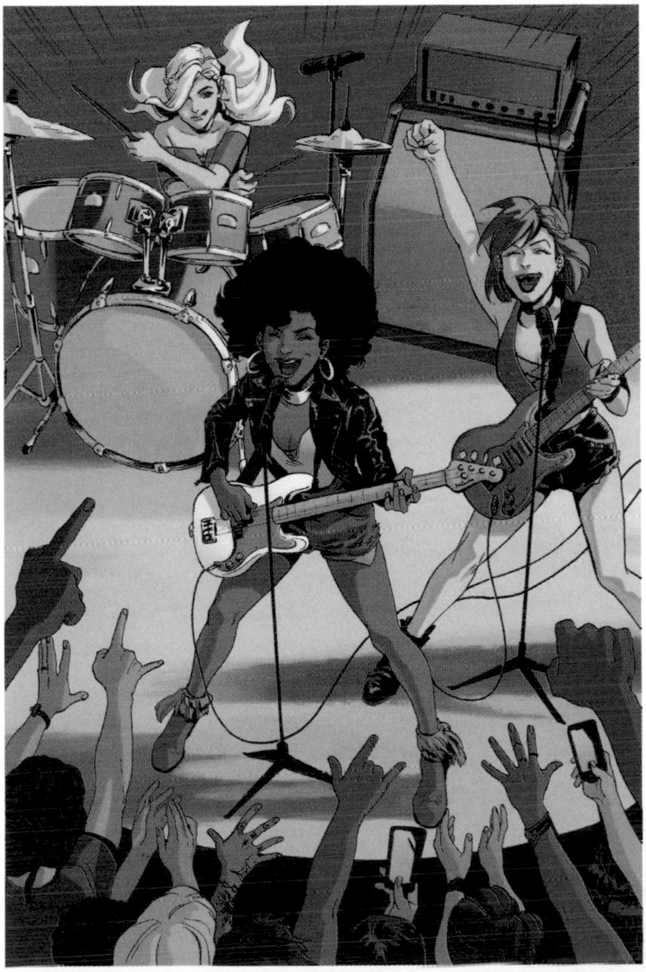

Josie, Valerie and Melody rocking out, from *Josie and the Pussycats* #1. Art by AUDREY MOK.

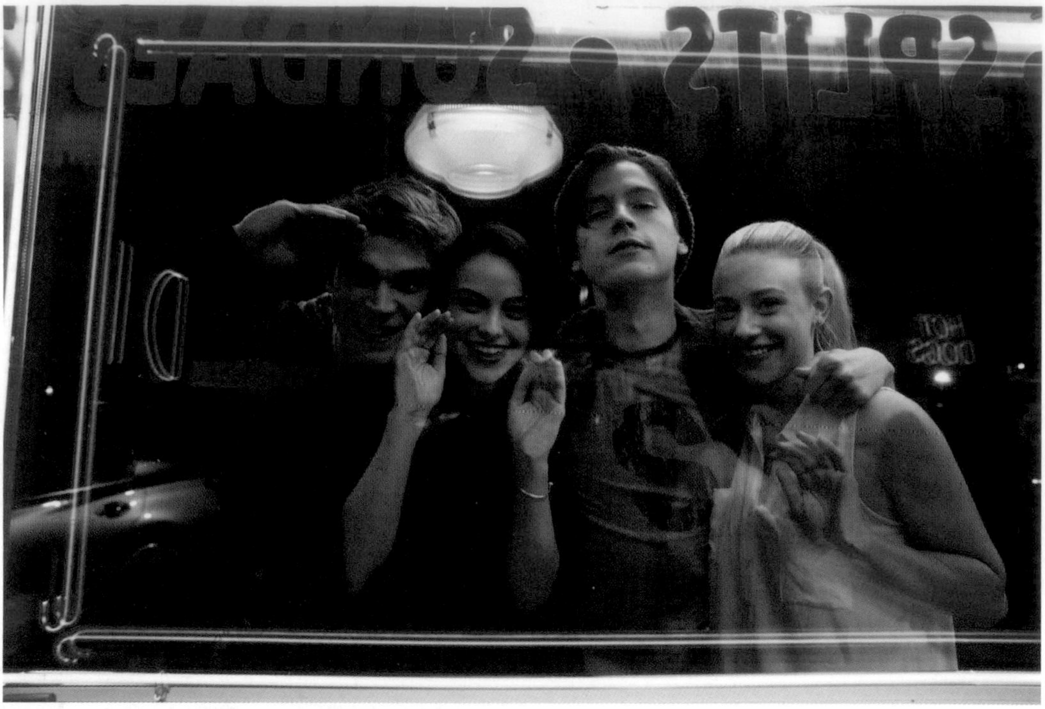

Archie, Veronica, Jughead and Betty outside Pop's.

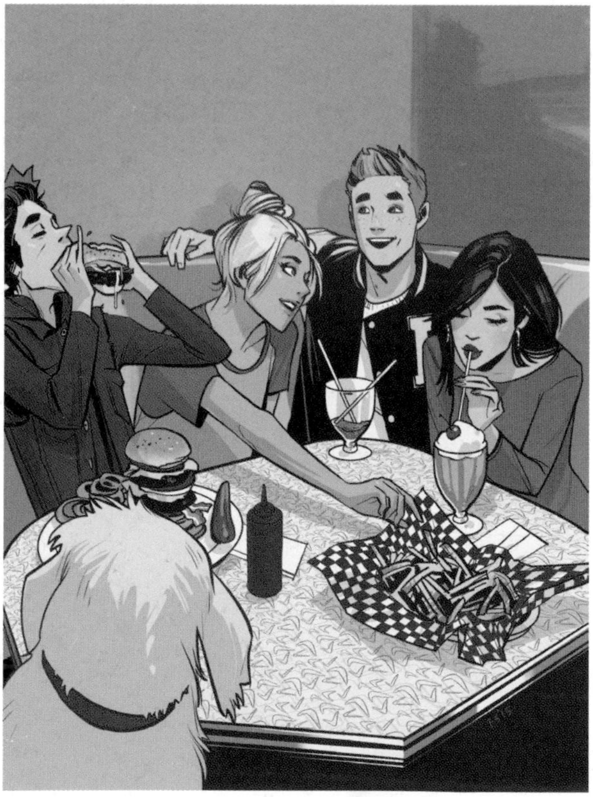

Archie, Betty, Veronica and Jughead at Pop's. Cover by FIONA STAPLES for the *Archie: Collector's Edition*.

Watch RIVERDALE on the CW network, premiering January 26.
For more details, check your local listings and ArchieComics.com.